Criticism and
the Nineteenth Century

# CRITICISM

## and the

# NINETEENTH
# CENTURY

*by*

GEOFFREY TILLOTSON

With a new preface
by the author

ARCHON BOOKS
1967

PR
463
.T5
1967

*First published 1951*
*University of London*
THE ATHLONE PRESS

*Reprinted 1967 with permission*

LIBRARY OF CONGRESS CATALOG CARD NUMBER: 67-17251
PRINTED IN THE UNITED STATES OF AMERICA

*In Memory of*
*H. Gordon Jackson*
*Friend and Master*
*of*
*Birkbeck College*

# PREFACE

THE pieces that make this book, and make it I think a book having some sort of unity, are now appearing for the first time, or reappearing (*a*) in a form that can be called 'revised', or (*b*) in a form so changed in substance and structure as to require a term more declaredly thorough-going. The pieces that have been printed before are as follows—and I am grateful to the institutions and publishers whom I name below for permission to use them to this new end. 'Matthew Arnold: The Critic and the Advocate' was delivered on 30 March, 1942, as the Tredegar Memorial Lecture of the Royal Society of Literature, and was printed in the Transactions of the Society—*Essays by Divers Hands*, new series vol. XX, edited by Gordon Bottomley, 1943. 'Matthew Arnold and Eighteenth-Century Poetry' was included in *Essays on the Eighteenth Century Presented to David Nichol Smith in Honour of his Seventieth Birthday*, published by the Clarendon Press, 1945. The essays on Pater were printed in the volumes put out by the English Association—*Essays and Studies*, vol. XXXII, 1946, edited by Basil Willey, 1947, and *Essays and Studies 1949*, edited by George Rostrevor Hamilton, 1950. 'Newman's Essay on Poetry' was included in *Newman Centenary Essays*, edited by Henry Tristram, and published by Burns, Oates and Washbourne Ltd., 1945; and, much changed, in *Perspectives in Criticism* edited by Harry Levin, Harvard University Press, 1950. 'English Poetry in the Nineteenth Century' was an Inaugural Lecture delivered on 4 December, 1945, in the University of London, Birkbeck

College; in revised form it was privately printed by the College. Much of it has been again rewritten for the new occasion, but I have retained the opening patter appropriate to a lecture.

*    *    *

It will be seen that I have given my essays notes and that I have placed them at the foot of the page. The other courses open are not to have them or to place them at the back of the book. The former alternative does not attract those who have either benefited from the notes of any book or been put to the trouble of hunting for an undivulged source. Nor does the second alternative attract those who have ever wished to consult a note that lurks somewhere in a jungle occupying twenty pages placed before the index.

The matter of the notes, other than of those giving chapter and verse, is of two sorts: (1) that of last minute discoveries which if made in time would have affected the text; and (2) that which having no claim to a place in the text suggests new lines of enquiry. The former sort is bad, but better than nothing; the latter good.

The above arguments will seem pedantic to those who have not heard debates on the matter. At the word 'notes' donnish passions stir. And with reason. For an attitude to the past, to scholarship, to truthfulness may be bound up in their presence or absence. One way of dividing up the English departments of the universities is by testing their allegiance to the principles in and behind the note, wherever placed, however dry. I shall speak more persuasively perhaps if I say that as soon as notes are slighted or banished the text itself suffers. For confirmation I appeal to anyone who has ever checked a quotation copied out by his own hand or another's. How often when its source is turned up is the transcript found accurate? Not very often.

Men, said Newman, can never be too suspicious of themselves. Certainly not when they are copying another's words.
There are occasions when the checker finds his transcript so
badly wrong that it could only serve the present occasion if
kept wrong—see below, p. 91. To check the transcript of a
quotation is sometimes to discard the quotation. Further, even
if the transcript is accurate, turning it up may lead the checker
to find that he has so far forgotten its context as to have come
to misunderstand what the writer of the quotation intended
it to mean. To re-examine the context of a quotation is sometimes to discard the quotation. The supplying of footnotes,
therefore, is a habit that helps keep the author straight. It also
gives the reader, along with the advantages I have already
named, the handy means of checking the straightness for
himself.

*      *      *

I wish to record my thanks to my wife, Kathleen Tillotson.
The help she has given me has been mainly that of her example,
by being herself actively and closely concerned in the
literature of the nineteenth century, as of several others. So
much more thoroughly versed in its multitudinousness than
I, she has taught me much. She has also enriched my book at
particular points, especially in the essay on Henry James.

I also wish to thank my brother, Arthur Tillotson, for the
collation of *The New Republic* which I have drawn on below
at p. 131.

G.T.

*Birkbeck College,*
*University of London.*
*20 August* 1950.

# PREFACE—1967

The re-emergence into critical esteem of the literature of the English mid-nineteenth century has been one of the post-war excitements for students and 'general' readers, and I am pleased to have done something to help it on the course that cannot even now be said to have proceeded further than a fair beginning. Mid-nineteenth-century literature is not simply the best body of literature the English have produced. It happens also to be the literature that has most practical interest for ourselves. We live so plainly in its wake. The problems being faced a hundred years ago are the problems still facing ourselves. Chief among them is the problem raised by the continued supremacy of science and its methods, and the consequently progressive disappearance of what was called the supernatural. Nature we believe, as many of our great grandfathers did, to be all there is. Meanwhile, like them, we are finding it to be more and more complex. We are still feeling a sense of wonder as deep as that felt by our remoter ancestors before their theological dogmas, but it is now a wonder prompted by the atom and the distant heavens.

On pp. 4f. below I give some instances of century-old problems that are still with us, and the reader may be amused, as I have been, to prolong the list—as, for instance, with the following. In *Macmillan's Magazine* (IX, Nov. 1864-April 1865) one F. E. Anstey discusses 'state medicine'; Carlyle airs the problem of river pollution; and Mrs. Gaskell notes that we shall soon have to start burning our own smoke; Ruskin pillories 'advertisement frescoes', and in *Modern Painters* is moved to the exclamation:

> Not the old hospitable innkeeper, who honoured his guests, and was honoured by them, than whom I do not know a more useful or worthy character; but the modern innkeeper, proprietor of a building in the shape of a factory, making up three hundred beds; who necessarily regards his guests in the light of Numbers 1, 2, 3–300, and is too often felt or apprehended by them only as a presiding influence of extortion;

John Addington Symonds, collaborating with Havelock Ellis in their book *Sexual Inversion* (the first and only volume of their *Studies in the Psychology of Sex*) anonymously contributes his own case history; and a day or two ago Mr. Michael Hurst quoted *The Times* of 25 October 1873 to this effect:

> The present is a time of universal, however unreasonable, discontent. All classes, all employments are wanting better pay, less work, more money, more for the money, quicker promotion, earlier retirement and larger superannuations. All complain of rising prices and wages. For good or ill there is a universal rising in the rate of expenditure and there is probably not such a thing in these isles as a man content to live as his father did at the same age and under the same circumstances.

Mr. Hurst continued:

> A true story of the 1820's in Ireland also rings an all too familiar bell. "My good friend", said a gentleman to a peasant standing idle in the road, "you seem to be doing nothing". The man negligently began striking the stones. "Oh, that won't do. Do you call that hard work?" "Sure", answered he to this expostulation, "sure, isn't it time now, and not labour we are bound to give the master!" (*Letter from the Irish Highlands.* Anon. 2nd edit. 1825)

Some of our newspapers have taken to devoting a few inches of space to giving us a still topical example from *The Times* etc. of a hundred years ago to the day. The sub-editor who searches them out must often hesitate over alternative choices.

Not all my instances are by poets and novelists or by those who produced classics of the prose-of-thinking kind, but they well suggest the world in which nineteenth-century literature was produced, and to the current problems of which it contributed. The only quite new problem is that posed for us by the atom bomb, and how much we wish that we had a Carlyle or a Ruskin alive to fulminate about it.

Nineteenth-century literature, however, is interesting for other reasons than its extended topicality. On pp. 30–3 below I have suggested the infinite riches it offers of the aesthetic sort proper to great literature.

The reappearance of my book allows me to correct the misprints of the first edition:

> p. 17, *l.*4: *for* seing *read* seeing
> p. 19, *l.*30: *for* Leonato *read* Leonatus
> p. 32, *l.*5: *for* Rosamond's *read* Rosamund's
> p. 76, *l.*1: *for* that *read* than
> id., *l.*11: *for* The essay . . . attack *read* 'The Study of Poetry' attacks
> p. 77, *l.*16: *for* -awn *read* -awns
> p. 86, last line of text: *for* an *read* as
> p. 100, *l.*4: *for* administering *read* ministering
> p. 151, last line of text: *for* at *read* an
> p. 193, *n.*4: *for* 1854 *read* Jan.-June 1854
> p. 228, *n.*4: *for* 1849 *read* Jan.-June 1849
> p. 241, *l.*27: *for* when *read* where
> p. 258, *l.*25: for Ladislav . . . Rosamond's *read* Ladislaw . . . Rosamund's

June 1966                                                        G.T.

# CONTENTS

## I (a)

### The Critic and his Material: The Return to the Nineteenth Century

THE collecting of scattered pieces of criticism invites the collector to justify himself by discerning as much unity in them as he can.

One sort of unity he knows in advance they cannot but have and have, it may be, *ad nauseam*. The style is the man— the style that exists in a sentence as strongly as in a book. But though there is unity in a style, no book gets credit from what can be claimed by all books equally. On that score any credit comes from the worth, not from the inevitable uniqueness, of the style. And though at a certain pitch the goodness of a style—the soundness and grace, that is, of a mind directing a sensitive pen—can launch a volume of heterogeneous pieces, the pitch is discouragingly high.

What unity a volume of essays has additional to that of style will not usually lie in the objects of the essays, the objects patent in their titles. Usually essays that exist scattered exist in that condition just because they do not cohere into a close historical or philosophical sequence: if they did, they would exist as chapters in a book having a single theme. But the essays collected here do have a degree of unity in their objects. That is the first sort of unity I would claim for them. They all concern English writers of the nineteenth century. And they form separate segments long enough to be curved enough to suggest a circle, however enormous. Within that enormous suggested circle, some of the essays draw smaller circles more completely. And four of them—Numbers II-IV —conspire to grasp a unity completer still: they bring together across four essays two literary critics who between them represent the best—or at least the most influential—in English criticism over half a century. The circle sketched by these four essays is surely almost complete.

For the essays here collected, however, I claim another ground of unity, that of critical method. To explain which I resort, in the first place at least, to autobiography.

## II

DURING the last war, I was one of those many thousands of readers who turned gratefully to the literature of our despised nineteenth century. I say despised, but of course thousands of twentieth-century readers had never ceased to admire the literature of their grandparents. The great nineteenth-century novels in particular have remained so magnificent as re-creations of human experience that they have become, as it were, part of the map or of the weather; they are unignorable. The masterpieces of the nineteenth century were despised only by such writers or readers as found the despising of them the condition of doing anything new, of living, on their own account. When, in a moment of exasperation, Rupert Brooke called Tennyson 'that old fool',[1] when Aldous Huxley announced in the early twenties that the value of Ruskin as a 'dictat[or of] aesthetic Law' was the boost he gave to principles opposite to his own,[2] when Osbert Sitwell compiled his *Victoriana* in the early thirties[3]—

[1] In a letter to Mrs. Cornford, February 1911, quoted in Sir Edward Marsh's *Memoir*, 1918, p. 56.

[2] *On the Margin*, 1923, p. 175.

[3] *Victoriana. A Symposium of Victorian Wisdom*, ed. Margaret Barton and Osbert Sitwell, 1931.

on those occasions, we now see, new writers were battling for their lives. People who cared very much for the novelties of the new age—say, for new fashions in chairs, wall colours and cretonnes—despised the mahogany and woven horse-hair of their grandparents. And people who cared very much for James Joyce, and even for D. H. Lawrence and Virginia Woolf, despised Dickens and Thackeray simply because of 'the expulsive power of a new affection'. Then at last when the scarlet flush subsided, Dickens and Thackeray were found to be standing just where they stood always, Joyce, Lawrence and Virginia Woolf having come to stand in some sort of amiable relationship to them. But those people who felt no passionate affection for the new novelists went on reading the Victorian masters. When therefore I say the nineteenth century was despised, I merely mean it was despised by those who were driven as by a biological necessity to despise it. Its being despised was not to its discredit.

During the war, then, I for one took up the serious reading and re-reading of some of the numerous masterpieces of the nineteenth century. Alternatively, I might have gone back-wards into the seventeenth century, a century which at the time and in certain quarters was being advertised loudly. Perhaps it was partly a matter of what books were available. There was no chance of visiting the British Museum in those long days spent in handling files in a government office. But a lunch-time chance of visiting the London Library. That library is overwhelmingly rich in the literature of the century through which it has flourished since Carlyle helped to found it in 1841. It offered the books.[1] But that would not

---

[1] I also wish to thank my friend, Professor F. P. Wilson, for the long loan of a shelfful of Arnold's works, almost all of them in first editions; and also the City Librarian, Westminster, for a similar kindness.

have recommended it unless I had been eager to take them. Along with thousands of other readers in those years of the war, I felt an eagerness to read Victorian books. In time of stress, when the body cannot escape, one needs to let the mind escape. But many found, as I did, that escape must not be too far, not far enough to cut one off from the present. The escape that seemed best was escape into a time when our own public problems had begun to trouble—the private ones remain eternally the same—but had not yet troubled to the pitch of bombs, or, rather, not to the pitch of bombs on London. The Victorians had faced public problems recognisably similar to our own. And of course—this was their hold over us once we had looked at them—had faced them with so massive an intelligence, with so towering a height of capacious brow. It was a century sharply modern, when —to limit myself to half a dozen sentences from the thousands of them—when the American stranger, warmed by Shelley's praise of George Washington, declared that

there is dry rot in all the main timbers of the Old World, and none of you will do any good till you are docked, refitted, and annexed to the New[1]

(which Arnold for one countered with

I see a wave of more than American *vulgarity*, moral, intellectual, and social, preparing to break over us;[2]

and Burne-Jones, for another, with

If ever I travel it shall be to Chicago. I don't want to have my heart broken by the East [his correspondent was in Constantinople]; better one's head broken by the vulgar West);[3]

---

[1] *Trelawny's Recollections of . . . Shelley and Byron*, ed. Edward Dowden, 1923 edition, p. 57.
[2] Letter of 7 March, 1848 (*Letters*, i. 4).
[3] Frances Horner, *Time Remembered*, 1933, p. 131.

it was the century in which Carlyle declared that

There is no end to machinery;[1]

and Ruskin that

we old Reds fall into two classes, differing, not indeed in colour of redness, but in depth of tint of it—one class being, as it were, only of a delicately pink, peach-blossom, or dog-rose redness . . .[2]

and Newman that

Birmingham people have souls;[3]

and Mill that

Nothing can deserve the name of a good education which does not include literature and science too;[4]

and Clough that

> Thou shalt not covet, but tradition
> Approves all forms of competition;[5]

and Arnold that

Those who cannot read Greek should read nothing but Milton and parts of Wordsworth: the state should see to it;[6]

and George Eliot that

Even in that conservatory existence where the fair Camellia is sighed for by the noble young Pine-apple, neither of them needing to care about the frost or rain outside, there is a nether apparatus of hot-water pipes liable to cool down on a strike of gardeners or a scarcity of coal;[7]

and Hopkins that

I am afraid some great revolution is not far off. Horrible to say, in a manner I am a Communist.[8]

[1] 'Signs of the Times', *Edinburgh Review*, xcviii, 1829, p. 442.
[2] *Fors Clavigera*, Letter vii (1 July, 1871), p. 13; *Works*, xxvii. 122.
[3] See p. 184 below.
[4] *Inaugural Address Delivered to the University of St. Andrews*, 1867, p. 12.
[5] 'The Latest Decalogue', ll. 19 f.
[6] *Arnold to Clough*, p. 97. I have expanded Arnold's abbreviations.
[7] *Felix Holt, The Radical*, ch. 3.
[8] Letter of 2 August, 1871; *The Letters of Gerard Manley Hopkins to Robert Bridges*, ed. Claude Colleer Abbott, 1935, p. 27.

It was a century startlingly like our own. Only having so much more recognisable wisdom pouring out of its so many more oracular mouths. Dean Inge has called it 'the *saeculum mirabile*, the most wonderful century in human history'.[1] More recently the claim has been made that the world had seen two great ages of the human intellect, one being the age of Pericles, and the other the age of Victoria. That claim was made by Mr. G. M. Young on the occasion which produced No. VII below, and he remarked further that he had won the assent of the Sorbonne to it. Such a claim from such a source reverses a thousand taunts that the present century—quite legitimately on the indulged plea of filial ingratitude—has discharged at its predecessor. Of all except a few—we of the twentieth century can permit ourselves the laugh at Matthew Arnold, for instance, who was always decrying the contemporary England in favour of the contemporary France. That he was hopelessly wrong in his reading of the particular signs was discovered by at least one person, on at least one occasion: when in 1875 Henry James tried to settle in Paris, he was checked by finding

the circle of literature tightly closed to outside influences; it seemed to exclude all culture but its own . . . [James spoke] sarcastically on one occasion of having watched Turgenev and Flaubert seriously discussing Daudet's *Jack*, while he reflected that none of the three had read, or knew English enough to read, *Daniel Deronda*.[2]

Henry James, therefore, settled in Matthew Arnold's England: it would be so very interesting to be in England when the British Empire was dying:

even the 'decline' of England seems to me a tremendous and even, almost, an inspiring spectacle, and if the British Empire is once more to

[1] W. R. Inge, *The Victorian Age*, 1922, p. 7.
[2] *Letters*, ed. Percy Lubbock, 1920, i. 42.

shrink up into that plethoric little island, the process will be the greatest drama in history![1]

In our warring 'forties the astonishing thing was not so much the greatness of the Victorians, as that we had not seen it before, or that not enough of us had seen it before, or seen it clearly enough, or seen it and said it. But we had seen it at last. And seen it to keep on seeing it. Surely Mr. John Sparrow erred the other day when he called George Eliot 'a writer as much overrated today as she was underrated yesterday'.[2] That remark, I submit, is not a pin proving that our excitement is a bubble, but a pin thrust childishly into a giant oak. One cannot easily overrate *Middlemarch*: one could only do that by saying that it was easily the best of the half-dozen best novels of the world.

It was Matthew Arnold's poetry I found myself reading. Much reading was done, and much writing, in those 'blacked-out' evenings. But you cannot read Arnold's poetry without reading, or re-reading, the prose. Much reading, therefore, in the prose. Out of the much writing came No. II, and later No. III. The former of these two essays built itself round a sentence met in Arnold's *Lectures on Celtic Literature*, a work which Robin Flower made delightful fun of—

Matthew Arnold . . . having attended an Eisteddfod on a holiday and read a few translations of Welsh and Irish literature took upon himself the task of defining [the 'Celtic note'] and discovering it in some of the most admired passages of English poetry[3]

—but which has been saved by a certain American scholar who claimed it as the originating force of the poets of the Celtic twilight: Arnold had got the Irish badly wrong,

[1] Letter of 15 December, 1877; *Letters*, ed. cit., i. 58.
[2] *Spectator*, 24 February, 1950, p. 252.
[3] *Byron and Ossian* (The Byron Foundation Lecture of the University of Nottingham), 1928, p. 6.

but the new Irish were bent on living up to his inspiring mistake.[1]

But another temptation to rove sprang from Arnold's *Discourses in America*, where in the lecture on Emerson he evoked the memory of the strong influences playing on him as a young man. There like many others I was arrested—as Arnold intended me to be—by this account of Newman's preaching:

Forty years ago, when I was an undergraduate at Oxford, voices were in the air there which haunt my memory still. Happy the man who in that susceptible season of youth hears such voices! they are a possession to him for ever. No such voices as those which we heard in our youth at Oxford are sounding there now. Oxford has more criticism now, more knowledge, more light; but such voices as those of our youth it has no longer. The name of Cardinal Newman is a great name to the imagination still; his genius and his style are still things of power. But he is over eighty years old; he is in the Oratory at Birmingham; he has adopted, for the doubts and difficulties which beset men's minds to-day, a solution which, to speak frankly, is impossible. Forty years ago he was in the very prime of life; he was close at hand to us at Oxford; he was preaching in St. Mary's pulpit every Sunday; he seemed about to transform and to renew what was for us the most national and natural institution in the world, the Church of England. Who could resist the charm of that spiritual apparition, gliding in the dim afternoon light through the aisles of St. Mary's, rising into the pulpit, and then, in the most entrancing of voices, breaking the silence with words and thoughts which were a religious music,—subtle, sweet, mournful? I seem to hear him still, saying: 'After the fever of life, after wearinesses and sicknesses, fightings and despondings, languor and fretfulness, struggling and succeeding; after all the changes and chances of this troubled, unhealthy state,—at length comes death, at length the white throne of God, at length the beatific vision.' Or, if we followed him back to his seclusion at Littlemore,

---

[1] John V. Kelleher, 'Matthew Arnold and the Celtic Revival', in *Perspectives of Criticism*, ed. H. Levin, Harvard University Press, 1950, pp. 197 ff.

that dreary village by the London road, and to the house of retreat and the church which he built there,—a mean house such 'as Paul might have lived in when he was tent-making at Ephesus, a church plain and thinly sown with worshippers,—who could resist him there either, welcoming back to the severe joys of church-fellowship, and of daily worship and prayer, the firstlings of a generation which had well-nigh forgotten them? Again I seem to hear him: 'The season is chill and dark, and the breath of the morning is damp, and worshippers are few; but all this befits those who are by their profession penitents and mourners, watchers and pilgrims. More dear to them that loneliness, more cheerful that severity, and more bright that gloom, than all those aids and appliances of luxury by which men nowadays attempt to make prayer less disagreeable to them. True faith does not covet comforts; they who realise that awful day, when they shall see Him face to face whose eyes are as a flame of fire, will as little bargain to pray pleasantly now as they will think of doing so then.'[1]

This passage proved a temptation in Oscar Wilde's sense— he cynically defined the word as an attraction that one yielded to. So an 'earnest' reading—how the Victorians loved the word—of Newman set in. Not everybody was reading Newman in 1942: when, for instance, I applied to the Oratory at Birmingham for permission to print a transcript from one of the Newman manuscripts, Father Tristram, their custodian, assured me that, contrary to my assumption, the Oratory had no policy governing permission: I was the first to enquire after it—the first of a line now, in 1950, already a long one. Reading Newman meant reading his letters—the most telling evidence left by any author, thought Newman.

---

[1] The method Arnold invented here is as interesting as his matter. The passages quoted come from Newman's sermons. Ordinarily the making of quotations cannot but seem rather a pompous business. Arnold evades that defect by floating his in what he makes a sort of vision. The method used here and that used in his introduction to the lectures on Celtic literature have helped the 'higher journalists' to write about literature with so pleasant a 'creativeness'. Henry James and Virginia Woolf owed him a great debt on this score as on others. Nor is it without significance that Arnold's quotations are inaccurate!

And reading his letters—the printed ones of the Anglican period—meant coming on his poems, many of which are transcribed in them. Much was written on his poems. But how write on his poems without writing on his essay on poetry? And there I stuck long enough to write a first version of No. VI below.

Much the same thing happened over Pater. A reading of him almost complete ended with considering closely a few sentences.

There has been constantly at work, then, a principle of reduction: what we call glibly 'the nineteenth century' reduced to certain authors, reduced to certain small patches in them, even to a single sentence. That has proved the method of working, and a single method employed over several essays is a means of unification. My book of essays is something of a whole.

# I (b)
## The Critic and his Material: On Critical Method

IF at last I have come to rest on the small thing, it is usually after spending some time in exploring the country in which it lies. You do not find things worth finding by rotating blindfold, running at large, and falling on what offers. Treasure is found by means of an exploration. But explorations can be narrow or wide, scamped or close. And it is how these qualifications are mixed that will determine not only what it is that is found, but what the thing found means to the finder, and so to those to whom it is offered.

In considering ways of writing criticism I propose to rule out at once whatever ways may be favoured by critics who have scamped their exploration. The realms of gold are vast and of a daedal complexity. Masterpieces of writing, even those written in English, are innumerable. The writings of a single author often run into scores of books. And into his books he puts his best. His mind is at its most intense when he is holding the pen. Talk streams out of him like breath, but it is with sweat, with blood and sweat, that good writing achieves existence. Carlyle was of the opinion that

You cannot, if you are going to do any decisive intellectual operation —if you are going to write a book—at least, I never could—[do it] without getting decidedly made ill by it....[1]

Or there was Newman for whom the producing of each of his books had been 'a sort of operation',[2] 'in point of pain, a mental

[1] *On The Choice of Books. An Inaugural Address* [*at*] *Edinburgh*, 1866, p. 93.
[2] Ward's *Life*, i. 296.

childbearing'.[1] And for the critic the resulting book must be as close and warm and complicated and intense as for its author. The exploration that is scamped is therefore no exploration at all. Critics who scamp it are merely Count Smorltorks: a fortnight's visit was all he gave to preparing to write on England.

I cannot claim that all the criticism in this book is the result of explorations both wide and close. In particular No. VIII declares its lack of context. *No Name* is simply a piece of an author's works cut off. Wilkie Collins wrote novels and stories with Trollopean pertinacity, writings of which I have read three only. In writing of the novel read last, I cannot but treat it as something of a peninsula instead of as the busy inland place it was for its author, and for its tens of thousands of readers in the nineteenth century, and as it must be for the critic of Wilkie Collins who has proper authority. For me *No Name* exists almost as if Wilkie Collins were a 'single-novel author', an Emily or an Anne Brontë—or, to keep him among detective novelists, an E. C. Bentley. How then did I come on a novel which having little general fame is so well worth reading? The pointed answer is that my choice was indeed the result of a wide exploration, but not of one made by me—my friend, Professor Howard Mumford Jones of Harvard, asked me on one occasion if I had read *No Name*, describing it as a novel which if once started on is read and finished in wild career. My essay, therefore, reaped the advantage of another's exploration. But though one may be handed a good book like an apple on a plate, its goodness cannot be so savoury as if one had climbed the great tree—in all its Preraphaelite detail—for oneself. To the critic of Wilkie Collins complete my essay on *No Name* must look

[1] Op cit., ii. 204.

silly. If it escapes his jibe that is because he does not exist—
which indicates the degree to which the Victorians have been
neglected.

II

IF his exploration has been wide and also close the explorer
has three main methods open to him:

1. To write an account of the journey through the whole
   country;
2. To write of the small trove—a village or rich valley—in
   the light of the whole country tramped over;
3. To write of the whole country as if, at the end of tramping
   it, he were to take a helicopter and view it from a chosen
   altitude.

Of the three methods the first gives him least trouble. To
the writer of a travel book, keeping a diary and writing it up
afterwards presents few difficulties. And if you are a critic it is
easier to allow chronology to present you with an organisation than to achieve an organisation by standing, as it were,
at the last page of your author's works and bracing yourself
to discern them as they form a piece in your mind—about
which I shall have more to say. Method 1 is popular: it does
not call for much intensity of mind.

But to recount the author's journey through time can be
a task of great difficulty if his progress is seen not merely
as sequence but as that process of organic change which in the
nineteenth century came to be called 'development'. To
discern a development in an author's progress calls for subtle
powers indeed, and few critics have given proof that they
possess them. It is the word rather than the power to discern
the thing that during the last hundred years has been so much

in evidence. I suggest that the word be dropped except by those who having read, say, Newman's *Essay* on the thing as he saw it working in one field, have come to share the subtleties I have tried to summarise as 'organic change'. Furthermore, no one should use the word who cannot discern the root nature of what it is that is supposed to be undergoing the growth. How tired one is of the critics who talk 'of the development of, say, Shakespeare without stopping to ask what existed apart from any development it underwent, and without seeing that, even if development did take place, it threw off, when the developer was Shakespeare, a long series of works each of them perfect, or pretty well so, in themselves; I should not like to have to account in terms of development for the differences between *Love's Labours Lost* and *Othello*—plays that can only be seen as connected, let alone connected as early and inferior to later and superior, by critics who do not get very deep into either. Before they see their author's works as showing a development, critics choosing method 1 must grasp his root nature in the way that, say, Dr. Johnson (before the word 'development' was invented) grasped it and put it into words in the preface to his edition of Shakespeare or on hundreds of occasions in the *Lives of the Poets*: they must penetrate to the still hearth and home of their author. And if they are not too much exhausted by that feat, they can then go on to watch their author undergoing his modifying growth and to tell us what they see. Method 1, however, as usually seen and followed offers the critic the easiest course.

Methods 2 and 3 attract by looking more difficult. Critics are drawn to 3 by its promise of power. Who would not see the whole from above? The prospect flatters one's conceit, and would-be cartographers rise up numerously as birds in thunder. But critics choosing method 3 are open to the dangers that usually await those who choose 1. Often the plodders who choose 1 know that plodding is unworthy, and try to make amends by closing their book with a big generalisation. But often it is merely a repetition in briefer form, heavier with a valedictory intonation. It evinces no fresh return to the country, no fresh look at the object. Similarly the critics choosing 3 exclusively often seem to be merely expanding the heavy generalisation achieved by critics choosing 1. They often write 'out of touch', as we say, with their object: the great danger of choosing 3 is that of losing hold of the country you once explored closely as well as widely. To the airborne eye a country's flora, for instance, disappears. And to the traveller on foot the flora is delightful. Hovering in his helicopter the critic tends to see merely as green what once he saw as the feathery green and white and red of a meadow. Of course the colour of a meadow when seen from the helicopter will not be the same green as that offered at the same distance by a cricket-pitch, but in practice there have been few critics who, choosing 3, have managed to name the distanced colours with a due subtlety. Critics choosing 3 sometimes seem disembodied as well as remote. They forget the vividness of their responses when they were formerly exploring phenomena on foot. Great remote tracts of literature have the sad property of inducing drowsiness. Critics often write of them as in their sleep, as if their heli-copter were a balloon drifting in conditions of haze. Their own condition may be gathered from this: that what they write seldom contains quotations. They dream of poetry, and we have only to confront them with a vivid line of it to see them start as if at the smell of ammonia. If they were to fall harmlessly overboard they would not recognise the country they were purporting to be surveying. Dick Minim, cooing that Waller was sweet and Denham strong—what a shock if he could suddenly have been confronted with the mere presence of a poem of either of those remarkable poets. Certainly there have been few good critics who, having chosen 3, have not mixed the survey from above with a pedestrian account of certain tracts of the country.

III

IT WILL be observed that I am on the defensive, that I am speaking as one who has chosen method 2.

A critic works as he can, or perhaps merely as he does. Luckily for him the conditions of his working are not altogether those of solitary confinement. He does not feel much more isolated than the worker at an office desk, much less so, I should say, than the house-to-house vendor of this or that. He knows with some degree of certainty that if his wares prove unsaleable that is because he has not made them good enough, and it follows that if he cannot make them better, he had better leave off being a critic and carry out his own version of Polonius's threat to 'keep a farm and carters'. Good criticism is saleable—that he cannot but believe: so long as literature is read, criticism of it will be read also since to read literature is to feel the need to respond with words— to respond in celebration or disapproval, with words that are like the clapping that at the close of the song the hands jump to, or like sighs, embarrassment, or outraged catcalls. Yet though the critic does not feel unnecessary to his fellows, he knows the necessity of solitude, that he must leave them if only to justify his return. However warmly he belongs to the world while he is educating his talents or experiencing his

object—in the theatre, at the fireside, in the public library—
he must retreat at times into a solitary trust of himself: his
writing, at least, must be done in solitude. As a thing written
his criticism is the result of seing more clearly what his own
mind has made of his object. He is at the mercy, then, of
himself, of his lonely capacities. The dispensations that critics
have to accept vary widely. One finds he reads fast, one
slowly, one writes piecemeal as reading proceeds, and ends
by sewing the bits together; another reserves writing till late,
and races the clock in great sweeps. One can think without
ink; another not. One goes for poetry first, another for prose;
one for drama, another for novels. One, gifted with tongues,
takes the novels or the plays of Europe; another remains as
insular as would befit a critic of Jane Austen. One knows much
of music and painting; another of bibliography or the
principles of textual criticism, or history, or philosophy or
science or psychology. Whatever the critic—whatever his
endowment, taste and equipment—it is out of him that his
criticism proceeds.

Taking myself as I am, I find I read slowly, write piecemeal
and without big gaps . . . and so on. And since these practices
seem ingrained, for good or ill, I must accept the results of
them. And so must my reader. His act of reading is his
acceptance. To read with approval or without it is alike to
accept: only by not reading does he reject.

I have said 'for good or ill'. But the tossed coin comes
down to the benefit, I think, of the critic who reads slowly.
Not necessarily, of course, to the benefit of the present
critic. A critic may be slow because feeble. There is no virtue
in slowness unless its rate is fixed by strong virtues requiring
slowness for their exercise. In seizing on speed as a differentia
I am seizing on the obvious: we can all tell a fast reader from

a slow by comparing the speeds of the eye along the lines. And I am assuming that the fast and slow readers are critics worth the name, and that a certain sort of literary intelligence goes with the slow speed, and a certain other sort with the fast. As I see it the slow reader has the better chance of attaining to good criticism and the fast reader to good literary history. The best literary criticism, it goes without saying, would be the work of a slow reader whose mature intellectual life was long enough to allow him to read with his minute perceptiveness all the books that go to make up that history; obviously good literary history, speaking ideally, would proceed *pari passu* with good criticism. But, as a matter of practice, it often seems to get on quite satisfactorily without that benefit. With little repining we accept as literary history what is mainly an account of literary matters at their most graspable; it is often a record of surfaces—of titles, dates, 'kinds', foreign models, stanza-forms, and the like. We do not expect, or Englishmen do not, that it should show the sequence of mental events that the sequence of books produced for their readers. Only a slow reader could manage to guess what those events were, and he would not find life long enough to read enough books to see enough of the sequence. Life being brief, it is to the fast reader we look for such literary history as we get: only he can read enough to make more than a beginning. But for attaining to criticism, which has nothing to do with sequence unless it so chooses, slow reading would seem to provide more favourable conditions.

I might argue the case in this way. There are certain occasions when a slow-reading critic wishes he could read fast. If that means merely that he wishes he could get through more books, the wish is childish—an adult sense tells him that the wish would continue to haunt him however great

the number of books he had read. It is a wish that has nothing
to do with criticism: it merely protests against the conditions
of our existence. Standing in the twentieth century and
looking around us and back into the past, whether we read
fast or slow, the books we 'ought to have read' are piled
so mountainously as to make the few more or the few less
scarcely worth computing. But if in wishing he could read
fast the slow-reading critic means that he is not getting
enough out of the book he is reading slowly, that is a sign
that he is reading the wrong book. And, I should add, a book
not worth criticising at the pitch I am considering. All good
books are worth reading slowly. Yes, but the fast reader,
you may say, has this advantage, he can find more such books
than the slow reader, which he can proceed to read slowly
when found: a fast reader, it may be held, can read slowly on
occasions. But here I appeal to my original assumption that
the sort of critical intelligence that goes with slow reading
differs from the sort that goes with fast. A fast reader cannot
get out of a book what a slow reader gets merely by slowing
down—what a fast reader gets by going slower is aches and
pains. A fast reader makes a poor slow reader. A slow reader
is gifted and trained to discern a range of literary phenomena
which the eye of the fast reader is largely unaware of and
which a mere slowing down is not a sure means to acquiring
the organs to discern. Only a reader who is contentedly and
rejoicingly slow comes close to the nature of literature. For
only he sees literature as of necessity composite, an aggregate
of *minutiae*, a coral-reef of thought and writing. A book may
be a big thing, but it is small things that make it so: it does
not come into existence like the lettered tablet that Leonato,
after the departure of Jupiter, found on his breast; it does not
assume its shape at an explosion or supernatural *fiat*. What it

has of instantaneity is the rapidly repeated instantaneity of a string of moments, drops of water in a stream which, even when a torrent, is composed of separate words, combined in groups, however strictly contributory the smaller to the larger. A writer—any writer—is a purveyor of small things, however large they mount up to in sum. And few small things strike a fast reader hard enough to induce him to pause and have a good look at them.

I pause myself at this point to help give small things their due. They are in no danger of lacking homage, and from quarters that command our best respect. Nor need we fly to priests and professional moralists to have their general importance confirmed. On every hand secular literature is strewn with a sad recognition of their crucial importance for us—sad because of the many unresisted temptations to deal with things immense, vague and distant. Our merely secular writers have issued many warnings. At their strongest the warnings concern conduct. There is Blake's:

> He who would do good to another, must do it in Minute Particulars.
> General Good is the plea of the Scoundrel hypocrite & flatterer.[1]

And on many occasions Dr. Johnson: for instance the paragraph on the moral of *The Rape of the Lock*, or this

Life is made up of little things; and that character is the best which does little but repeated acts of beneficence,[2]

which Wordsworth recalled in the 'little nameless un-remembered acts' of 'Tintern Abbey', and on which Dickens's Mrs. Jellyby provides a complicated gloss. To care for detail is one of the first requisites of living well, and so of learning well (see Newman's sample of 'a sufficient examination' that

---

[1] *Jerusalem*, ch. 3.
[2] Hesther Lynch Piozzi, *Anecdotes of Samuel Johnson*, ed. S. C. Roberts, 1932 edition, p. 60.

got no further than trying a pupil's awareness of the ramifications of a single word),[1] and so of writing well (and so of criticising well).[2]

If we follow the words of a book slowly there is nothing odd in this procedure: we are not the first to do so. The writer was slow before the slow reader. And if for some accidental reason he did not read his manuscript slowly several times, he had read it slowly while he was writing it. Writing is done more slowly even than slow reading. Even Defoe and Trollope wrote slowly comparatively to reading even when reading is slow. And we have enough evidence to guess how slowly poets like Milton wrote, or prose writers like Pater. One line, for instance, of the MS. of 'Comus' tells a tale of what may be long stretches of minutes: Milton first wrote (and this presumably when writing up the poem in fair copy):

& every bosky

Having proceeded so far, having pushed out so far into the silent whiteness of the paper where no writing ever came before, he paused and erased 'bosky'. He then ventured out a little further, but only with new ink-marks not with new thought, though he was now more certain of the rightness of his previous thought. The line now stood

& every ~~bosky~~ bosky

---

[1] *The Idea of a University*, pp. 336 ff.

[2] In his chapter 'Of the Foreground' in *Modern Painters*, Ruskin with all his lucid conciseness has much to say on the matter:

'The higher the mind, it may be taken as a universal rule, the less it will scorn that which appears to be small or unimportant; and the rank of a painter may always be determined by observing how he uses, and with what respect he views the minutiae of nature. Greatness of mind is not shown by admitting small things, but by making small things great under its influence. He who can take no interest in what is small will take false interest in what is great; he who cannot make a bank sublime will make a mountain ridiculous' (*Works*, iii. 491).

c

The process was then repeated. The completed line reads

& every ~~bosky~~ ~~bosky~~ bosky bourne from side, to side.[1]

Even slap-dash writers usually have slowness thrust upon them at some point. When they are lucky that point comes before publication. If not, afterwards, when they are revising for a later edition. At some stage or other they become conscious of their writing as having to stand the gaze of the public and so look at it slowly in order to look at it critically. We can take it that a writer is thoroughly, and perhaps painfully, conscious of his performance, and conscious of it, therefore, as a shepherding of *minutiae*. In his turn the critic must go slowly if he is to be aware of the thinking as thinking that is thought and of the writing as writing that is written. To take the second point first. Only slow reading provides the conditions for becoming closely aware of the written writing, of the expression. For however spacious are the means of a book in conception, they are necessarily small scale in execution. A book takes on its being as the pen progresses along the score or so of lines that there is room for on each page. A slow reader, therefore, has most chance to be aware of what outsiders, or the authors themselves in self-mockery, call 'the tricks of the trade'. Of the facial conformation, as it were, of a piece of writing a fast reader cannot have more than a hazy notion—of its diction, the straight or angular run of its sentences, its embedded verbal debt to other writers (what debt can be sincerer?), its terms so repeated as to form a terminology, its imagery, and so on through niceties by the score—all those tell-tale delicacies which, if he has chosen his book well, are the work of a mind subtler than his own and which call for his best attentiveness. And missing all this,

[1] *Comus*, l. 312. *Facsimile of the Manuscript of Milton's Minor Poems* [*at*] *Trinity College Cambridge*, 1899, p. 15.

or missing it in its due exactness, the fast reader will miss what these things have to tell him, their intimations of things that even fast readers consider of moment. If he is interested in the man, then we have excellent and much-supported authority for saying that the man exists in the style. If he is interested in the matter, then we have Wordsworth's penetrating remark that 'The matter of style very much comes out of the manner'.[1]

Which brings me to the second of my points: the thinking. What an author's thinking amounts to in the mass of a book is, no doubt, as discernible by the fast reader as by the slow. Perhaps more so. But is the sum of the thought the proper object of reading? Surely not when we are considering such books as are the object of the critics I am considering. The sum of the thinking is a *précis* of it—in other words, a rethinking. And so another thing—a reduced diagram in black and white doing duty for a canvas 'vast and of a daedal complexity', and, moreover, a diagram that pays little attention to how a canvas painted by Turner differs from one painted by Hogarth or Constable. It is surely the barefoot journey traced by the thought that is the interesting thing, a journey which a slow reader accompanies at an appropriate pace, attending and participating in its perils and calms as the squire in the romances accompanied the knight.

IV

I HAVE indulged in this justification of slow reading because method 2 is more easily chosen by a slow reader than by a fast one. But in any event method 2 must have something to commend it to every reader since to write criticism in accordance with it is to respect the conditions under which

[1] Quoted by Bagehot, *Physics and Politics*, 1872, p. 96.

reading proceeds at whatever pace. It is one of the recommendations of method 2 that it respects the conditions under which any sort of reader reads a book and during and after reading 'possesses' it. To explain what I mean I propose to invade in amateurish fashion the territory of the psychologist.

For the bibliographer and textual critic—not to mention the book-collector—the conditions of possession are enviably concrete. For the one the book is a material object to be examined and described, for the other a means, single or in combination, for arriving at the right words in the right order. But for the reader a book is an entity more elusive. Though like the bibliographer he holds it in his hand, the conditions of his possessing it are more wholly abstract. If the reader is also a critic and a critic who writes, his written criticism will be his attempt to possess it also on paper. However solid his possession may seem to himself and to some of his readers, it must in the nature of things be much less graspable, much less explicable, than the possession achieved also on paper by the bibliographer and textual critic.

First to distinguish the possession of a book that may be called 'moral' possession. Readers vary as man from man— but not more than that. Most of them feel they possess the contents of a book most thoroughly as they have 'judged' it. By that I mean reached an opinion about its soundness, about the degree of soundness of its matter when tested against the reader's own knowledge. And usually, since we are considering works of literature, against the reader's own knowledge of common life, his experience of it that is either sound already or on the painful way to becoming so. That sound experience provides the standard by which the matter of any book of literature is tested, however widely it enlarges

the reader's experience or suggests new aspects and evalua-
tions of it. The reader forms a judgment, pronouncing—the
confidence of that word!—the book good, bad or in-
different. This judgment is usually held to be a satisfactory
possession after reading; having formed it the reader feels he
possesses the book as practically, if as merely that, as he
possesses a dog he holds by the leash. Unless he is a critic,
he will not formulate his judgment in detail, or examine on
what it rests. But he is confident he grasps it as a practical
thing. I shall say no more of this. Obviously it concerns all
critics, whatever method they choose of writing of the object.
They have all judged a book before they write of it, and they
are best employed—I note in passing—in explaining what
they have judged to be good.

But there is a further sense in which the reader can say
he possesses a book. He possesses it as a mental image. When
I think of this read book or that my memory throws up what
I can only call a cloud, a cloud not very luminous, sometimes
merely a darkness more or less 'visible'. If I think, say, of
*Hamlet*, which like most students of English literature I know
almost by heart, the nearest I can come at any one moment to
seeing it as a whole is to see a cloud, rich like shadows painted
by Matthew Smith, a cloud that strikes awe as if it were of
incense, but vague and ungraspable, a thing possessed clearly
only in so far as I recall details of the play during the time I
devote to musing on the cloud. The details recalled, apparently
at random, 'spring to mind' one at a time, however fast they
succeed each other. That is what a piece of literature so short
as *Hamlet* means to me in retrospect; and it follows in general
that the bigger the piece the hazier the cloud and the more
widely scattered the details springing out of it as I muse. It
was because of the imprecision of the vast object in the

memory that when Garrick, trying to rise to an occasion, wrote 'An Ode upon Dedicating a Building, and Erecting a Statue to Shakespeare, at Stratford upon Avon' he was obliged to rely on the typographer for the sublimities he did not filch from Gray:

> Prepare! prepare! prepare!
> At once pour forth the choral song,
> Roll the full tide of harmony along;
> Let Rapture sweep the trembling strings,
> And Fame expanding all her wings,
> With all her trumpet-tongues proclaim,
> The lov'd, rever'd, immortal name!
> SHAKESPEARE! SHAKESPEARE! SHAKESPEARE![1]

And the pious yell is repeated. We know how detailed and exact is an actor's knowledge of the text of a play—or much of it—if he can give his memory time to recall it word by word. And yet the play as a whole, even for an actor, is as ungraspable as Garrick found Shakespeare.

The cloud I have spoken of we can observe forming as we experience the act of reading. Literature begins for the reader as an impression on the sense of sight, an impression upon which the mind works, depositing the result in the memory (I need not strive to speak more accurately than the present purpose calls for). It is at this first point—the point of contact with its words—that literature is most vivid for us. But such are the conditions under which writing communicates itself that the eye can see only a short span of it at any one moment. With a picture it is otherwise: when we look at a picture we can take it in as a whole as if its total coloured square were pushing more or less evenly into our consciousness. But a piece of literature is, so to speak, a league-long stretch of

[1] 1769, p. 2.

ribbon moving out of total darkness across a beam of light
into what at best is luminous cloud. The beam of light is
narrow. All that is lighted of the ribbon at one time is an
inch or two of the leagues. The vivid lighted beginning of
even so short a piece as a page is already passing into the
twilight of memory by the time its lighted close is making
its own vivid impression on the sense of sight. And when
literature exists to the length of a book and we bring down the
cover on the vivid last page, what we recall of the first is
so dim as almost to be atmospheric. And if we convert this
cloud back to vivid experience by a fresh contact with
chapter 1 we find the memory of the close of the book,
the vivid immediate experience of a few moments ago,
already starting to fade.

It follows from this that, existing complete only in the
memory, a piece of literature longer than a short lyric or
epigram can never be discerned as a whole distinct enough
to have a shape. The notion that it could may well come from
Aristotle who said that no piece of it intended to stand by
itself should be larger than can be taken in by the mind's eye;
pieces that offended by being too big he compared to animals
so huge as to stretch out of sight. Perhaps he was again basing
too much on that favourite play of his: *Oedipus Tyrannus*,
as Newman saw, was no fair measuring rod for other Greek
tragedies.[1] Certainly it is an exceptional play and may well
be one of the few sizable pieces of literature that come near
to having a shape for the memory of reader and play-goer:
the stages in the action are so strong and simple as to stand
out in the memory like the shining bones of a skeleton,
refusing to fade to the degree that those of other plays fade.
*Oedipus Tyrannus* may have encouraged Aristotle to generalise

[1] See pp. 150 ff. below.

too readily, to think a book read by a critic as seizable as a book held in the hand by a bibliographer, a play sat through as sizable for the mind as a horse for the eye. Take for instance the evidence of Gray's 'Progress of Poesy'. Like any other piece it gives us the vivid moments as we read ahead. Like the best pieces of literature its course is agreed to be sound: Matthew Arnold praised its 'evolution' as 'sound' as well as 'noble'.[1] Looking back on the poem, we see it as a rich blur starting into detail as we go on gazing, and this despite the egregious care Gray expended on its patterning on paper—the poem consists of three identical metrical sections each comprising three exquisitely varied sub-sections: one might compare it to three tricolors extended side by side after all three of them have been identically cut into an elaborate pattern. As an elaborate and scrupulously contrived shape on paper it is unique in English poetry except for the other big ode of Gray. But so far as the reader goes this care is largely wasted. Speaking for myself I read and re-read the poem over years without suspecting the existence of the pattern, and now I know of its existence I can only keep it in mind while reading by an effort of will which detracts from the attention I am paying the moments as they come. My knowledge that the scheme on paper is what it is may have the effect of making me think that my memory of the poem has some unusual degree of shape blocked out in the blur. But even so, it is not a shape I can experience as vividly as I experience its details. Gray's exquisite tripartite tallying is a pattern for the typographer rather than the reader. When the poem is read it is for its moments and the sound and noble evolution that carries them on its back.

[1] *Essays in Criticism: Second Series*, p. 99.   Cf. *Discourses in America*, 1885, pp. 156 f.

There is no need for us to be surprised at this. After all, the main reason why we read a book is to meet the moments in their vividness. We do not read it to have a memory of it, but to accompany its sentences from cover to cover. We do not go to the theatre *to have been*, to look back on an experience, even so strong and shapely a one as that provided by a performance of *Oedipus Tyrannus*: we go to see the 'two hours' traffic of [the] stage', to go through a long experience fluctuating in interest, of necessity and by design, but rising repeatedly to crests of present vividness.

v

VAGUE as is the memory of a whole book, it must be faced by the critic. No two clouds are alike since the books producing them are unique. The critic must be aware of how the vagueness of one book differs from the vagueness of another. And it is partly because he feels an inexplicable but reliable confidence in his capacity to keep all these vague and subtle things apart that he is a good critic. It is for this reason that a critic is, among other things, some part of a poet. A poet describes the sky over Helvellyn or Suffolk, a critic the cloud of a book. He feels he possesses a mysterious means of grasping the cloud enough to persuade his readers that they, too, discern what he is speaking of. When Coleridge criticising *Antony and Cleopatra* finds the phrase 'happy valiancy of style',[1] he carries his reader with him: at least it is clear that something has been seen in the style of the play that is not to be seen in that of *Julius Caesar* or *Much Ado* or most of the other plays of Shakespeare. When the critic achieves this degree of sound poetry we accept it, vague as it is—or rather vague as it may seem to those on whom much of

[1] *Coleridge's Shakespearean Criticism*, ed. T. M. Raysor, 1930, i. 86.

poetry is lost. Its achievement is one sign that the critic is a good one, one sign that he is trying to go a step further than that bold step taken by Mozart when he said that he could hear each of his symphonies as one note. For the critic tries to find a means for making the reader hear that mysterious nexus of a note. What he proceeds to say of the symphony or the poems must be said, as it were, in the key that note establishes. Impalpable as the cloud is, his awareness of it governs what he writes. For a poor critic all clouds are alike; he has one piece of criticism which serves all turns by having stuck in it first the name of one author and then that of another. Conversely if a good critic were to leave out of his piece of criticism all names of men and books we ought to be able to insert them for ourselves. It is because Pater when speaking of individual works and their producers makes them out as rather like his own and himself that on those occasions his criticism is autobiographical poetry, and only good criticism of himself. Striving to master the cloud with words, the critic cannot forget a certain number of the moments when, with that forming cloud as background, a vivid bit of the book lay before his eye.

## VI

THE details of literature, then, are the most vivid things about it especially when, the detail being a climax in paragraph, page or chapter, the mind is participating most actively with the glittering eye. To snatch up at random a few such 'climaxes' from the literature of the nineteenth century —into my list I do not recommend the reader to do more than dip—there is Wordsworth's record of the star-shaped shadow cast by a daisy on a naked stone;[1] or his words describing

[1] 'So fair, so sweet . . .' ll. 5 f.

Charles Lamb, 'the frolic and the gentle';[1] or Coleridge's
'one red leaf';[2] or Carlyle's headshake at the stars, 'Eh! It's a
*sad* sight!';[3] or Tennyson's calling a scholar (who shall
remain nameless because inoffensive) 'that louse on the locks
of literature'; or his lines about the ships in the Channel that

> . . . on thro' zones of light and shadow
> Glimmer away to the lonely deep;[4]

or Thackeray's phrase for Lady Kew, again in London,
'tramping about in her grim pursuit of pleasure';[5] or his sharp
injunction 'excavate your heart';[6] or Dickens's 'Talent,
Mr. Micawber has; capital, Mr. Micawber has not';[7] or his
'smoke, which is the ivy of London';[8] or his 'Fruits is in, cats
is out';[9] or Browning's 'but don't jog the ice';[10] or Clough's
'grave man, nicknamed Adam';[11] or that Johnsonian flash and
rumble from F. H. Bradley, 'the unearthly ballet of bloodless
categories';[12] or Lear's 'Runcible Spoon',[13] and his 'purpledi-
cular crags';[14] or Arnold's

> . . . unplumb'd, salt, estranging sea;[15]

or his 'powerful, but at present somewhat narrow-toned organ,
the modern Englishman';[16] or *Punch*'s charades and riddles offer-

[1] 'Extempore Effusion upon the Death of James Hogg', l. 19.
[2] 'Christabel', i. 49.
[3] R. H. Horne, *The New Spirit of the Age*, 1844, ii. 280.
[4] 'To the Rev. F. D. Maurice', ll. 27 f.
[5] *The Newcomes*, ch. li.
[6] id., ch. xxviii.
[7] *David Copperfield*, ch. xvii.
[8] *Bleak House*, ch. x.
[9] *Pickwick Papers*, ch. xix; Sam Weller is recalling his acquaintance with a pieman.
[10] 'Bishop Blougram's Apology'.
[11] *The Bothie*, i. 20.
[12] *Principles of Logic*, 1883, p. 533: cf. such phrases of Johnson's as 'this lagging
race of frosty grovellers' (*Lives*, i. 138.)
[13] *The Complete Nonsense of Edward Lear*, ed. Holbrook Jackson, 1947, p. 211.
On p. 219 a raven is runcible, on p. 250 a goose and a wall.
[14] id., p. 230.
[15] 'Isolation', last line.
[16] *Essays in Criticism*, p. xiv.

ed as easy enough for solving in a heat-wave;[1] or Swinburne's

> Life is the lust of a lamp for the light that is dark till the dawn of the
> day when we die;[2]

or the turning long neck of Ethel in *The Newcomes*,[3] and that
other neck, Rosemond's in *Middlemarch*, lofty and consciously
revolved;[4] or the conclusion of one of Dodgson's examples
in his *Symbolic Logic*, 'No hedgehog takes in *The Times*';[5] or
Newman's words 'the stars of this lower heaven were one
by one going out' and equally his sentence of most familiar
English: 'The table was then shoved back a bit';[6] or this:[7]

or Morris's

> Many scarlet bricks there were
> In its walls, and old grey stone;[8]

---

[1] Vol. lviii, 1870, p. 248: e.g. 'Why is a man who, when at Dover, is *going to
Deal*, like a gentleman at a card-table, going to deal for whist? *Answer:* Because
he is going to deal.' It was during this heat-wave, by the way, that Dickens died.

[2] 'Nymphelidia', l. 16.        [3] ch. xxv.

[4] e.g. in ch. lviii. 'Martinus Scriblerus' in the *Memoirs*, ch. x, 'charg'd all
Husbands to take notice of the Posture of the Head of such as are courted to
Matrimony, as that upon which their future happiness did much depend.'

[5] Part I, 1896, p. 157.        [6] *Apologia*, Part V, and *Loss and Gain*, Part II. ch. xix.

[7] *H.M.S. Pinafore: or, The Lass that Loved a Sailor. An Entirely Original Nautical
Comic Opera in Two Acts. Written by W. S. Gilbert, composed by Arthur Sullivan*,
1878, p. 14.

[8] 'Golden Wings', ll. 5 f. *The Defence of Guenevere*, 1858, p. 202.

or Meredith's

> Sharp as a sickle is the edge of shade and shine;[1]

or Hopkins's

> It is Margaret you mourn for;[2]

or Kingsley's

> . . . my child's laugh rang through me;[3]

or the pattern to which Miss Prism constructed her three-volume novel:

The good ended happily and the bad unhappily. That is what Fiction means;[4]

or Henry James's nurse who suggested 'a combination of the barmaid and the nun';[5] or Max's 'ideal of happiness' as 'a four-poster bed in a field of poppies and mandragora'.[6]

## VII

TO STRING out these details is to come very close to literature, to feel close to it as it is a thing written, almost to see the manuscript of it as still wet. With a detail such as these under his eye the critic must feel at least as close to literature as the youngster with a spoonful of salt who approaches the tail of a robin. And when he chooses method 2, part of his set purpose is to place details of the object actually under the eye of the reader. As he reads the criticism, the reader finds his moments vivid with the vividness of the

---

[1] 'Love in the Valley', l. 118. Meredith is indebted to Ruskin here: cf. the chapter on 'The Truth of Chiaroscuro' in *Modern Painters*, II. II. iii, especially such a remark as 'For no outline of objects whatsoever is so sharp as the edge of a close shadow' (*Works*, iii. 304).

[2] 'Spring and Fall', l. 15.

[3] 'A Lament', l. 4.

[4] Oscar Wilde, *The Importance of Being Earnest*, Act II.

[5] *The Tragic Muse*, ch. xxxii.

[6] Recalled as having been written by him 'as a youngish man . . . in some newspaper, or in some book' (Max Beerbohm, *Mainly on the Air*, 1946, p. 51).

object itself, not simply with the vividness, the competing or usurping vividness, of the critic's prose. Having details of the object itself before him, he can 'follow' the critic, a critic of his critic: the material is visible as well as the comment on it. His hands like the critic's are green with the poet's meadow. Whether he comes nearer still or recoils, he has had a sharp experience. It is a great thing for a critic to make his reader touch the object, where alone it is touchable, at points on its career. The critic, of course, has other things to do besides touching details, and making his reader touch them. But that other work is done on materials that have come to him detail by detail, and if dull instead of sharp, his memory of them will not even be a cloud that has luminousness, a blur that is rich—it will be fog. Details like the ones I have snatched from their context remain bright 'jewels five words long'. They invite the critic to perceive them truly. The style which is the man exists in them as surely as in a book. Of each of them it could be maintained that only their author could have written it just so. The uniqueness of literature even down to its *minutiae* is a measure of one of the critic's difficulties.

As I have said, the critic has also other work to do. His beloved details are parts of a whole. Bright as they are when detached, they are not merely jewels, aphorisms, memorable phrases, striking points. To be details that satisfy us where they live in the midst of a piece of writing, they must satisfy us as men for whom life itself has 'made sense' by running in accordance with the logic—accepted as firm if seen as obscure—of cause and effect. They must satisfy what I spoke of earlier as our judgment. If the writer is worth his salt, the vivid details are not tossed at random into space: they are allotted fixed places on the ribbon. And the welcome we accord them will depend on what has gone before, on the strength of a causal relationship. If moments existing on the first page of a book are vivid, are already 'climaxes', that is because their predecessors lie available and 'tickle o' the sere' in our stored experience of life. Sterne's famously vivid first sentence—'They order, said I, this matter better in France'—is a detail strong enough to imply predecessors: it calls out the ghosts of the passions of Agincourt, and other passions too. The details I have just set out can all of them be immediately related to excitable past experiences. Even so, remarks comparable in force will be more forceful still if they come late in their respective books, always provided that the writer has used his opportunities for satisfying our judgment that causes are working forward to their due effect. The remark quoted above about Lady Kew has more force in *The Newcomes* than when taken out of the book, and more force in the fifty-first chapter than it could have had in the first—part of its sad ferocity lies in the old woman's being seen as *again* on the tramp. Even the refrain line that ends a villanelle has the chance of being more forceful than its predecessors. (And the reverse is true: if the poet has failed to interest us by satisfying our judgment, its last appearance will be the weakest.) Newman—to revert to his essay once more—did not allow for this. Rightly seeing the value of the moments, he failed to appreciate how much of that value accrued from what had preceded them; he did not discern that the moments of dramatic or poetic vividness pierce us as the play has prepared us to be pierced. It is because of the weight that foregoing details can add to later that authors have often done what they could to keep the memory of the reader aware of certain atoms in its cloud. Powerless by means of words to create in the memory a great shape, they

have used numerous devices in the midst of their writing for
harking back—recapitulations, reminders, reiterated phrases
and images, patternings, wheels coming full circle, dramatic
irony, runs of short words which force themselves back on
the consciousness, and which, making a crucial distinction,
we call 'memorable'.

And so the critic puts back his details where he found them.
The bright particulars are returned to the huge and vague.
But to write criticism according to method 2 is not to let
details fade again. Indeed it is to use them as a means of
making the cloud itself as vivid as possible. I have said that the
critic choosing method 3 and writing at a distance from his
object does not often distinguish the image of his author's
works with due subtlety, that he often merges the green of a
meadow with that of a cricket field. And I have also said that
the good critic feels a confidence that he can make just such
distinctions. To make them, however, is more difficult even
for a good critic when he is stationed far from the object.
It is safer to keep close, to examine detail, and re-examine it,
not to be afraid of the text in all its moment-by-moment
actuality. After all, both poets and men in general prefer
concrete to vague. Operating to the advantage of the vivid,
method 2 is a means of satisfying that preference. And without forfeiting the vague. To choose method 2 is, as I have put
it, 'to write of the small trove—a village or rich valley—in
the light of the whole country tramped over'. Inevitably,
therefore, to write also of the whole country in the light of the
detail. And according to the detail chosen to write of it well or
ill. Any detail whatever cannot but exist in a relation to the
whole of which it is part. Some details, however, are related
more vitally than others, and the critic choosing method 2
tries to discover which those are. Well chosen, the detail

represents the rest; it is detail as emblem and symbol of the whole, as *locus classicus* where the whole concentrates itself, the clue to its maze, the 'key' to its great wards, the 'secret'[1] of its huge unwieldy being. The critic can lay hold on the cloud as he can show it existing in the part. For the part, unlike the whole, is quotable and can be seen whole and vivid at one and the same time.

The choice of the detail is a momentous one to make. It represents an act of criticism over and above theirs who choose methods 1 and 3. Much depends on its rightness. If it is too light it lets down the author's works, if not square tilts the whole structure. Off-hand we should say that Aristotle's *Art of Poetry* shows a critic choosing 3. But in part at least he may have chosen 2 under the guise of choosing 3: he may have seen Greek tragedy through *Oedipus Tyrannus*. And, therefore, if we are to believe Newman, he saw it wrong. Nearer home there is Arnold's unhappy choice of the *vice essentiel* of Gray: the nature of Gray's achievement was seen falsely in so far as it was seen in the light of the words 'He never spoke out'.

## VIII

I HAVE used the words 'whole works' repeatedly, and too· glibly. It will appear to many of my readers, as it sometimes appears to myself, that, having chosen method 2, my worst

---

[1] As a term in general criticism 'secret' has had a longish history, not yet ended. Carlyle and Newman used it. Arnold was fond of it. And Pater too: see pp. 121 and 144 below. It strikes a modern reader as rather too coy a term. It struck Henry James so: he laughed at it; on p. 117 below he fires it out as part of the battery of Mrs. Church, the cheerful pathetic culture-getter. Mr. T. S. Eliot has laughed at it, and with reason—Arnold had gone so far as to speak of the secret of Jesus. Arnold was fond also of the expression 'to put the finger on', which he may have learned from Newman, an expression denoting that you think you have caught something small but of huge importance—an insect either terribly noxious or of a scarab-like sanctity.

failing is not having applied the principle bound up in choosing it to an object that is as complete as its author made it. Instead of writing of Arnold whole—on the author who stretches from *The Strayed Reveller* to *God and the Bible* and *Discourses in America*—I have written on him mainly as a literary critic. And so of Pater, though of him more completely. And so of Newman. Granted that it is unwise to choose method 3, and stick to it, I admit that I should think better of myself if I had proved myself equal, having chosen the standpoint and, I hope, the vantage-point of a part of them, to viewing my author's writings as a whole. A writer's work is a whole, and should be written of as such.

Ideally it should, whatever the author. But in practice authors differ in the range of demands they make of their critics. Some make one sort of demand only, and if the critic has elected to criticise such an author at all, he can criticise him whole: he has drawn to this author rather than that because of mutual congeniality, and to the critic's powers each separate work in the complete works of the author is congenial equally. One such author is Jane Austen: another, Emily Dickinson: to be able to criticise *Emma* with authority is to be able to criticise with authority the rest of her novels and stories, and the poems of Emily Dickinson are flowers on the same tree, or gaudies on the same Christmas tree. They can be written of complete by one and the same critic. But the writings of many authors are various enough within themselves to outwit any single critic. There are no critics equal, singly, to giving them criticism that has a uniform authority. Even the powers of critics who are great critics are limited. For all the domes of brow of Bradley and Ker—to name two recent giants—had they fingers that tapered finely enough to touch the quick of small things?

Or to name another, had Raleigh, with all his boyish energy and adult judgment, enough fineness? He himself confessed to a degree of puzzlement before the mysteries of the lyrical which to certain other critics seems an unduly high degree:

The worst of it is you cannot lecture on really pure poetry any more than you can talk about the ingredients of pure water—it is adulterated, methylated, sanded poetry that makes the best lectures.[1]

In a letter about the same date he made a slight recovery:

I have been reading Christina Rossetti—she is wonderful. I am very glad I have not to lecture on her, for it is pure poetry. I want to quote this little poem to you as a contrast to fubsy old Browning's *Any Wife*:

> 'Shall I forget on this side of the grave?
> I promise nothing: you must wait and see,
>       Patient and brave.
> (O my soul, watch with him, and he with me.)
>
> Shall I forget in peace of Paradise?
> I promise nothing: follow, friend, and see,
>       Faithful and wise.
> (O my soul, lead the way he walks with me.)'

I think that is very splendid, especially in the device of the brackets to express a half articulate prayer.[2]

But surely certain critics can hope to penetrate further into that piece of pure poetry than Raleigh did on this occasion, as the scientist penetrates into pure water. Even Bradley, Ker and Raleigh had their limitations, Raleigh here admitting as much. Lesser critics, outwitted like him but not so frank, 'cover the ground', as the phrase is, regardless of whether they are trespassing or not. One way of admitting to powers narrower than the powers called for by your object complete

[1] Letter of 11 January, 1892, in *The Letters of Sir Walter Raleigh* (1879-1922), ed. Lady Raleigh with a preface by David Nichol Smith, 1928 edition, i. 164.
[2] op. cit., i. 164 f.

is to reject some of it. But if lacking the due powers, you do
retain it whole, the sum effect is that in your hands it trims
itself. You cannot assume powers you have no right to
without being (to a fine judgment) embarrassed by them.
What you say about the part of the object that lies beyond
them is words-words-words. I have tried from one point of
vantage to write on Henry James whole (except for the plays).
This was possible for me because Henry James—perhaps
even when the novels are completed by the plays—is a
writer who makes the same sort of demands from first to
last. But Arnold is another matter. I cannot say that as a
critic I have boxed his compass, though as a reader I have
read him almost complete—who now reads, who ever read,
*Merope*? Arnold began his career with *The Strayed Reveller*
and ended it with *Discourses in America*. The poem which
gave its name to his first book contains these lines:

> . . . the dark ship
> On the foamless, long-heaving
> Violet sea.

The *Discourses in America* contain this sentence:

And Isaiah was right, as Plato was right.

Can we, I ask, imagine a critic endowed to criticise with
equal authority and insight the books these fragments come
from and the books that come between their limits, to have
discovered with the mind as well as the eye the product in all
its fulness? We are all critics with blind spots big or little. Nor
can we take comfort in the knowledge that Arnold himself
lacked authority to deal with his huge and varied object
whole. Some of the many fields he entered he entered over
the hedge. But the critic of his earnest theological jollifications
who has authority must enter those fields through the gate,

and also enjoy the sight of the hay that Arnold made in them. Arnold must not only be shooed away but delighted in. His gay and graceful mixture of poet, philosopher and pamphleteer may well outwit any one critic. All critics can come by the sight of any piece of literature, can attain to an image of it, but not all can get 'moral' possession of all kinds of pieces: as authors depart from the matter that all men are expert in, the matter of common life, they speak to fewer readers—only to those who have the right sort of knowledge to judge them by.

# I I
## Matthew Arnold: The Critic and the Advocate

IN HIS lectures *On the Study of Celtic Literature* Matthew Arnold settled for a moment on this distinction:

the difference there is between an interested and a disinterested critical habit. [The scholar concerned] deals with this fragment [Arnold is speaking of 'the *Juvencus* manuscript at Cambridge']; but, in spite of all his great acuteness and learning, because he has a bias, because he does not bring to these matters the disinterested spirit they need, he is capable of getting rid, quite unwarrantably, of a particular word in a fragment which does not suit him; his dealing with the verses is an advocate's dealing, not a critic's.

This distinction is a clear one, and it is drawn here at its clearest. The distinction between black and white is scarcely clearer than that between a critic who sees what is there and an advocate who chooses to miss what is there. But the distinction is harder to draw clearly when the object is a bigger and subtler matter than the presence or absence of a series of pen strokes in a manuscript, when the object is a piece of literature, when we leave scholarship for literary criticism. But to draw the distinction is still possible. We can draw it between some of the criticism of Dryden and the criticism of Coleridge. Coleridge had a gift for penetrating into the object (to use the terms Arnold liked), for losing himself in finding the content of written words and of the mind behind them, for finding, say in the writings of Shakespeare or of Wordsworth, qualities subtle and massive which later readers have agreed to be fairly and squarely there. If Aristotle presides over the object like a sun pouring down unobstructed beams, Coleridge is like the wind licking in and out of the object, knowing it thoroughly, knowing (to use Keats's words about him) even the 'Penetralium of [its] mystery.'[1] Aristotle and Coleridge are, in this more complicated sense, critics, not advocates.

Arnold saw that Coleridge was a critic of this quality. In his essay on Joubert, he compared the two men, finding the essence of their likeness [to consist] in this,—that they both had from nature an ardent impulse for seeking the genuine truth on all matters they thought about, and a gift for finding it and recognising it when it was found.[2]

And though he noted further that 'the impulse for seeking it is much rarer than most people think', and that 'to have the gift for finding it is, I need not say, very rare indeed' yet there is ample evidence that Arnold could have been this kind of critic substantially, as well as brilliantly, if he had wanted to. When it is a matter of this kind of criticism, and especially when the object lies in certain fields—I shall revert to this —everybody would agree that Arnold's criticism can be as disinterested as it is penetrating. Arnold can be so good a critic of this kind that he can make us feel that the object of the criticism is itself speaking with his words, saying, 'This is my nature: my "secret", for better or worse, is out.' The following, for example: Arnold's perception of the impure bravado of much of Burns's bacchanalian poetry, his perception of Wordsworth's having encouraged poets to think aloud rather than to make something, his perception of Tennyson's curiousness even in 'simple' passages.[3] And in the Homer lectures this power of perception is pinned down by an elaborate pattern of hard thinking. In these four lectures Arnold's power of co-ordination, of *architectonice*, is

---

[1] *Letters*, p. 72.
[2] *Essays in Criticism*, p. 222.
[3] *The North British Review*, 1853, p. 320, had cited 'Dora' as 'simple'.

probably more complicated than anything he demanded of the architectonic powers of the poet. In those lectures he resembles a champion chess-player who has taken on half-a-dozen opponents each with his board, and moves from one to the other with the minimum of visible effort. His power of penetration, here functioning along with a remarkable architectonic power, is the power of all good critics, and Arnold takes his place with perfect ease among them. But he is not mainly a critic of this kind. For this is literary criticism, and Arnold claims to write criticism. Indeed, whenever he speaks of literary criticism or of the literary critic, he prefixes, like Keble, Newman and Ruskin, a derogative and speaks of 'mere' literary criticism, the 'mere' literary critic. Literature was a criticism of life, and the critic of that criticism was a critic of literature and life together. Arnold's *Essays in Criticism* are criticisms of literature and life together. But as soon as Arnold left 'mere' literary criticism for this larger field, he ceased to be disinterested though he did not cease to claim to be disinterested.

The essay placed in the forefront of the *Essays in Criticism* is an essay on criticism. That essay is not entitled 'The Nature of Criticism' nor even 'The Function of Criticism'; it is entitled 'The Function of Criticism at the Present Time'. Its purport is clear enough for us who can read it alongside *Culture and Anarchy*. But it was not found clear enough at the time, and, together with the essay 'Sweetness and Light' which followed three years later, earned Arnold some notoriety as an ineffectual angel.[1] He had certainly been made to look foolish—on some counts if not on all—by Fitzjames Stephen. And promptly. 'The Functions of Criticism at the Present Time'—its title first had a plural—had appeared in

[1] *Culture and Anarchy*, pp. 72 f.

the distinguished first number of the New Series of the *National Review*, that for November 1864, and Stephen's reply, 'Mr. Matthew Arnold and his Countrymen', followed in the *Saturday Review* for 3 December. This champion of the rest of England allowed Arnold all his liveliness but hoisted him as a transcendentalist self-duped into believing that 'reason'—'absolute, unchanging, of universal validity'—had power to touch the field of practice. Arnold's plea made more sense than Stephen saw, but Stephen did see that it was with practice that, for all his transcendental stuff, Arnold was concerned. To see this was to see Arnold more truly than at some points Arnold had shown himself. For at the centre of his essay he had summed up the virtue of his advertised 'criticism' in the word '*disinterestedness*'. Promising 'functions' he proffered academic remoteness, and he flaunted his abstraction in italics as if he meant by it not enlightenment about facts but unconcernedness with them. No wonder British anger was roused. No wonder Stephen replied with proper strictures—strictures which Arnold was to joke about rather than face when he printed the article (with a singular 'Function', a preface and a few footnotes) in his *Essays* of the following year. Yet the dearest end Arnold had set himself he had achieved: it had become widely known that there had been an explosion. To Arnold's countrymen the lively essay with its score of topical hits proclaimed a rebel in the midst. And to have a rebel in the midst was to have to think, if only about defences.

What was clear and remained so was that Arnold had little disinterestedness himself. His own criticism flouted its rule of 'keeping aloof from practice', 'steadily refusing to lend itself to any . . . ulterior, political, practical considerations'. The very act of taking all that is known and thought in the world and marking off from it 'the best that is known and thought in the world' was itself partisan and 'interested'. Indeed it was only because in this particular island and at that time—as at others—practical matters were being steadily seen to that Arnold was free to affect to be disinterested. The words I have just quoted are followed up with a rush of contemptuous subclauses: 'criticism', Arnold said, steadily refuses

to lend itself to any of those ulterior, political, practical considerations about ideas which plenty of people will be sure to attach to them, which perhaps ought often to be attached to them, which in this country at any rate are certain to be attached to them quite sufficiently, but which criticism has really nothing to do with.

Contemptuous, yes. But it was because practical interests were already quite sufficiently secured that Arnold was free to pose as an ineffectual angel beating his luminous wings in an empyrean of pure ideas. At bottom, he had no wish to stop any fight that was going, but a great wish—if not always enough of a right—to improve, by however small a fraction, the end being fought for. Stephen, indeed, seeing through the mirage, spoke boldly of Arnold's 'mission':

His self-imposed mission is to give good advice to the English people as to their manifold faults. . . .

If we cut out the Arnoldian 'vivacity' from these words— the fun of 'self-imposed' and 'good'—they represent Arnold so fairly that they could stand on his tombstone. The vendor of the Frenchified disinterestedness was a hard-working school inspector with a national mission.

II

SPEAKING generally, however varied were its objects, Arnold's highly interested disinterestedness had a single aim: to produce a certain effect on the British middle class.

Great Britain, as Arnold saw it, badly required reinstating in a Europe dominated by the democratic intelligence of the French and by the regimented vigour of the Germans. The British aristocracy had ceased to count; their heyday had ended when the last, or at least the tallest, candles of the eighteenth century went out in 1832, and they now deserved the nickname *barbarians*. If their class had still held power, Arnold no doubt would have offered a different criticism; his aim would have been to cajole them into effective sympathy with the industrial masses, the 'populace'. But they had ceased to count. And, on the other hand, the power of the populace had not yet begun to count. They were shifting, they were even kicking, in their sleep, but they were still, like Shelley and perhaps himself, ineffectual, and, in Arnold's prophetic eye, were doomed for a long time to remain so. If this class had been in power, no doubt Arnold would have offered a different criticism again: his aim would have been to induce them to save what could still be saved of the toppling culture of the eighteenth century. But they had not yet begun to count. What had begun to count, and to count only too patently, was the middle class, 'the kernel of the nation.'[1] It was this class which was in power and the career of Arnold's criticism was determined accordingly. In his essay on 'The Future of Liberalism', he contrasted his own field with that of Cobbett:

Cobbett's politics were at bottom always governed by one master-thought—the thought of the evil condition of the English labourer. . . . The master-thought by which my politics are governed is rather this—the thought of the bad civilization of the English middle class.[2]

'Improved conduct', Lecky was to say,

[1] *Essays in Criticism*, p. 170.
[2] *Irish Essays and Others*, 1882, p. 141.

and improved circumstances are to an English mind the chief and almost the only measures of progress.[1]

And a later historian:

The English bourgeoisie had never been isolated long enough to frame, except in the spheres of comfort and carnal morality, ideals and standards of its own.[2]

This lack Arnold set himself to remedy. Seeing that 'our middle class and its civilization require to be transformed',[3] he set himself the task of refining that class, 'the great representative of trade and Dissent',[4] of arnoldifying it;[5] of endowing it with 'culture . . . by means of reading, observing and thinking'.[6] The position is elaborated in *Culture and Anarchy*, its practical remedy being well aired in Arnold's books on education, and applied, as he could, in his profession.

### III

WHEN Arnold spoke of literature he spoke as he did because the middle class were in power. Mill had descried,[7] and

---

[1] *The Map of Life*, 1908 edition, p. 10.

[2] G. M. Young, *Victorian England; Portrait of an Age*, 1937 edition, p. 85.

[3] *Irish Essays and Others*, 1882, p. 77.

[4] Cf. *Culture and Anarchy*, p. 75.

[5] Cf. *Culture and Anarchy*, p. 48: 'The individual is required, under pain of being stunted and enfeebled in his own development if he disobeys, to carry others along with him in his march towards perfection, to be continually doing all he can to enlarge and increase the volume of the human stream sweeping thitherward.'

[6] Op cit., p. 89. Mallock laughed at the cultural reading done conscientiously by his Lady Ambrose (*The New Republic*, ii. 36 f.) Cf. Henry James's Mrs. Church, p. 117 below.

[7] Mill spoke of 'the two influences which have chiefly shaped the British character since the days of the Stuarts: commercial money-getting business, and religious Puritanism. Business demanding the whole of the faculties, and whether pursued from duty or the love of gain, regarding as a loss of time whatever does not conduce directly to the end; Puritanism, which looking upon every feeling of human nature, except fear and reverence for God, as a snare, if not as partaking of sin . . .' (*Inaugural Address Delivered to the University of St. Andrews*, 1867, p. 89).

Arnold after him, what Weber and Tawney have regularly proved, that the middle-class Briton of the nineteenth century was descended from the Puritan of the seventeenth.[1] In the descent he had lost both his manly fire and his scars and had gained all that paraphernalia of prosperity which the satiric eye of Arnold was so quick to turn against him. But he was still interested in the old questions; in practical morality, in solid demonstrable values, in ways of succeeding, in religious questions when those questions were tied up with something—indeed with 'something or other'—in the Bible. And because of this, Arnold the advocate could rest confident that his agenda included nothing hopeless. If, in his poems, he had rebelled against the buoyant, though solemn, mood of Rugby, in his prose he was his father's son busying himself cheerfully and optimistically. This course was possible because of his fundamental sympathy with much that lay in and around the 'bad civilization' he sought to improve. He was himself a member of the class he addressed: in the preface to *Essays in Criticism* he acknowledged himself 'a feeble unit' of it. Like his audience he was interested in practical morality—as he read of 'the occurrences of Shelley's private life', the exclamation that broke from him, as it broke from them, was 'What a set! what a world!'[2] He, too, admired and shared the wish to succeed, and to succeed by means of hard work; he, too, revered the Bible and even took up Hebrew to study it more closely. And so, for all his high-hat persiflage, he descended among them not to destroy but to fulfil. In offering the middle class the beautiful high-serious poetry of the world he offered it not as the rival of their Hebraic male religion, but as its

[1] Cf. *Culture and Anarchy*, pp. 55, 56.
[2] *Essays in Criticism: Second Series*, p. 237.

queenly complement. He did not ask them to change their ground so much as to see that their chosen oasis was part of a rich plain. Poetry was religious, too. If consolation and joy were the products of religion, they were also the products of poetry. Arnold had long believed this. In the preface to the 'Poems' of 1853, his first prose piece and the map of so much of his mind, he had quoted Hesiod's divination that 'the Muses . . . were born that they might be "a forgetfulness of evils, and a truce from cares".' Words on this subject came powerfully from a writer whose poems had earnestly sought to console the tedious questionings of a young man's intellect. And, in addition to consolation, the best poetry offered joy. The 1853 preface had also quoted the dictum of Schiller that 'All art . . . is dedicated to joy, and there is no higher and no more serious problem than how to make men happy.' Newman wished religion to suck all things into its fearful and purifying furnace. Arnold wished religion to spread its intensity more widely, even though more thinly, so as to play like a happy breeze over the pleasant savannahs of all human thinking and feeling.[1] Newman offered a deferred white throne of God, but Arnold a paradise at least as accessible as the city of dreaming spires. Poetry is presented as the fulfilment of a lack which Arnold recognized elsewhere:

> And yet men have such need of joy!
> But joy whose grounds are true.

Poetry alone seemed fixed true in a world of changes. It is

---

[1] Arnold had his whole mind behind him here. While he was still in the twenties he told Clough that the

religious sentiment . . . now, I think, is best not regarded alone, but considered in conjunction with the grandeur of the world, love of kindred, love, gratitude, etc., etc.

(*Arnold to Clough*, p. 115.) In a further letter to Clough (id., p. 143) and in the preface to the 1853 *Poems*, the view was applied to modern poetry. And it was pushed further in the Celtic lectures.

founded in the heart of man. Arnold, therefore, did not
present its powers as accidental or miraculous: its 'grounds
are true'. Like Shelley, he believed the doctrine of Longinus
for whom great poetry was literally sincere, the direct echo
of a great soul. Poetry, the source of all this consolation and
joy, was, after all, the speech of members of the British middle
class, i.e., of members purified and ennobled, and speaking,
equally with English, the tongues of Europe. Since it was
understood that man was working towards perfection, here
was not only a handy vehicle to take him nearer his destina-
tion, but a vehicle reassuringly home-made. Different things
had been believed in the eighteenth century; Swift had only a
momentary illusion that *Gulliver's Travels* would 'wonder-
fully mend the world', Pope ceased to write since he could
not hope 'to amend . . . any', and Dr. Johnson agreed that the
moral poetry of 'neither Boileau nor Pope had made the
world much better than [it] found it'. At the close of his
brilliant essay 'Democracy', Arnold admitted, like so many
others, that 'Perfection will never be reached'. But the
British middle class was obviously capable of marching a
good deal nearer to it than it had marched so far.

If Arnold's mingling of religion and poetry slighted
religion as Newman understood religion, it slighted also a
great deal of poetry as everybody understood poetry. For
the religious functions which Arnold attributed to poetry
entailed the rigid corollary that what did not exercise them
might well be other 'excellent and indispensable' things, but
was not poetry. If poetry shared the functions of religion,
only poetry of a certain kind could be allowed the name. By
its fruits of joy and consolation ye shall know it. Authentic
poetry was solemn as church. Charles Lamb's fancy that we
should say a grace before opening *The Faerie Queene* had been

translated into earnest. But though Arnold could say a grace before opening Spenser or Milton or Dante, he felt a difference, almost a guiltiness, when his fingers touched the binding of his Chaucer; Chaucer seemed to resist being put on his honour by the priest. And so Arnold had to rule out Chaucer, and with him all poets lacking 'high seriousness', from among the greatest, the religious, 'the glorious class of the best';[1] and Molière, and the poets of the eighteenth century, who were dismissed below stairs to join the prose writers (poets who looked to satire seemed mean and dirty beside Arnold's angels); and the metaphysical poets, poets already part of the mind of Browning and a number of others. No more than the satirists did Donne offer consolation. Nor could he be said to offer joy. For, as Arnold saw it, joy was a primary human emotion, Wordsworthian, four-square, sane, bland, harmonious—and the joy we get from Donne is more alarming than this Hellenic 'sunshine of the breast.'[2]

We can see Arnold as a clever salesman, a 'portly jeweller from Cheapside', a Bottles as clever as any of those he sought to charm into hearing him. We can see him creating the

[1] I quote below an instance of Henry James's amusement over what happened to Arnold's category of 'the best' when it dropped lower down the intellectual scale: see p. 117. Even as late as 1899 reference to it could still be found amusing as a means of 'placing' people: Anthony Hope made subtle use of it in *The Dolly Dialogues* (1899, p. 37): Mr. Carter is speaking to Miss Sophia Milton whom Mrs. Hilary wants him to marry:

'The Empire wants gentlemen; that's what it wants', said I. . . .

'Men and women', said she, 'who are acquainted with the best that has been said and thought on all important subjects.'

At the time I believed this observation to be original, but I have since been told that it was borrowed. I was delighted with it.

[2] I cannot support my argument by noting Arnold's omission of the life of Cowley from his edition of six of Johnson's Lives. A life of Cowley and its discussion of 'metaphysical' poetry would have been out of place in a book intended as 'a school-edition'. Arnold did, however, entitle the book *The Six Chief Lives from Johnson's 'Lives of the Poets'*.

demand for those particular goods of which he held stock. If 'no race needs . . . refining and elevation . . . more than ours',[1] why did Arnold speak almost solely of poetry when there were also the other potent influences of art and music? The answer is, of course, that Arnold had only poetry and criticism to sell; he betrayed his ignorance whenever he spoke of painting or music. The need of England, her critic-advocate simultaneously warned and tendered, was a need for criticism if she did not want to see herself left behind in the European 'march towards perfection'. If criticism was needed, so was literature and poetry (Arnold did not always trouble to discriminate them), which at their 'best' are also a criticism, a 'criticism of life'. How could the Philistines fail to oppose demand to supply? If they bought—and buy many of them did—they bought because they had been got at by a salesman as expert as themselves. For Arnold drew on all the machinery of salesmanship to carry through his great deal. He was a great selling 'personality', the Shaw of his age; and, as Mr. Garrod has seen,[2] what were the constantly recurring phrases—'grand style', 'high seriousness', 'primary human emotions', 'sweetness and light'—what were they but the slogans that undermined resistance to sales? Undermined resistance at least for a time: it is not long before any catch-phrase drops dead and stinks.

IV

WITH all this at stake, then, Arnold could scarcely be less disinterested as a critic, could scarcely be more an advocate. Criticism was the means for advertising the best and for

[1] *Essays in Criticism: Second Series*, p. 64.
[2] *Poetry and the Criticism of Life*, 1931, pp. 72 f.

making it prevail. It was not in Arnold to be disinterested with
Coleridge's degree of purity. His bent towards advocacy was
the bent of his whole nature, and even when the advocacy
seems to be blowing less like a trade wind, it is not often that
we are given disinterested criticism, even disinterested
literary criticism.

For one thing, Arnold was a satirist. His limited view of
poetry did not allow his gifts full scope in his poems. We
know that his friends were surprised to find the dandy
publishing poetry at all; they had been led to expect something more dashing and brilliant, more waggish, something
in Peacock's vein, perhaps a *Coningsby* or the *Friendship's
Garland* which they got later. Arnold christened his first
volume after one of its constituents, 'The Strayed Reveller'.
The reason for this preference is obscure unless the words
were promoted as a sort of *apologia*, Matt Arnold the reveller
having strayed into poetry. Arnold's view of poetry was,
from the start, Wordsworthian. From the start poetry for
him was solemn as church. But prose was delightful. Arnold
was solemn as a steel bar by nature, and by nature also he
was flippant, gay, loud. He had it in him to be a delicious
satirist. He had all the necessary sensitiveness (despite everything else, he was one of the first of the aesthetes), and he had
the wish to inflict pain. And this potential satirist was
actualised in flashes and stretches of his prose. We are all
familiar with the satire in his social criticism, but satire exists
in the more purely literary criticism too. Whereas Pope put
most of his literary satire into verse, Arnold put almost all
of his into prose. Arnold dubbed Macaulay 'the great apostle
of the Philistines', which, being already a 'heroic' line, might
have gone straight into a satire, say, of Dryden's. Or, from
among the other digs at Macaulay, there is the Popian dig

at his 'pinchbeck Roman Ballads'.[1] Or we read of 'an abyss of platitude . . . and the German nation swimming calmly about in it'. Or Arnold tells Clough that their fellow poet Burbidge sits apart from the general stream of poetry 'under a little gourd'. And so on. We have to discount from Arnold's disinterestedness the element of his vivacity—it is his own word for the dangerous element—discounting it as fun first and criticism, if at all, only after that. It is regrettable in the Homer lectures; regrettable simply because out of place—in itself it is delicious:

'To grunt and sweat under a weary load [sic]';—that does perfectly well where it comes in Shakespeare; but if the translator of Homer . . . were to employ . . . this figure of 'grunting' and 'sweating', we should say, *He Newmanises.*

That, in its context, is one of the most risible moments in the literature of criticism; the metamorphosis of a cranky professor into a household word, a verb.[2] The unpleasantest pages in Arnold are those in which he pleads that no offence was intended. What he meant was that no offence was intended consciously. That he could be so offensive without knowing it is final proof of the force of this most un-scrupulous of talents. Powers were working in him deeper than his famous politeness and his notorious disinterestedness.

Arnold's wicked gifts, suppressed in verse, jetted in prose. The gift of the satirist, however, is no solid help to the critic because the satirist sees things too quickly, too summarily,

---

[1] *On Translating Homer*, p. 50.

[2] The old formula [proper noun] +*ize* was a favourite one at the time. To the instances noted in the *O.E.D.* (s.v. -*ize* § 5), I add three more: in 1836 Harriet Martineau was invited by an American publisher to 'Trollopize' her transatlantic adventures, i.e., write them up as Mrs. Trollope had done hers (J. C. Nevill, *Harriet Martineau*, 1943, p. 64); in 1841 Newman used 'Benthamizing' in 'The Tamworth Reading Room' (*Discussions and Arguments*, p. 263); in 1843 Ruskin recorded the determination of J. B. Pyne, the painter, 'to Pynise everything' (*Works*, iii. 479).

with little of the loafing sympathy that ends in understanding.

And there were other subtle deflections from disinterestedness. Arnold, as I have already said, was an egotist. There is always a strong presence in his essays. His way of writing compels attention, but that attention is directed, not on his object, but on himself and his object together. In the essay on Amiel he stands like an unyielding rock washed around by the waves of Amiel. His essays are monologues. We cannot imagine him employing, as Dryden did, the dialogue form. Arnold's egotism accounts for the high-pitched conversational tone, the ripple of inspired extemporisation, the French grace, the lizard slickness. It accounts for the posturings. We sometimes find him hovering in pretended apprehension when his theme nears a knot that he is perfectly well prepared for. And there are the aesthetic shrinkings. Newman is the only earlier writer I know of who publicly 'shrinks back into his shelly cave with pain' when his sense of the beautiful and the fitting is too rudely brushed.[1] It all makes away from criticism, because you cannot show off and be disinterested at the same time.

Then again, speaking relatively, there was Arnold's ignorance. Obviously Arnold knew a great deal. Nevertheless, placed against Dr. Johnson or Coleridge, he was unlearned. He freely confessed so himself. One of the means to understanding him lies in the phrase he used in a letter to Clough: 'my . . . want of intellectual robustness'; the negatived noun is beautifully chosen. Elsewhere, this time in public, he called himself 'an unlearned belletristic trifler', and

---

[1] There is a discussion—lively if a little portly—of Arnold's 'over-fastidiousness' by his successor in the Chair of Poetry, Francis Hastings Doyle, in *Reminiscences and Opinions*, 1886, pp. 178 ff.

his evident pleasure in the phrase prepares us for those occasions when he not only admitted his lack of robust intellect and knowledge but made light of it. Which is scarcely the Arnold who subscribed to Joubert's remark that 'ignorance in intellectual matters is a crime of the first order'. (At this date, by the way, Arnold preferred to go abroad for a good remark, but on this occasion there was one nearer home, made by Johnson.)[1] No critic, we feel, was ever the worse for knowledge so long as he remained a critic.

There is still another deflection. For Arnold, unlike some at least of his contemporaries, had almost no sense of the historical. He thought he had. But what he possessed was a much flimsier thing—a sense of 'the spirit of the age'. Arnold preferred reading books that philosophised about the past rather than books that doggedly recorded or re-created it. If one has an active mind, a creative mind, nothing is easier than to let it draw coloured fume out of a few 'significant' facts and to treasure that distorting mirage as history. And accordingly there are times when one feels that Arnold knew as much about the English past as a foreigner does. When he wished, for example, to show how well the Elizabethans liked the fantastic, he mentioned the testimony afforded by their portraits, but relied otherwise on Scott's *Kenilworth*. And we find him comparing a hymn in an idyll of Theocritus with the canticle of St. Francis. His comparison takes the form of knocking their astonished heads together. Anyone who really understood those two religious lyrics would edge them together after years of preparation, perhaps after half a volume of print. Arnold lacked an adequate sense of the places originally occupied by old things and by things in

---

[1] 'Ignorance, when it is voluntary, is criminal' (*Rasselas*, ch. xxx).

foreign lands, and when he criticised them, he was a critic not so much of them themselves as of his personal reactions to them. The data were his *ad hoc* reactions. He would group together lines from Homer, Chaucer, Milton, because they had in common a capacity to make a similar impression on Matthew Arnold in the nineteenth century. It follows that Arnold was a good critic, a good literary critic, only within limits—i.e., when the quality of the things criticised had not suffered the almost inevitable fate of deteriorating along with the quite inevitable fate of ageing, or when, criticising contemporary things, he was an authentic historical critic without knowing it.

Arnold's sense of the nineteenth century was historically sound because he had lived in it and was still engaged in doing so. Outside his memory and his sense of the present, history scarcely existed. But within those shining limits, it existed comprehensively, substantially and vividly. Arnold was extraordinarily sensitive to his times, to what he called 'the modern spirit', 'how the world is going'.[1] His pages, whatever their stated object, are a sort of meteorological chart tracing the intellectual weather of Europe and especially the intellectual weather of Britain (or at least some of it: he shows little interest in science). To take one small instance, from his essay on Heine:

The modern spirit is now awake almost everywhere . . . almost everyone now perceives [this] . . . people are even beginning to be shy of denying it.

Later, in the preface to *God and the Bible*, we read that people grow more shy of recourse to the preternatural.

Though the direct connection between literature and morals

[1] *Culture and Anarchy*, pp. 76, 83.

had been seen by Shelley, he did not see with Arnold's almost journalistic eye (or is it still the eye of the diner-out and the satirist here well employed in the service of criticism?) how intellectual matters, literature and poetry, affect not only morals but manners, and manners even at their most delicate, how they can have their say in bringing the blood to the cheek. It is this sort of sensitiveness to a quite new area of intellectual and literary evidence that compensates for Arnold's lack of a robust intellect. He began catching his worms before it was known that the dawn had broken.[1] It seems that here Arnold often gives us criticism and not advocacy. He tells the contemporary truth as a barometer does. Or rather as a seasoned sailor, since for the detection of these conditions of opinion there are no mechanical short cuts; the weather-wise work by instinct.

v

ARNOLD ended his 'Last Words' on Homer with his noble testimonial to the virtues of Clough, his dead friend and dear enemy. Arnold drew the substance of that testimonial from layers of thinking and feeling which make 'Thyrsis' seem, in comparison, a turning to favour and to prettiness:

And how, then, can I help being reminded what a student of this sort we have just lost in Mr. Clough, whose name I have already mentioned in these lectures? He, too, was busy with Homer, but it is not on that account that I now speak of him. Nor do I speak of him in order to call attention to his qualities and powers in general, admirable as these were. I mention him because, in so eminent a degree, he possessed these two

---

[1] Arnold's tombstone bears the words 'Awake, thou Lute and Harp! I will awake right early' (see *D.N.B.*). Cf. *Matthew Arnold's Notebooks*, 1903, p. 48 where, on the death of his son Tommy, the same text is entered up; and his *Letters*, ii. 222, on a commonplace but vivid occasion: 'You may imagine I was on deck with the first light'.

invaluable literary qualities,—a true sense for his object of study, and a single-hearted care for it. . . . In the study of art, poetry, or philosophy, he had the most undivided and disinterested love for his object in itself, the greatest aversion to mixing up with it anything accidental or personal. His interest was in literature itself; and it was this which gave so rare a stamp to his character. . . .

That particular stamp was not the stamp given to the character of Arnold, though some part of his praise of Clough may be transferred to the author of the superb 1853 preface and of the superb Homer lectures which that testimonial rounds off. Arnold, who at thirty avowed that he was three parts iced over, did not freeze any further. He did not shrivel up into the desolate carcass foreseen in his poem 'Growing Old'. Instead of shrivelling, he knit and suppled his frame till it stood that of a hero, indefatigable, more striking than Clough's, vivid with a passion rather than a 'love', a Puritan passion for what he saw to be best, and a missionary passion for making what he saw to be best prevail. What Arnold saw drew a multitude of eyes the way his were looking; and still draws our eyes; for the Victorian age, despite all the jibes of its grandchildren and all the bombs and tanks of its great-grandchildren, recedes from us very slowly.

# III

## Matthew Arnold and Eighteenth-Century Poetry

WHEN we read the writings of Matthew Arnold we should remember that the better part of his working day went in attending to his profession of school inspector, and that the volumes of his collected works are the product of what time was left over from that. All adverse criticism of their contents should be prefaced by the acknowledgment that those volumes do exist, and that they exist to the number of fifteen.[1] Such acknowledgment is, as I say, prefatory: we praise Arnold's achievement as an unusual one, as an instance of authorship against odds. But we cannot choose but proceed to examine his writings as unaccommodatingly as if, like Henry James, he had poured out his whole working day into them. Criticism, trembling with sympathy, cannot but be ruthless. An author offers his wares to the public, and takes the consequences, however hard. After all nobody *asked* Arnold to be an author. Being an author against odds he receives our moral esteem as a man. But to have that as a man is not also to have favour as an author: he qualifies for moral esteem only because he asks no special quarter for the writings. Our knowing that they are by-products, or, if not that, co-products, merely provides their shortcomings with a convenient explanation. Those shortcomings are particularly noticeable when Arnold is dealing with the past, when he is employed in glancing back at older civilisations,

[1] Three of the fifteen volumes of the *Works*, 1903-4, are taken up with letters. If letters do not count as 'work', we could substitute for these three volumes Arnold's uncollected writings, and the passages he discarded from later editions of his books.

at the world's poetry and theology. On those occasions we cannot help wishing that he had studied closely enough to strike the proper balance between interpretation and facts, between intelligence and its material. That balance is well struck whenever he spoke of his own age, since in that field an adequate number of facts came his way inevitably. But he tells us little that we cannot dispense with about earlier ages, about the mysteries (for instance) of the Elizabethan age or of the eighteenth century. Arnold is a first-rate commentator on Victorian times (and an interesting one on our own, since he saw not only 'how the world is going', but also how the world 'must go');[1] but when his theme is times anterior to the Victorian, the hungry sheep look up, and are given merely the 'fragrant steams' of cooking.

## II

A R N O L D 's being a writer who is charming does not pre-clude his also being a writer given to pontificating: the charm is often priestly. He is found perpetuating the formula favoured by the *honnête* critics of the eighteenth century—the formula 'the most [beautiful] in the world',[2] which both delights us with its indulgence and enthusiasm, and also disturbs us (as critics of a critic who, asking to be taken seriously, should weigh his words) with its assumption of a supernatural omniscience and infallibility. Arnold's pontifical manner persists even when he is confessing that he is out of his depth. Usually he makes no such confession, and we therefore cannot usually tell when he is giving out what he has tested, and when he is giving out what he has seized on trust for the sake of a brilliant paragraph, a paragraph to 'startle', to shock, or to enchant, and so to contribute to the

[1] Letters, i. 309 f.                    [2] See e.g., p. 90 below, n. 2.

propaganda to which he devoted his life. In 'The Literary Influence of Academies' there is a passage (it is almost a melodramatic incident) which, when linked, say, with remarks in the preface to his selections from Burke, suggests that he did not always hold his views about the eighteenth century as responsibly as his manner suggests. The former essay is dated 1864 and the latter 1881. In the former the eighteenth century in England is called provincial and second-rate, and the best that it can show is given as the 'Attic prose' of Addison. The Augustan age, and the whole English eighteenth century with it, drops into the category of provincial and second-rate because the peg of Addison's prose, though pretty, proves too light in substance, and collapses. Why, one asks, does not Arnold take Swift for his peg, a peg of oak from which the intellectual greatness of any age could hang in any wind? If my three answers are right answers they discredit Arnold's worth as an authority. The first is that Sainte-Beuve had made no use of Swift in the essay 'Qu'est-ce qu'un Classique?' to which Arnold at this point was indebted. That essay places Addison among the 'Attics of every tongue and every nation', but alludes to the author of *Gulliver's Travels* only casually as the recipient of a certain letter from Bolingbroke. Perhaps, then, Arnold omitted Swift through reliance on his hero Sainte-Beuve. And the second possible reason. Arnold sometimes seems to be accepting the lazy assumptions of those of his contemporaries who were under no obligation to think.[1] It

---

[1] Evidence supporting this interpretation comes in the essay on Wordsworth, which is as late as 1879. In that essay Arnold exalted Wordsworth above all English poets since Chaucer, with the two exceptions of Shakespeare and Milton, but did so by reference not to those rivals who alone count, but to a list of 'our chief poetical names' (i.e., the poets who in 1879 were thought to be poets by the man in the street) a list which includes Scott, Campbell, and Moore.

was different, of course, where foreign literature was concerned: for instance, in 1887 Arnold predicted a future for Russian novelists which promptly came true, and there is plenty of up-to-date knowledge of contemporary French literature (though Arnold seems unaware of Baudelaire).[1] Arnold came near to confessing that in the former essay he had overlooked Swift, and overlooked him because of his acceptance of man-in-the-street opinion, when, in the preface to Burke, he put himself in the position of having known no better than his grandfather on a subject about which his grandfather was mistaken:

Shakespeare and Milton we are all supposed to know something of; but of none of our prose classics, I think, if we leave stories out of the account, such as are the *Pilgrim's Progress* and the *Vicar of Wakefield*, are we expected to have a like knowledge. . . . Our grandfathers were bound to know their Addison, but for us the obligation has ceased;[2] nor is that loss, indeed, a very serious matter. But to lose Swift and Burke out of our mind's circle of acquaintance is a loss indeed, and a loss for which no conversance with contemporary prose literature can make up, any more than conversance with contemporary poetry could make up to us for unacquaintance with Shakespeare and Milton.[3]

The third reason is a fine remark of Bagehot's. Arnold admired Bagehot, and no doubt read his exploratory *Physics and Politics*, which appeared first in 1872 and was much reprinted. Bagehot, on his side, admired Arnold, and paid his poems a strong compliment in this very book.[4] Of Addison and Swift Bagehot wrote as follows:

If you will endeavour to write an imitation of the thoughts of Swift

---

[1] It seems that it was Saintsbury who introduced Baudelaire into English criticism; his copy was brought him from Paris in 1866 (see Dorothy Richardson, *Saintsbury and Art for Art's Sake in England*, P.M.L.A., vol. lix, 1944, pp. 246, 251).

[2] Cf. 'who now reads Addison?' (D. C. Tovey, *Reviews and Essays*, 1897, p. 98).

[3] *Letters Speeches and Tracts on Irish Affairs by Edmund Burke*, 1881, pp. v f.

[4] See p. 213 below.

in a copy of the style of Addison, you will find that not only is it hard to write Addison's style, from its intrinsic excellence, but also that the more you approach to it the more you lose the thought of Swift. The eager passion of the meaning beats upon the mild drapery of the words.[1]

There seems, then, to be no more responsible reason for Arnold's final estimate of Swift than that time had brought about a general improvement in his popularity, an improvement from which Arnold had benefited as well as everybody else.[2] And benefited up to the hilt: two years earlier in *Mixed Essays* Goethe's prose in the 'Memoirs' is said to have

none of those positive qualities of style which give pleasure, it is not the prose of Voltaire or Swift. . . .[3]

and in that late piece, the lecture on 'Emerson' comes this question 'Who are the great men of letters?' and this answer to beat the prose of Emerson with:

They are men like Cicero, Plato, Bacon, Pascal, Swift, Voltaire,—writers with, in the first place, a genius and instinct for style; writers whose prose is by a kind of native necessity true and sound.[4]

### III

IT IS perhaps because so much of Arnold's day went in school inspecting, and so much of his leisure in keeping abreast of his own age, that he achieved only a vague notion of the past. Vagueness is a disabling disease of the historian because the one thing certain about the past (we infer this from our own experience of the present) is that it was lived

---

[1] *Physics and Politics*, 1872, p. 96.

[2] Arnold told Thomas Hardy that 'the best man to read for style—narrative style—was Swift' (Florence Emily Hardy, *The Early Life of Thomas Hardy*, 1928, p. 175). If Arnold intended the remark as a home-truth, it was lost on Hardy, who had made his own style for his own purposes, and very properly regarded both style and purposes as sacred.

[3] p. 308.

[4] *Discourses in America*, 1896, pp. 159 f.

through particular by particular. It is the business of the historian to discover these particulars for himself and for us. He will not always, of course, present them as particulars; he will sometimes generalise. But generalisations are concrete things when derived from an adequate number of particulars. They are the pattern made by the particulars; they are the expression (to adapt a phrase of Wordsworth's) on the countenance of knowledge. Arnold's generalisations are not pattern, expression: they are the speculations of a mind interested in ideas independently of the material that alone should generate and govern them. When Arnold gives us the phrase, 'blank with all the ennui of the Middle Ages',[1] we ask him for his evidence that there was more ennui at that time than at any other; we ask him to search for it in, say, Chaucer, i.e., in a piece of 'the Middle Ages' which is sufficiently big and detailed to count as an adequate represent-ation of the life of the time. We ask Arnold if what he read as blank ennui was not rather the blank left by records which have disappeared, and the blankness of his own unfamiliarity with what medieval records have survived: these records are not so plentiful as those of later ages, and accordingly Arnold came across few of them in the general reading which was all he had time for. In so far as adequate records exist, ennui seems to have been no more endemic in the Middle Ages than in any other age, and what did exist should not have been called by that name, a name which had developed new connotations during the nineteenth century.

And then there are all Arnold's abstract terms. It is no business of the historian to deal in abstractions so near to no-meaning as many that Arnold dealt in: 'the great open stream of the world's history', 'the mental history of mankind',

[1] *Essays in Criticism*, 2nd ed. 1869, p. 282.

'universal history', the 'Middle Ages', the 'eighteenth century', 'things as they are', 'the way the world is going', 'tendencies', 'influences', 'the Zeitgeist'. And take the term 'century'. I do not know when the term was first used by historians and critics, and became the specious term of generalisation which it often still is: but prior to Arnold's day people had preferred to manage smaller quantities, to speak of the age of Elizabeth, of the reign of Queen Anne, and so on. But the enormous held no terrors for Arnold. Burke, we remember, recoiled from pitting himself against odds that were too great: when faced with the American Rebellion, he did not know how to draw up an indictment against a whole nation. No such arresting sense of personal insignificance, of being dangerously in a minority, struck Arnold, who saw no difference between attacking a line of Goldsmith, or F. W. Newman's translation of the *Iliad*, or the *Daily Telegraph*, or the eighteenth century, or the Middle Ages. Occasionally when speaking roundly of the eighteenth century he did find it necessary to distinguish the later from the earlier part, to insist on the contrasts between the age of Swift and of Burke.[1] But his usual practice was to bulk all the multitudinous detail surviving from those hundred years under the bombinating term 'the eighteenth century'.

One good result of his later theological studies was that they jolted him into seeing that the abstract, the enormous, and the vague were deceptive quantities. In *God and the Bible*, for example, he made this discovery:

To such a degree do words make man, who invents them, their sport! The moment we have an abstract word, a word where we do

[1] The age of Burke pleased him much more than its predecessor. Being one when 'new wine' was flowing, it belonged in effect to the succeeding century. See *Essays in Criticism*, p. 154, and cf. the quotation from *The Six Chief Lives from Johnson's Lives of the Poets*, p. 210 below.

not apprehend both the concrete sense and the manner of the sense's application, there is danger. . . . And [a certain term] is . . . a dangerous term, because without clearly conceiving what it means, we nevertheless use it freely . . . we talk of our idea of a myriagon or ten-thousand-sided figure . . . but it is not a clear idea, it is an idea of something very big, but confused.[1]

This, of course, is excellent sense, a sense so excellent that it is beyond the power of any critic to live up to it altogether. It is useless, however, to argue that if Arnold had made the discovery earlier it might have effected his salvation as a secular historian. There is no evidence that, as a secular historian, he had reached the point of wanting to be saved: he delighted in his vague quantities.

## IV

ARNOLD therefore was not a victim: it was not a lack of leisure which imposed vagueness on him, but a preference for seeing vague things. The verse shows it equally with the prose, though vagueness, of course, is not necessarily so fatal to verse as to prose. (The distinction between Arnold's verse and prose is sometimes merely one of rhythm, and sometimes even that distinction is very nearly a distinction without a difference: see, for instance, such a poem as 'Heine's Grave' and such a prose-poem as that which concludes the essay on Falkland.) A gift for clarity of manner is often expended on presenting vague thoughts and a vague conception of the concrete. As a secular historian he remained vague to the end. With the result that much of his history exists in a sort of poetical sanctuary. Its impressionistic vagueness makes it inaccessible to argument. This being so there is no need to examine his grandiose generalisations about the eighteenth century either when he praises it or,

[1] *God and the Bible*, 1875, pp. 85, 100.

more often, when he attacks it as 'second-rate', 'provincial', 'arid of air', 'touched with frost', 'an age of prose', an age whose greatest poet conceived his poem in the 'wits' rather than in the 'soul'. We must interpret such vague charges as 'poetry', as the outcome of fits of dislike, or, to adopt more of his theological words, as 'language *thrown out* at an object of consciousness . . . which inspired emotion.'[1] They are expressions of individual distaste which differ from the following expression of it in one of his letters only by being direct:

I am glad you like [my essay on] Gray; that century is very interesting, though I should not like to have lived in it. . . .[2]

They shed light on the subject feeling the distaste rather than upon its object. They expressed the distaste of Arnold and those of his contemporaries who were 'modern' enough to resemble him, of people who had only just managed to effect an escape; they are a part of Arnold's attempt to get rid of that streak in his intellectual ancestry which he found 'retarding', to push himself and his fellows farther into what remained of the nineteenth century. For instance, if he called the air of the eighteenth century arid, that was because his own sense of freshness had been finely improved. We can observe that sense of freshness improving as a general thing over the hundred years which separate Arnold from Gray, who, like so many after him, sought out mountains in the Lakes and Scotland.[3] Later poets followed Gray on foot and

---

[1] *Literature & Dogma*, 1873, p. 41.

[2] *Letters*, ii. 187.

[3] It seems to have been Thomson and Gray who reintroduced the use of the term 'fresh', which became so popular in the nineteenth century, and which led to the use of such phrases as Arnold's 'torrent of freshness' (applied to his father's contribution to English thought: see *Letters*, i. 311). It was Gray's 'Ode on the Pleasures arising from Vicissitude' that Hurrell Froude quoted (or rather misquoted) when, away in the Barbados, he longed for a sight of the English spring: 'I wish I could be in England now, and see a little of "Nature's tenderest, freshest green", etc.' (*Remains*, Part I, 1838, i. 367).

F

in imagination, and Wordsworth and Scott reaped the benefit of being born and bred in the midst of country then at last properly appreciated. The sense of 'freshness' seems to have been specially cultivated by the Rugby circle. Thomas Arnold and his favourite pupils spent all their available holidays in the Lakes or in Scotland, and fostered a need for the air of fell and mountain which made the normal air of eighteenth-century haunts seem stuffy in comparison—the air of town, village, highroad, park, and garden. But the air of the eighteenth century was arid only by the northern standards of those holidaymakers whose nose had become sharp as a pen. And, again, when Arnold speaks of the eighteenth century as provincial and second-rate, he tells us little about the Englishmen who in that century led Europe, or greatly influenced it, in theology,[1] philosophy, industrial invention, geographical discovery, imperial expansion, trade, landscape gardening, domestic architecture, an age which produced Alexander Pope who seemed to Voltaire to be the greatest poet living,[2] an age which produced European household words like *Robinson Crusoe*, *Gulliver's Travels*, the *Essay on Man*, *Pamela*, the *Night Thoughts*, *Ossian*,[3] *The Vicar of Wakefield*. Instead of telling us anything about the eighteenth century, Arnold tells us about his own dislike for parochialism, and about his own wish that his fellows would take to bathing more freely in that boosted Ganges of his, the current of European ideas.

---

[1] It was only in the second half of the century that the leadership in theological thought passed from England to the Continent (cf. J. M. Creed and J. S. Boys Smith, *Religious Thought in the Eighteenth Century*, p. xxvi).

[2] See J. W. Mackail, *Pope*, 1919, pp. 15 f.

[3] Arnold was well aware that 'All Europe felt the power of [the] Melancholy [of Ossian]' (*On the Study of Celtic Literature*, 1867, p. 154).

V

ARNOLD, however, did not always write about the eighteenth century as a vague quantity. He wrote about it also at particular points. For example, when he praised what its writers did for English prose, he provided instances which enable us to appreciate his praise closely. When he blamed the lapses of Burke, whom he regarded as the greatest of English prose-writers, he quoted the lapses for all to see. We can also follow him closely when, commenting on eighteenth-century poetry, he centred his comment in a quotation. On that subject, however, it is usually a matter of following not praise but patronage.

There is enough evidence to show that Arnold knew eighteenth-century poetry fairly well,[1] and that to begin with he paid it at least that amount of respect which the ordinary reader of his time felt to be its due. At his most handsome the young Professor of Poetry could even write of it in this way:

Every one will at once remember a thousand passages in which . . . the ten-syllable couplet [proves itself] to have nobleness. Undoubtedly the movement and manner of this;

> Still raise for good the supplicating voice,
> But leave to Heaven the measure and the choice—

are noble.[2]

But as he grew older he grew less ready to allow due value to the kinds of poetry Pope wrote, and in the end could only speak of them as the kinds of poetry that a 'true' poet like

---

[1] He knew it better than Professor Lowry recognised, who, when editing his letters to Clough, added an '[e]' to the name of Green under the impression that Arnold meant the author of *Friar Bacon and Friar Bungay* and not the author of *The Spleen (Arnold to Clough*, p. 99.)

[2] *On Translating Homer*, p. 69. The instance is from Johnson's *Vanity of Human Wishes*, ll. 351 f.

Gray needed to be rescued from, rescued by means of a critic's fantasy of what might have been. To begin with, Arnold perceived that Pope had 'a quick and darting spirit'— a spirit Coleridge must have allowed to be Shakespearean[1] —and 'real nobleness',[2] but later could see him only as stiff, pompous, and inhuman, as a splendid high priest, as the splendid high priest, indeed, of an age of prose.[3] The results of Arnold's patronage are still with us, of course: in his later days his prestige as a critic was so high that his brilliant epigrams established themselves in the minds of younger critics as dogmas, and in the minds of the incurious mass of readers as assumptions. The critics and readers who relied on his critical scheme—glorious Shakespeare, glorious Milton, an age of prose, fairly glorious Wordsworth—did not understand how precariously he climbed to the point at which he found mockery of eighteenth-century poetry possible. For like most nineteenth-century poets and readers, Arnold never got clear of eighteenth-century poetry. Most nineteenth-century poets and readers were in two minds about it, hating it one moment because it strangled what was new in their own poetry, and admiring it the next because it was so much a part of them. Tennyson avowed that he would rather have written Gray's 'Elegy' than the whole of Wordsworth; and Pope he saw as rival to himself in the minute interpretative observation of what he found beautiful, or beautiful and interesting, in external nature. And to take a smaller instance, the poet David Gray, whom Arnold set beside Keats whom he set beside Shakespeare, freely exclaimed that when he opened his Thomson he despaired.

[1] In contrast to Milton, Shakespeare 'darts himself forth' (*Biographia Literaria*, ii. 20).

[2] Both phrases come from *On Translating Homer*, p. 67.

[3] *Essays in Criticism: Second Series*, p. 40.

## VI

IN SO far as Arnold's remarks on eighteenth-century poetry are concrete ones, comment is possible, and here are comments on three of them.

1. In the essay on Gray, Arnold, seeking something of Goldsmith 'in retaliation' for Goldsmith's disparagement of Gray, hit on the line,

> No chearful murmurs fluctuate in the gale,

and commented expansively:

there is exactly the poetic diction of our prose century! rhetorical, ornate,—and, poetically, quite false.

And he proceeds to 'apply', as a deadly touchstone,

> In cradle of the rude, imperious surge.

But if we turn to the *Deserted Village*, we find that the line belongs inseparably to a context remarkable for its fidelity to a complicated recollection, the recollection of an experience which for the senses was blurred, but which for the apperceptive intellect (sorting out and naming the 'mingling notes') was clear; a recollection of an experience of the senses and intellect which is prompted by a general emotion of pity for the decay of a society:

> Sweet was the sound when oft at evening's close,
> Up yonder hill the village murmur rose;
> There as I past with careless steps and slow,
> The mingling notes came softened from below;
> The swain responsive as the milk-maid sung,
> The sober herd that lowed to meet their young;
> The noisy geese that gabbled o'er the pool,
> The playful children just let loose from school;
> The watch-dog's voice that bayed the whispering wind,
> And the loud laugh that spoke the vacant mind,
> These all in soft confusion sought the shade,
> And filled each pause the nightingale had made.

But now the sounds of population fail,
No chearful murmurs fluctuate in the gale,
No busy steps the grass-grown foot-way tread,
But all the bloomy flush of life is fled.
All but yon widowed, solitary thing
That feebly bends beside the plashy spring;
She, wretched matron, forced, in age, for bread,
To strip the brook with mantling cresses spread,
To pick her wintry faggot from the thorn,
To seek her nightly shed, and weep till morn;
She only left of all the harmless train,
The sad historian of the pensive plain.[1]

Arnold expressly concerned himself with the 'poetic diction' of the line which he tore from its place. I cannot believe he included in his dislike the word 'fluctuate' (a word which he had used more than once in his own poems): the accuracy of Goldsmith's use of it was as obvious in 1880 as it had been in 1770 and as it remains to-day. It was against 'cheerful' and 'gale', then, that Arnold levelled his charges. The word 'cheerful' was as necessary to the poets of the eighteenth century as the word 'lone' was necessary to Arnold. It was an inevitable word for poets who were conscious of the social group, and who fully prized the consolations to be got from being accepted by the normal run of one's fellows. Much of their poetry was built on the assumption that the happiness of men glows most steadily in the family and in a group of friends. Like so many other things, it is all there in Gray's *Elegy* where the warm precincts of the cheerful day are set against dull forgetfulness and the solitude and melancholy of

And leave the world to darkness and to me.
Goldsmith's poems are related to society as if by a fascination.

[1] *The Deserted Village*, 1770, pp. 7 f.

They concern the emotions of the stranger, the guest, the exiled, the turned-away, the forsaken, the wanderer, the native returning. And so the 'cheerful' was what he longed for most.

If the eighteenth-century poets used the word too much, that was because they were preoccupied with the thing it signifies. To have denied them this word would have been to cut them off from the source of their best poetry. It would be as if we denied to modern poets the word 'history'.

Then the word 'gale'. By Arnold's time this word had come to have a new and narrower meaning, that of a wind which is strong. For the seventeenth and eighteenth centuries, however, its connotation was more neutral: it meant 'a movement of air'; and the preciser meaning of the context it appeared in springs from the epithet which almost invariably accompanies it. We find a nautical writer in 1621 making a list of the following degrees: 'A calme, a brese, a fresh gaile, a pleasant gayle, a stiffe gayle'.[1] And Milton has the lines:

> . . . and winds
> Of gentlest gale *Arabian* odors fann'd
> From their soft wings, and *Flora*'s earliest smells.[2]

Elsewhere Goldsmith himself wrote:

> . . . sea-born gales their gelid wings expand
> To winnow fragrance round the smiling land,

[1] See *O.E.D.* s.v. 'gale'. The *O.E.D.*'s treatment of this word proceeds on the assumption that 'gale' has always meant what it means to-day, i.e., a stiff wind. But in most of its many instances the word is qualified by an epithet, and where not, means a movement of air rather than a brisk movement of air. When the word is qualified by an epithet connoting gentleness, the editors consider it to be used 'poetically', but where the poetry comes in is in the epithet, in the gentleness, poets requiring to speak of gentle gales more often than of stiff ones.

[2] *Paradise Regained*, ii. 362 ff.: it is worth remarking that when the twentieth-century reader encounters 'gales' and cries 'poetic diction!' he should equally, when he encounters 'smell', cry 'how unpoetic!'; and then go on to discover the historical conditions which explain a great poet's use of both words.

where 'gales' can no more mean high winds that 'gelid' can mean icy.

Goldsmith's line therefore does not exhibit poetic diction at all. It exhibits eighteenth-century usage, whether in prose or verse. Arnold's quarrel is with the history of the English language, which is as unavailing as a quarrel with your family tree.

Moreover Arnold had no right to speak of the line as typical of eighteenth-century poetry. At the most it is typical of certain poems, and kinds and parts of poems.

2. The essay proceeds to attack Dryden's ode *To the Pious Memory of . . . Mrs. Anne Killigrew*, citing Johnson's praise of it as 'the noblest ode that our language ever has produced'. Arnold quotes a few lines, and comments:

The intellectual, ingenious, superficial evolution of poetry of this school could not be better illustrated,

and out comes a strip of litmus from Pindar.

Arnold does not trouble to weigh the remark of Johnson. Unlike Johnson, he admitted too few categories, and so did not appreciate the restriction implied in Johnson's words 'noblest' and 'ode'. Johnson did not care for the ode as a kind of lyric poem, and praise from him on this subject amounts to little more than saying that Dryden's ode is the best of a poor lot. Missing this shade of emphasis Arnold offered as the normal poetry of 'this school' what is most abnormal. Dryden's ode exhibits his breaking out into a baroque floridity which he manages as beautifully as Rubens managed that of his royal portraits. But the poetry which Dryden wrote habitually was otherwise. Instead of being florid, it was a sort of Adam and Eve poetry, masculine and feminine together, both on the grand scale and both on that grand scale which is also simple. Arnold saw this habitual poetry

as so much admirable prose. Fortunately he supported his
charge with an instance, the instance of

> A milk-white *Hind*, immortal and unchang'd,
> Fed on the lawns and in the forest rang'd.

In the last resort we can rely only on our own reaction to this
couplet: if we do not welcome it as poetry, poetry for us it
cannot be. But before rejecting it as poetry Arnold might
have seen that at least it is not prose in the means it uses.
Prose cannot achieve that degree of economy, cannot give
such weight as in this instance to the word 'and'—a word
which Dryden makes heavy with the fate of Tithonus, who
lived on and on only to age *pari passu*. Nor can prose convey
so much by means of sound. We do not think of Dryden
as a poet concerning himself overmuch with subtleties of
sound. And yet how smooth the repeated [long vowel]+n:
*hind, -anged, -awn, -anged*. And a further subtlety: *lawns* is a
Janus having the 'aw' sound of *immortal* and the *n* of *ranged*.
The music of the couplet, subtle without being fussy,
substantial without being heavy, securely divides it off from
prose. These things are only means, it might be objected.
But in poetry means are vital to the sensuous pleasure which,
however faintly, poetry must give us before it can exist.
And it is given us generously by the means used here. If
pictorial suggestiveness, especially when subtle, takes us
nearer to content, and to content considered poetical,
Dryden's couplet makes its claim. His hind may not have the
mystery of Wordsworth's white doe of Rylstone but ranges
alive in the imagination and is set in a landscape: and
*milk-white* is so much more tender, and appropriately so,
than *white*, and *lawns* so much more tender to the tread than
'grass' or 'fields'. And finally the enrichment of the allegory:
the hind is a lovely creature in its own right: but over and

above its animal being it represents the Catholic Church, and so aroused, and still arouses, passions. I do not say that these particular passions have much to do with poetry, or with prose. But passions at least remove us from the stuffy air that Arnold closed round poetry such as this. To use words like 'admirable' and 'indispensable' for sense like this of Dryden's is absurd.

3. In his lecture on Milton we get this paragraph:

Thomson, Cowper, Wordsworth, all of them good poets who have studied Milton, followed Milton, adopted his form, fail in their diction and rhythm if we try them by that high standard of excellence maintained by Milton constantly. From style really high and pure Milton never departs; their departures from it are frequent.[1]

I have ranged this among Arnold's particular criticisms of eighteenth-century poetry, but, apart from his using names, its place is among his vague ones. Of course Thomson and Cowper studied Milton: so have almost all English poets since Milton's day. But they did not adopt his 'form' (by 'form' I take it Arnold means the blank verse of *Paradise Lost* with its characteristic use of pauses, and perhaps also the diction and syntax which are sometimes latinate). With his usual decisive subtlety Dr. Johnson saw that

[Thomson's] blank verse is no more the blank verse of Milton or of any other poet than the rhymes of Prior are the rhymes of Cowley.[2]

The same is true of Cowper, also. And if Thomson and Cowper did not adopt Milton's form, they cannot be said to depart from it, and the only sense in which they can be said to fail is the absolute sense: they may be said to be inferior to Milton as poets only in the way that, as a dramatist, Jonson may be said to be inferior to Shakespeare. Discipleship

[1] *Essays in Criticism: Second Series*, p. 62. Arnold had already stated this view in *Mixed Essays*, pp. 267 ff.
[2] *Lives of the Poets*, iii. 298.

of Milton is precluded for Thomson and Cowper by their subject and by the literary kind which it required. Thomson is following Virgil, the poet of the *Georgics*, and Cowper the mock-heroic and Georgic poets. And in writing more humbly than epic poets, they succeed thoroughly. Both Thomson and Cowper wrote latinately, and did so as deliberately as Milton did; but for other ends. Arnold had raised an easy laugh against Cowper when he warned off the would-be translator of Homer from Cowper's latinate diction:

It must not be Cowper's blank verse, who has studied Milton's pregnant manner with such effect, that, having to say of Mr. Throckmorton that he spares his avenue, although it is the fashion with other people to cut down theirs, he says that Benevolus 'reprieves The obsolete prolixity of shade'.[1]

But that line is not taken from Cowper's own translation of Homer: it is taken from *The Task*. Of course no translator of Homer should imitate the verse and diction of *The Task*: Cowper himself had said as much by not doing so himself. Arnold's instance, therefore, serves no purpose except that of raising a laugh against Cowper, the sort of laugh we associate with the lecture room. But Cowper had laughed before Arnold, and so laughs after him. The point of Cowper's line and of the many appropriately like it in a poem beginning 'I Sing the Sofa', is that Cowper's words are selected fastidiously, haughtily, amusedly, and were recognized at the time as being so selected. Arnold spoke as if Cowper did not know that he was writing with exquisite cleverness, and so missed the chance of recognizing the quality of the product. *The Task* (especially when we remember that while writing it Cowper was *very often most supremely unhappy*')[2]

---

[1] *On Translating Homer*, p. 74.
[2] Letter to Lady Hesketh, 16 January, 1786. The italics are Cowper's.

demonstrates the quality of the particular civilisation of the eighteenth century. At times Arnold fully appreciated this civilisation, but he did not see that Cowper's writings were an instance of it equally with the 'culture, lofty spirit, and greatness' of Lord Granville,[1] and the heavenly beauty of Esher.[2]

Arnold confounded the distinctions of times in his concern with absolute standards. But though Cowper is inferior to Milton when those doomsday standards are evoked, his deficiency, as I have said, is not so much one of style, of diction and rhythm, as of subject-matter. Cowper accepted the absolute deficiency of his subject-matter as inevitable. He knew he could not pile up the sublimities, and so, unlike a hundred foolish poets of his times, did not try to. Instead, he did what he knew to be within his varied capabilities as Milton did what Milton knew to be within his own. The discrepancy, therefore, lies rather in the capabilities than in the degree of their fulfilment. One of his capabilities was for expressing his thoughts accurately and according to the 'kind' of the poem he was writing. Cowper, therefore, was strong at the point where Arnold attacked. He has several subtle discussions on style, and claimed that he never wrote any line negligently, but made each line as good as possible before proceeding.[3] And the goodness on most occasions satisfied, and satisfies still, others besides himself.

In discussing these instances I have done no more than indicate that Arnold gave sentence in ignorance of the nature of the fact.

---

[1] See *On Translating Homer*, pp. 16 ff. Cf. *Mixed Essays*, pp. 20 ff., and *Friendship's Garland*, 1871, pp. 80 ff.

[2] 'And Esher is a heaven upon earth for beauty' (*Arnold to Clough*, p. 89). Arnold was echoing the praise which Pope and Walpole had accorded this famous eighteenth-century garden (cf. Pope, 'Twickenham' ed., iv. 367).

[3] Letter to John Newton, 18 September, 1781.

## VII

I HAVE already quoted his discovery that Pope, the translator of Homer, had 'a quick and darting spirit'[1] and contrasted that discovery with the image of him later as a splendid high priest. About the same time as Arnold hit on this ecclesiastical image, he also made the statement that while 'genuine' poetry is conceived and composed in the soul, Pope's poetry 'is conceived and composed in the wits'.[2] 'Spirit', 'soul', 'wits': Arnold is still being vague. But vagueness about an individual is at least preferable to vagueness about a century, and I think we can make something of his terms.

If it is true that Pope conceived and composed his poems in his 'wits', he could still be said to have 'a quick and darting spirit' if the word 'spirit' were used in the sense of the spirit which issues in a witticism or a bagatelle. But this is not the sense of the word as Arnold applies it to Pope, because his 'quick and darting spirit' is seen as an appropriate endowment for one who is tracking down 'the swift-moving spirit of Homer'. If Pope had 'spirit' in this superior sense, then one would have thought that he had the beginnings, at least, of the 'soul' which Arnold denied him. Arnold, one concludes, has not worked out his meaning fully enough (I am assuming that his view of Pope had not changed during the twenty years that separate the former judgement from the latter two).

No one would trouble to deny that Pope's poems were

[1] Although in his letters Pope made the most of the painful enormity of his task of translating Homer, he repeatedly described himself as 'spirited' and 'in spirits' over it.

[2] *Essays in Criticism: Second Series*, p. 95. Arnold may have owed to Schiller the introduction of the term 'soul' into his critical vocabulary: 'Goethe's *Iphigeneia* . . . that noble poem which Schiller so exactly characterised when he said that it was "full of soul".' (*Merope*, 1858, p. xl.)

conceived and composed in the wits if they were all made up of couplets like that instanced, confessedly at random, in Arnold's 'Study of Poetry':

Do you ask me if Pope's verse, take it almost where you will, is not good?

> 'To Hounslow Heath I point, and Banstead Down;
> Thence comes your mutton, and these chicks my own.'

I answer: Admirable for the purposes of the high priest of an age of prose and reason. But do you ask me whether such verse proceeds from men with an adequate poetic criticism of life, from men whose criticism of life has a high seriousness, or even, without that high seriousness, has poetic largeness, freedom, insight, benignity? Do you ask me whether the application of ideas to life in the verse of these men, often a powerful application, no doubt, is a powerful *poetic* application? Do you ask me whether the poetry of these men has either the matter or the inseparable manner of such an adequate poetic criticism; whether it has the accent of

> 'Absent thee from felicity awhile. . . .'

or of

> 'And what is else not to be overcome. . . .'

or of

> 'O martyr souded in virginitee!'

I answer: It has not and cannot have them; it is the poetry of the builders of an age of prose and reason. Though they may write in verse, though they may in a certain sense be masters of the art of versification, Dryden and Pope are not classics of our poetry, they are classics of our prose.[1]

We need not take Arnold's list of indispensable qualifications too seriously since most people agree that they discredited themselves in discrediting Chaucer. But, as it happens, Pope's poetry does satisfy three of Arnold's arbitrary, or at least inadequately argued, desiderata: it has high seriousness (if by high seriousness is meant the intense application of the mind to seeing human life as it is), poetic largeness (a handy

[1] *Essays in Criticism: Second Series*, pp. 40 ff.

witness is the ending of *The Dunciad*), and insight (no poet had it keener). Passages have even got benignity if it comes to a pinch (Pope certainly claimed that satire 'heals with Morals what it hurts with Wit')[1], though benignity is the desideratum that stands most in need of argument. But the piling up of abstract terms does not take us very far. It is more helpful to look at the couplets.

If all of them were like the couplet Arnold quoted, we could call Pope, for all his versification, a prose writer. But even that prosy couplet (I am viewing it as an isolated poem since that is what Arnold, for the occasion, made it) is not the blankest prose. Even that couplet exhibits a stealing out if not a darting out, of the 'spirit', a perceptible stirring of the 'soul'. 'And these chicks my own' is, surprisingly, a tender, an emotive phrase. The mood of the couplet begins as though Pope were merely versifying a scrap of, say, Defoe's *Complete Tradesman*, but it becomes complicated at the end, and the syntax with it.[2] The couplet comes from one of the *Imitations of Horace*, and in this particular one Pope is adapting Horace quite pointedly since mutton and chicken, besides being typical English meats (Horace's meats were chicken and kid), were exactly those meats to which Pope had restricted Lord Oxford on the occasion of their dining together a few years earlier.[3] But in the Latin there is no flicker of tenderness like that with which Pope ends his simple couplet. That small subtlety is insinuated at a point where his poem is demanding

[1] *Imitations of Horace*, Ep. II, i. 262.
[2] The method of his complication owes something to Milton's in *Paradise Lost*: cf. ix. 433:
> From her best prop so farr, and storm so nigh;
and ix. 1106 f.:
> . . . a Pillard shade
> High overarch't, and echoing Walks between.
[3] See the 'Twickenham' edition of Pope, iv. 66.

as blank a prose as he could write. It demands blank prose because at this point it demands fact. (The closing paragraphs of Newman's *Apologia* are of interest here. Though they are planned as a great musical dedication, Newman does not hesitate to introduce at length the cacophonous names of his fellow Oratorians, aesthetic considerations being suspended as a matter of course where facts are sacred.) Pope's poem demands the fact whether poetical (in the ordinary sense) or not. Facts which happen to be more poetical (in the ordinary sense) follow in the next lines:

> From yon old wallnut-tree a show'r shall fall;
> And grapes, long-lingring on my only wall;

but their superior 'beauty' is not the first reason why they are there, either for Horace or for Pope. And yet, the fact of chickens is expressed with a stealing out of the spirit. So that I should hesitate to say that even the Hounslow Heath couplet was altogether conceived and composed in the wits. In the same way, to turn to a bigger matter, I should hesitate to say that the prose writings of the eighteenth century, which Arnold praised with such filial admiration, were conceived and composed in the wits, though Arnold assumed that this was so, assumed that prose is an absolute thing, prose. Even the prose of Swift is sometimes near to poetry—it rouses intense emotions of an aesthetic as well as of other kinds, though of a severely aesthetic kind. (If we look at Swift's escritoire, photographed in Elrington Ball's edition of the *Correspondence*, we see a thing which is eminently useful but also so strikingly perfect in its proportions that it gives tense pleasure.) And there is as much of the poet as of the prose writer in the writings of, say, Berkeley, Johnson, Goldsmith, Sterne, and Burke. But if the Hounslow Heath

couplet of Pope has its small element of 'soul', what about
the thousands of couplets Arnold did not cite which have
that element in plenty? Arnold's word is, of course, too
vague for us to be confident that we understand it in the sense
he intended (though his use of it in such a poem as 'The
Palladium' offers help), but I should have thought that, in
any possible sense of the word, 'soul' exists in Pope's poetry.
And since it is a poet we are dealing with, there is a more
concrete check on its presence: we can usually approach the
'soul' of a poet by way of observing the quality of his senses:
and Pope's senses are as fine, amorous, immediate, and
voracious as Keats's (though they range more widely and
are much more under control).

Since I am concerned to show that, whatever else he was,
Pope was a poet according to Arnold's own tests and
standards for a poet, there is another quality which it would
be well to claim for him if possible. In the lectures on Celtic
literature Arnold distinguished what he called 'natural
magic':

in the magical [handling of nature], the eye is on the object, but charm
and magic are added.[1]

Arnold's instances of this quality are various, and imply the
inclusion of some of Pope's poetry. Pope's way, of course, is
not to drown a poem in 'natural magic'. It is there like all the
elements in his poetry when the poem reaches the point of
needing it, or, rather, the point of needing the cluster of
elements of which it is one. But, as if he were giving Arnold
and his like every chance not to miss it, Pope sometimes
indulged its stay a little: his hands, like those of the village
organist, sometimes dwelt a little longer than was strictly

---

[1] *On the Study of Celtic Literature*, 1867, p. 164.

G

necessary on the trembling chords. The one instance I give is from the passage which describes the decline and fall of the young aristocrat on the grand tour, a passage from which I select the following:

> Europe he saw, and Europe saw him too.
> There all thy[1] gifts and graces we display,
> Thou, only thou, directing all our way!
> To where the Seine, obsequious as she runs,
> Pours at great Bourbon's feet her silken sons;
> Or Tyber, now no longer Roman, rolls,
> Vain of Italian Arts, Italian Souls:
> To happy Convents, bosom'd deep in vines,
> Where slumber Abbots, purple as their wines:
> To Isles of fragrance, lilly-silver'd vales,
> Diffusing languor in the panting gales:
> To lands of singing, or of dancing slaves,
> Love-whisp'ring woods, and lute-resounding waves.
> But chief her shrine where naked Venus keeps,
> And Cupids ride the Lyon of the Deeps;
> Where, eas'd of Fleets, the Adriatic main
> Wafts the smooth Eunuch and enamour'd swain.
> Led by my hand,[2] he saunter'd Europe round,
> And gather'd ev'ry Vice on Christian ground.[3]

The lines of 'natural magic' exist in this passage not only, of course, because of the luxury they pour on the senses, but also because of their necessary contribution to the account of the rake's progress: Pope rises to the poetic occasion now that he encounters it in the course of the observed biography (that is the best way of putting it since the satirist is dependent on what materials offer themselves). And his display of 'natural magic' is an authentic as anything in Shakespeare or

[1] The goddess Dulness.
[2] The hand of his tutor, who is speaking.
[3] *Dunciad*, iv. 294 ff.

Keats.[1] The same thing happened whenever his poem demanded it (or whenever he demanded it for his poem), which was fairly often.

An opportunity for understanding Pope's use of 'natural magic' was provided for Arnold by his own experiences over the 'New Sirens'. That poem, unlike any poem of Pope's is drowned in 'natural magic'. (It is that long lyric, almost flaringly sensuous, hauntingly trochaic, of which the final stanza is known to all readers of nineteenth-century poetry:

> Pluck no more red roses, maidens,
> Leave the lilies in their dew—
> Pluck, pluck cypress, O pale maidens,
> Dusk, oh, dusk the hall with yew! . . .)

Arnold's friends could not make out the gist of the poem, and Arnold wrote penitently to Clough:

Cumin also advises a running commentary for the New Sirens: and Shairp finds them cloudy and obscure: and they are, what you called them, a mumble.[2]

Arnold supplied a commentary, but without any confidence in its remedial power: '. . . your word is quite just—it is

---

[1] The reader may object to Pope's use of 'silver' with 'lilies' as having too metallic a light. If so, it is worth noting that Arnold would probably not have agreed with him. He himself ascribed something metallic to flowers. Austin Dobson quite rightly drew attention to the line from 'Thyrsis'
> Roses that down the alleys shine afar,
commenting, 'it may be questioned whether "shine" is absolutely inevitable as applied to a rose' (*A Bookman's Budget*, 1917, p. 129). Like any big flower, a rose can be seen from a distance, but not seen as shining. The same verb is used of the rhododendron in one of the late letters (*Letters*, ii. 341), but here Arnold may be describing leaves rather than flowers. Tennyson used descriptive words more accurately: cf. *Tennyson and His Friends*, p. 248: 'Gloriously crimson flowers set along the edge of the terrace . . . burn like lamps against the purple distance'. In *Maud* the daffodil, it is true, is called 'shining', but that surely is because the speaker, wandering at midnight, sees with the nightmare vision of one hectically near to madness. The 'glimmer' of the midnight is seen as 'ghastly', and the daffodil, therefore, as 'shining'.

[2] *Arnold to Clough*, p. 104.

exactly a mumble'.[1] He did print the poem, but only in his
first volume (1849). And that was the end of the matter till
Swinburne's repeated plea prevailed on him in 1876 to
reinstate it in the canon. The moral is clear. Arnold and his
friends of 1849 did not consider 'natural magic' a sufficient
ground for a poem's existence: sense, too, was necessary,
and this, in the 'New Sirens', Arnold had attempted but
failed to supply. When the poem was readmitted into the
canon, it was mainly to please Swinburne, that is, to please
one so unlike the rest of us as never to be happier than when
isolated from everything except 'natural magic'. After this
experience, and because of Arnold's general views on how
poems should be put together, one would have expected
him to value the achievement of Pope, an unusual one for an
English poet: his power of commanding this 'magic' into
being, of commanding it often, and his power of limiting
its life to the service of the larger matter in hand.

## VIII

ARNOLD does not seem to have given Pope's poetry the
attention necessary for experiencing it as it is. And one
reason for this may well have been his dislike of the heroic
couplet. This dislike was clearly formulated by 1862, the
date of his essay on Maurice de Guérin. After depreciating
the French alexandrine, Arnold continued:

The same may be said of our own poets of the eighteenth century,
a century which gave them as the main vehicle for their high poetry a
metre inadequate (as much as the French Alexandrine, and nearly in the
same way) for this poetry,—the ten-syllable couplet. It is worth
remarking, that the English poet of the eighteenth century whose
compositions wear best and give one the most entire satisfaction,—

[1] Op cit., p. 107.

Gray,—does not use[1] that couplet at all: this abstinence, however, limits Gray's productions to a few short compositions, and (exquisite as these are) he is a poetical nature repressed and without free issue. For English poetical production on a great scale, for an English poet deploying all the forces of his genius, the ten-syllable couplet was, in the eighteenth century, the established, one may almost say the inevitable, channel. Now this couplet, admirable (as Chaucer uses it) for story-telling not of the epic pitch, and often admirable for a few lines even in poetry of a very high pitch, is for continuous use in poetry of this latter kind inadequate. Pope, in his *Essay on Man*, is thus at a disadvantage compared with Lucretius in his poem on Nature: Lucretius has an adequate vehicle, Pope has not. Nay, though Pope's genius for didactic poetry was not less than that of Horace, while his satirical power was certainly greater, still one's taste receives, I cannot but think, a certain satisfaction when one reads the Epistles and Satires of Horace, which it fails to receive when one reads the Satires and Epistles of Pope. Of such avail is the superior adequacy of the vehicle used to compensate even an inferiority of genius in the user! In the same way Pope is at a disadvantage as compared with Addison. The best of Addison's composition (the 'Coverley Papers' in the *Spectator*, for instance) wears better than the best of Pope's, because Addison has in his prose an intrinsically better vehicle for his genius than Pope in his couplet.[2]

We can take it that the main reason for Arnold's dislike of the heroic couplet is its art, which, since variations between small units can be appreciated readily, is art that is patent rather than art that is hidden. In this matter we come up against a stolid deficiency in Arnold, a deficiency no doubt compensated by the presence of a complementary virtue. The pleasure which he derived from art was insignificant in comparison with the pleasure he derived from nature. By

---

[1] 'Does not use' becomes 'hardly uses' in the second edition, 1869, p. 78. In the meantime Arnold had recollected Gray's authorship of the fragmentary 'Alliance of Education and Government', 'Tophet' (the satire on the Rev. Henry Etough), and other small pieces written in the heroic couplet.

[2] *Essays in Criticism*, pp. 82 ff. Cf. *The Six Chief Lives from Johnson's 'Lives of the Poets'*, pp. xx f.

'art' I mean things accounted beautiful at the time concerned (in this instance the nineteenth century) and in the making of which human beings have played a decisive part. For all his humanism, Arnold does not value art. This lack is shown most clearly in his letters.[1] Aesthetically he experienced almost nothing when hearing music, and not very much when seeing painting (he only began to be excited by painting when he found that the Italian galleries gave dates on their labels and so allowed him to exchange the burden of aesthetic contemplation for the lively interest of constructing a private history of the art). And he freely stated that he could never see anything aesthetic in pottery and china. Only to architecture did he respond adequately (he responded also with remarkable catholicity, admiring Grecian buildings in Birmingham and Liverpool as well as dreaming spires and the cathedral at Florence).[2] If you do not care for art except when it reaches the scale of cathedrals and town halls, it is unlikely that you will care very much for the heroic couplet (or the French alexandrine). There is no need, at this date, to show up Arnold's mistaken estimate of the heroic couplet. If it is what he thought it, a mechanical means of achieving the prose virtues of 'regularity, uniformity, precision and balance', Pope who was blessed with a darting spirit would not have

[1] In the short introduction that he contributed to Edoardo Fusco's lecture 'Italian Art and Literature before Giotto and Dante' when it was printed in *Macmillan's Magazine*, xxxiii, 1875-6, Arnold declared his belief that the Italians think too much of these things: 'Fusco's treatment of his great subject is clear and instructive, although his point of view is, naturally, too Italian. An Italian is always apt to count literary and artistic achievement as all in all in a nation's life; to concentrate his thoughts upon this, which has been Italy's glory, and to forget what has been her curse—a relaxed moral fibre' (p. 228).

[2] *Letters*, ii. 163: 'to my feeling the most beautiful church in the world, and it always looks to me like a hen gathering its chickens under its wings, it stands in such a soft, lovely way with Florence around it'. It is interesting to find Clough more circumspect: 'I went . . . to Milan; saw the Cathedral, the most beautiful building I ever beheld . . .' (*The Poems and Prose Remains*, 1869, i. 90).

used it throughout his career. Nor is Arnold's citation of
Gray to the purpose. What he said of Gray in the first edition
was wrong, and instead of correcting it for the second,[1] he
should have scrapped it. When given accurately it told against
his argument. Gray used the heroic couplet for subjects and
'kinds' which needed it: for the satire on the Rev. Henry
Etough and for the fragmentary 'essay' on education. But,
like Pope, he did not use it for the odes and lyrics of which his
best work, unlike that of Pope, mainly consisted.

IX

I HAVE written at length of Arnold's estimate of Pope
because it is easier to defend an individual against charges
that are vague than to defend a century against them, and
because a defence of Pope contributes to a defence of the
eighteenth century itself, since his poetry is an obvious instance
of how thoroughly a poet's work can penetrate the thinking
and feeling of a country during a hundred years. Of his own
country and also of the countries of Europe; and during a
hundred years and beyond: it could be readily shown, for
instance, that Arnold's own thinking, like that of many of his
time, was not without its debt to Pope. Perhaps Arnold also
owed him a debt on the score of feeling. On that score, at
any rate, Pope's own century owed him a heavy one: even
those poets and critics who moved on to give their warmest
admiration to other sorts of poetry than the *Essay on Man*
first met and admired those other sorts in the poems of Pope.
For instance, if they admired Milton and his 'Gothick' glooms,
it was in the way that 'Eloisa to Abelard' had taught them to.

[1] See p. 89 above, n. 1.

# IV

## Arnold and Pater: Critics Historical, Aesthetic and Unlabelled

AT the end of his second lecture on translating Homer, Matthew Arnold subscribed to the view[1] that

the main effort [of the intellect of the continent], for now many years, has been a *critical* effort; the endeavour, in all branches of knowledge—theology, philosophy, history, art, science—to see the object as in itself it really is;

and he noted the laggardliness of English writers who continued to exhibit that obsolete and insular thing, a

strong tendency . . . to bring to the consideration of their object some individual fancy.[2]

Arnold felt himself enough convinced of the soundness of his view to make this passage the starting point of an essay written four years later, 'The Function of Criticism at the Present Time', an essay discussing this English failing as an introduction to his own widely ranging *Essays in Criticism*.

That phrase 'the object as in itself it really is' shows Arnold on one of the occasions when he advertised what he called the disinterested critic. This kind of critic was, and is,

---

[1] It was perhaps French in origin. In the same year, 1861, Nisard declared that 'Criticism is the general and dominating faculty of the nineteenth century' (I. Babbitt, *The Masters of Modern French Criticism*, 1913, p. 93).

[2] *On Translating Homer*, pp. 63 f. Cf. Locke, *An Essay Concerning Human Understanding*, ed. A. C. Fraser, 1894, ii. 227: 'It matters not what men's fancies are, it is the knowledge of things that is only to be prized: it is this alone gives a value to our reasonings, and preference to one man's knowledge over another's, that it is of things as they really are, and not of dreams and fancies.' Wordsworth may have had this passage in mind when he defined as an elementary requisite of the poetic mind the power 'to observe with accuracy things as they are in themselves, and with fidelity to describe them, unmodified by any passion or feeling existing in the mind of the describer . . .' (*Poetical Works*, ed. E. de Selincourt, ii (1944), 431 f).

impossible in practice. In Arnold's day, so he thought, too many critics were wearing their interestedness on their sleeves—the sectarian, political, and jingoistic, for instance. Arnold's own interestedness, nevertheless, was clear, even to himself. It was exhibited in the very vivacity of his writing. His bouquet of sweetness and light was discharged, as Newman said of an olive-branch of Pusey's, 'as if from a catapult'.[1] And it was discharged with a fillip because it was designed to produce an effect, and to produce it quickly. If Arnold's first concern was with the object as it really is, his second and last was with the object as it really *did*. He wanted his objects to produce a certain effect on the members of the British middle class as he saw them ranged, crude and stiff-necked, round about him.

There was evidence of his interestedness in the wording of the phrase in which he renounced it; the present tense showed his concern to be limited to himself and his living fellows. In so far as he was aware of the claims on the present made by an object surviving from the past, Arnold dismissed them from primary consideration. In that late essay, 'The Study of Poetry', he was at pains to protect what he called the 'real' estimate of poetry from two other estimates, the former of which was the 'historic':

A poet or a poem may count to us historically. . . . The course of development of a nation's language, thought, and poetry, is profoundly interesting; and by regarding a poet's work as a stage in this course of development we may easily bring ourselves to make it of more importance as poetry than in itself it really is, we may come to use a language of quite exaggerated praise in criticising it; in short, to over-rate it.[2]

Arnold was not concerned so much with the object as it

[1] *A Letter to the Rev. E. B. Pusey, D.D., on his recent Eirenicon*, 1866, p. 9.
[2] *Essays in Criticism: Second Series*, pp. 6 f.

originally was as with what it amounted to in the present. That phrase, ignoring time and its changes, sucked everything into the present moment when, for the moment, time obligingly seemed still. 'To see the object as in itself it really is' brought all objects on to the same mid-nineteenth-century footing whether they were old objects or new, whether they were poems of Milton or poems of Browning. Arnold did not see that to survive at all was to survive in a perpetual state of being modified. When the object was a poem of Browning, well and good: then Arnold met an object which had not 'had time', as we say, to change: he met an object, which like himself was a contemporary object. But when the object was a poem of Milton, there was the complication of a choice, since there were then, broadly speaking, two objects: the object as in itself it really *was* at first (*Paradise Lost* as it appeared to Milton and to the seventeenth-century reader) and the object as in itself it really is (*Paradise Lost* as it lay helpless after the latest of the modifications, the object as it appeared to the gaily unlearned[1] Arnold and the mid-nineteenth-century reader).

Arnold's criticism of the literature that was produced before the nineteenth century was criticism of objects as they appeared to a mind unaware that the date of a mind mattered. So that the amount of Arnold included in criticism of old objects is disproportionate to the amount included of the objects. But of course even when we recognize that this is so, we go on reading Arnold's criticism, and for two reasons in the main. It is, in the first place, that of its author: whatever Matthew Arnold touched he adorned. Our impatience—if in the increased fullness of time we see his shortcomings as an interpreter of past literature—dissolves away in the general

[1] See p. 56 above.

gratitude for a context as lively as a novel of Peacock's. Moreover, Arnold's writings now reap the supererogatory benefit of having belonged so vividly to their own age. His criticism of the past is saved for us the more completely for the paradoxical reason that it was so much of its own time. Nevertheless, being originally so modern in intention, it is a pity it drew as much as it did on the past. It was, and is, at its best when in frank dependence on the present. A novelist like Scott can take the past and make a brave new world of it for the entertainment of men and boys. But the critic should only touch the past in order to explain it. No critic who is concerned first of all with his own times will care to do this. Let such a critic, therefore, write essays like those making up *Culture and Anarchy* rather than essays on Marcus Aurelius, Milton, pagan and medieval religious sentiment.

Arnold was for dismissing the 'historic estimate'. Yes, by all means let the literary historian keep in his place. Let him give us correct dates and ample bibliographies, and let him point out good texts. And, further, let him do all this as if his materials were all of equal value. But do not let us confuse his place with that of the historical critic, the writer, that is, who to his critical sense and skill adds a close knowledge of the literature of the past, a knowledge complete with all the findings of the literary historian. Arnold's ideal critic who estimates the object in itself as it really is stands in some danger even from the literary historian, who by pointing out an inconvenient date or a correct reading can make him look foolish. But he stands in great danger from the historical critic who, as capable as any of dealing with a new poem, can add to that capacity a capacity to explain what in objects belonging originally to the past has become puzzling merely through the inevitable, accidental, and mindless distortions of time.

## II

WALTER PATER followed Arnold in honouring 'the object as in itself it really is'.

He quoted the phrase in the preface to the book we have come to call *The Renaissance*, his first book, and that which had more effect on his contemporaries than any later book of his:

'To see the object as in itself it really is', has been justly said to be the aim of all true criticism whatever. . . .[1]

And the sentence proceeds to include in the category of 'all true criticism whatever'—is it a wide or a narrow category?— that sort of criticism of which Pater himself, to take him at his word, was a practitioner: the category of 'aesthetic' criticism.

We might well have expected from Pater a preference for the object as it *was*. Since 1877 when his book attained its second edition, it has borne the title *The Renaissance: Studies in Art and Literature*, but when first published in 1873 its title promised more of the historical: *Studies in the History of the Renaissance*. Pater, then, began by offering himself as an historian, and several passages in the works repeat the offer. Moreover, in the course of the first essay in his book, 'Aucassin and Nicolette'[2] he produced the following:

To say of an ancient literary composition that it has an antiquarian interest, often means that it has no distinct æsthetic interest for the reader of to-day. Antiquarianism, by a purely historical effort, by putting its object in perspective and setting the reader in a certain point of view from which what gave pleasure to the past is pleasurable for him also, may often add greatly to the charm we receive from ancient literature. But the first condition of such aid must be a real, direct, æsthetic charm in the thing itself; unless it has that charm, unless some purely artistic quality went to its original making, no merely anti-

---

[1] *Studies in the History of the Renaissance*, 1873, p. viii. All further quotations from this book are taken from this edition and, unless otherwise stated, from this page.

[2] In the second edition, 1877, this essay was expanded into 'Two Early French Stories'.

quarian effort can ever give it an æsthetic value or make it a proper
object of æsthetic criticism. These qualities, when they exist, it is always
pleasant to define, and discriminate from the sort of borrowed interest
which an old play, or an old story, may very likely acquire through a
true antiquarianism.[1]

Here Pater offered a certain encouragement to the historian.
Provided the historian chose his object well, he could 'add
greatly to the charm we receive from ancient literature.' He
could not create 'charm' where none of that 'one thing
needful' seemed to exist already, but where it did, he could
add more. There is no reason to quarrel with this. Pater was
speaking as Arnold was to,[2] of the critic, not of the historian,
and no critic, however well versed in history, is going to
work on an object that looks unpromising when there exist
so many that, before he begins, look 'charming' and that
promise to prove so more and more as he comes to see them
as belonging more intimately to their time. Here there was
encouragement to the historian. And elsewhere. For instance,

every intellectual product must be judged from the point of view of the
age and the people in which it was produced.[3]

Or this smile at the 'scholars of the fifteenth century':

They lacked the very rudiments of the historic sense, which by an
imaginative act throws itself back into a world unlike one's own, and
judges each intellectual product in connection with the age which
produced it.[4]

All such remarks were encouraging to the scholar-critic. But,
alas, they lacked the support of Pater's practice. In the paragraph immediately following the last quotation Pater twice
used the word 'strange' and twice the word 'quaint', words,
that is, which no one uses who has made an effort to throw

---

[1] *The Renaissance*, pp. 9 f.
[2] Arnold's dismissal of the 'historic estimate' came eight years later.
[3] *The Renaissance*, p. 22.
[4] ibid.

himself back into a former age. One recalls the opening of
Kittredge's book on Chaucer with its good-humoured pillory-
ing of 'quaint' and other terms of patronage and antipathy.[1] In
practice, more often than not, the past is served up by Pater as
if it were the present. Far from going back to the Renaissance
through the crooked corridors of time, he preferred to see it as
it had wound its way through them into his beloved present.

### III

TAKE his remarks on pictures. Pater liked pictures not as
they were left by the artist, but as they had survived. He liked
them, that is, 'embrowned'. His taste, therefore, defeated what
we can go so far as to call his adequate knowledge of the facts.

The only source of the embrownment of Renaissance
pictures is varnish and the changes worked on it by time. To
begin with, no doubt, varnish was applied as we apply it to
modern pictures, as a preservative that is seen as both
necessary and defiling. But at some time we conveniently
think of as the eighteenth century, it was applied for its own
sake, as an enrichment, and applied generously as basting to a
duck. In other words, it was applied by some painters to their
new pictures, and by dealers and by owners to old pictures.
By the eighteenth century, varnish had become a prime
pigment. And the poets promoted it to a grade still higher.
They saw the autumnal effect it had on paintings as an effect
unconnected with chemicals and the hand of man, as an
effect that time had produced unaided on the picture as the

---

[1] 'There is no great harm in the air of patronage with which our times, in their
self-satisfied enlightenment, address the great who were of old; but we do use
droll adjectives! If these great ancients show the simplicity of perfect art, we call
them *naïf*, particularly when their irony eludes us; if they tickle our fancy, they
are *quaint;* if we find them altogether satisfactory, both in form and substance, we
adorn them with the epithet *modern*, which we somehow think is a superlative of
eminence. . . .' (*Chaucer and his Poetry*, Cambridge, Mass., 1933 edition, p. 3).

painter left it. This is what Dryden told Kneller to expect from a beneficent future:

> More cannot be by Mortal Art exprest;
> But venerable Age shall add the rest.
> For Time shall with his ready Pencil stand;
> Retouch your Figures with his ripening Hand,
> Mellow your Colours, and imbrown the Teint,
> Add every Grace, which Time alone can grant;
> To future Ages shall your Fame convey;
> And give more Beauties, than he takes away.[1]

As well as from the varnish pot, embrownment came to be asked of the palette. Even so late as the close of the eighteenth century, Sir George Beaumont was busy advising Constable to give his landscapes the glow of 'an old Cremona fiddle'.[2]

---

[1] 'To Sir Godfrey Kneller, Principal Painter to His Majesty', ll. 174 ff.

[2] 'Sir George thought Constable too daring in the modes he adopted to obtain the [quality of freshness]; while Constable saw that Sir George often allowed himself to be deceived by the effects of time, of accident, and by the tricks that are, far oftener than is generally supposed, played by dealers, to give mellowness to pictures. . . . Sir George had placed a small landscape by Gaspar Poussin on his easel close to a picture he was painting, and said, "Now, if I can match these tints I am sure to be right." "But suppose, Sir George," replied Constable, "Gaspar could rise from his grave, do you think he would know his own picture in its present state? Or if he did, should we not find it difficult to persuade him that somebody had not smeared tar or cart-grease over its surface, and then wiped it imperfectly off?" At another time, Sir George recommended the colour of an old Cremona fiddle for the prevailing tone of everything, and this Constable answered by laying an old fiddle on the green lawn before the house. Again, Sir George, who seemed to consider the autumnal tints necessary, at least to some part of a landscape, said, "Do you not find it very difficult to determine where to place your brown tree?" And the reply was, "Not in the least, for I never put such a thing into a picture".' (C. R. Leslie, *Life and Letters of John Constable*, 1896 edition, pp. 140 f.)

I am indebted for the reference to this passage to E. W. Manwaring's *Italian Landscape in Eighteenth Century England*, 1925, p. 16. Though Constable was rebelling against this age-old provision of brown colours, he retained a certain love for at least brownishness.

Ruskin in his brilliant discussion of the use of the word 'brown' by poets and the use of the colour by 'Sir George Beaumont and his colleagues' notes the remark of 'one of our best living modern colourists' that 'there is no brown in Nature[.] What we call brown is always a variety either of orange or purple' (*Modern Painters*, IV. v. §10).

In 1873, Pater was still admiring the fictions of varnish. It does not seem to have crossed his mind that his love for the 'minor tones'[1] of Renaissance pictures was a love for the tricks of dealers who were administering to a particular taste active well after the close of the period the 'history' of which he was making his 'study'. If it had, he might have been more eager to seek the object of the historian, the object as it *was* at first. If not, he could only have stuck to his love for the minor tones of Renaissance pictures as a man sticks to a woman who has deceived him, that is cynically and with what strong-minded pleasures come from the complexities of lost innocence. Certainly, Pater loved complexities. Even though he did not know about varnish, he contrived as much complexity as he could for the aesthetic benefit of his Renaissance pictures. For though ignorant of the last and sobering deception, he knew that time had worked changes. And he made the most of them—when he cared to, and for his particular purposes. He saw to it that he had enough knowledge to flirt with.

The embrownment of Time and his 'pencil'—Dryden's words are wise to both sources of change—was hugged by Dryden as a warmth. Pater, in one sentence and part of a footnote, felt it as a chill. Or so he said. At the beginning of his meditation on the Mona Lisa he remarked that

Perhaps of all ancient pictures time has chilled it least.[2]

[1] *The Renaissance*, p. 49. Pater's love of minor tones, while not exclusive, was stronger than A. C. Benson could understand: 'He was fond . . . of insisting upon some altogether unimportant detail . . . he used to pretend that he shut his eyes in crossing Switzerland, on his journeys to and from Italy, so as not to see the "horrid pots of blue paint", as he called the Swiss lakes.' (*Walter Pater*, 1906, p. 191.) In approving shades of blue, Pater went as far as he could when he furnished his rooms with blue and white china.

[2] *The Renaissance*, p. 116. 'Chill' in this sense Pater seems to have borrowed from Ruskin's *Modern Painters* (*Works*, iii. 249 n.).

Apart from 'perhaps' (which is no great fault, if we consider the difficulty of certitude in the matter) that sentence is worthy of the historian Pater had given himself out to be. 'Ancient' and 'time' show him taking the first step necessary for the historian, the step backwards; while 'chilled' shows him going still further and acknowledging time's changes; and further still, and acknowledging that the changes time works on a material object are changes to be deplored—acknowledging it apparently as a move towards remedying the damage by an exercise of the historical imagination. And there is another touch of the historical imagination in the footnote to this same sentence. Pater added the footnote at some point during the preparation of his manuscript—it is there in the article as first published, in the *Fortnightly Review*:[1]

> Yet for Vasari there was some further magic of crimson in the lips and cheeks, lost for us.[2]

I find this note disingenuous. Pater speaks as if he would like to have seen what Vasari saw. But if that crimson had survived till his day, what would have become of the minor tones of his description? Would the Mona Lisa have kept as much fallen day about her, would the eyelids have had the same weariness, if the cheeks had retained the merriness of those of Hogarth's Shrimp Girl? 'Perhaps of all ancient pictures time has chilled it least.' But time had chilled it enough, fortunately for Pater, to allow him to write a poem on *la femme fatale*, as it also had chilled the roses of Botticelli's

---

[1] 1869, p. 506.

[2] Pater does not say 'some crimson' but 'some further magic of crimson'. Mr. Empson has noted the Elizabethan fondness for such a construction:

What means [the warning of] this trumpet's sound?

(*Seven Types of Ambiguity*, 1930, p. 112.) Pater's uses of it would call for subtle analysis.

Birth of Venus to the exquisite point at which Pater could describe them as 'embrowned a little, as Botticelli's flowers always are'.[1] He banished from the body of his paragraph the crimson he knew of as the original, the Renaissance, colour. It was not, however, banished from his book. It was made to peep up into the minor tones which, if Pater had been an historian, it would have been made to banish as the usurpers they were. Pater knew history, that is, for his own ambiguous ends.

Pater quoted Vasari and made some use of him. Vasari's account of the picture takes us as near as we can get to knowing how Leonardo's picture was first received. Vasari considered it a most remarkable instance of a painter's fidelity to the appearance of a certain beautiful woman, whom he himself knew, or whom he knew by repute, and as a picture affording an intellectual satisfaction—the satisfaction of confirming the Aristotelian account of art as *mimesis*. And when Vasari did use his imagination, it was merely to imagine that the painting was real flesh with the pulse of blood in it:

This head is an extraordinary example of how art can imitate Nature, because here we have all the details painted with great subtlety. The eyes possess that moist lustre which is constantly seen in life, and about them are those livid reds and hair which cannot be rendered without the utmost delicacy. The lids could not be more natural, for the way in which the hairs issue from the skin, here thick and there scanty, and following the pores of the skin. The nose possesses the fine delicate reddish apertures seen in life. The opening of the mouth, with its red ends, and the scarlet cheeks seem not colour but living flesh. To look closely at her throat you might imagine that the pulse was beating.[2]

No doubt this account, even at the time, was an inadequate one. Even from the start any observer must have been taken

---

[1] *The Renaissance*, p. 49.
[2] *Leonardo da Vinci*, Phaidon Press, 1943, p. 11.

by the picture as a record of character and personality. But here was a contemporary criticism, and one would have expected a *soi-disant* historian to have schooled himself to approach his picture in accordance with its principles: Browning, one recalls, knew better: for the nonce he made himself a Vasari:

> That's my last Duchess painted on the wall,
> Looking as if she were alive. I call
> That piece a wonder, now. . . .

Vasari's criticism of the Mona Lisa amounted to the means of unvarnishing it. Pater saw that this was so, but through eyes deliberately kept half shut. In his own account all things needful for a right historical judgment existed: he knew that the Mona Lisa was old and that it had changed. All things needful existed, but to be perverted. Pater confused them all together in the interests of an ambiguous material lying halfway between history and the last exciting moment of the present. Speaking of his morality, Henry James was to say that he hunted with the hounds and ran with the hare.[1] The same was true of his historical criticism.

Pater, then, was not much more of an historian than Arnold was. We read him as we read Arnold, for his own sake rather than for the sake of understanding his object. Take away the object and there remain all the splendours of Pater. He is, for instance, a writer making constant use of similes. The major term to which they are tied may have been wrongly conceived, but the life in the minor term is unforgettable:

The white light on [the face of the Botticelli's Madonnas] is cast up hard and cheerless from below, as when snow lies upon the ground,

---

[1] I cannot recall the source of this quotation.

and the children look up with surprise at the strange whiteness of the ceiling.[1]

The same life is in his metaphors. His imagery usually leaves art for external nature. In that field time has had nothing to say—or rather, nothing to say to poets. And so nothing to say to Pater. Men, and what they have made, confuse him, but his eye for what comes issued from the hand of nature, as it is nature external to man, is a clear one. He is, therefore, more a painter-like poet than a critic. His claim to be an historian is mainly that time has thrust history upon him, as on any writer. His account of the Mona Lisa witnesses not so much to Leonardo as to the nineteenth-century idea of the fatal woman, and to the thorough poeticising of works of art which Gautier seems to have been the first to practise, and, falling between him and Pater, Swinburne.[2]

IV

PATER quoted Arnold's phrase, but he did not apply it to aesthetic criticism without stating it with a difference:

in æsthetic criticism the first step towards seeing one's object as it really is, is to know one's own impression as it really is, to discriminate it, to realise it distinctly.

The difference lay in that epistemological term 'impression'. It had not occurred to Arnold to use the term. As a critic, if not always as a poet, Arnold's business was with the world of every-day. And so with the common reader. 'The great art of criticism', he said on one occasion, 'is to get oneself out of the way and to let humanity decide'.[3] The words came oddly from one who was always fighting his fellows,

---

[1] *The Renaissance*, p. 46.

[2] See George Boas, 'The Mona Lisa in the History of Taste', *Journal of the History of Ideas*, New York, i (1940), 207 ff.

[3] *Essays in Criticism*, p. 208.

but not oddly in that to fight them was to honour them as worth fighting. In a later essay, that excellent piece introducing his edition of six of *The Lives of the Poets*, Arnold paid delighted homage to Johnson, to whose criticism he found himself coming back repeatedly as to a *point de repère*. There is nothing surprising in this homage. Johnson was a critic who could say 'I rejoice to concur with the common reader.'[1] If on occasions he could not get himself out of the way and let humanity decide, the occasions, important as some of them were, were exceptions. Usually Johnson stood with the common reader, whom he defined as using 'common sense' (i.e., drawing on the sense he shared with his fellows), as being 'uncorrupted with literary prejudices' and as holding opinions which remained firm 'after all the refinements of subtlety and the dogmatism of learning.'[2] This was a good description of Johnson himself. And a fair one of Arnold. When Arnold spoke of the object as in itself it really is he meant the object as it is seen by the common reader, who by definition has no more party and sectarian prejudice than he has refinements and dogmatism. In the eighteenth century, the number of such readers was as high as it ever was, and in the nineteenth century—such were the intellectual, political, religious divisions of the time—as low. Nevertheless, the count of common readers was only low comparatively. In standing among them, Arnold had a cheering sense of numbers. Like Johnson, he expressed his own distrust of the 'personal' estimate. I have quoted his dismissal of the 'historic estimate', and on the heels of that follows his dismissal of the 'personal':

a poet or a poem may count to us on grounds personal to ourselves.

[1] *The Lives of the Poets*, iii. 441.
[2] ibid.

Our personal affinities, likings, and circumstances, have great power to sway our estimate of this or that poet's work, and to make us attach more importance to it as poetry than in itself it really possesses, because to us it is, or has been, of high importance. Here also we over-rate the object of our interest, and apply to it a language of praise which is quite exaggerated.[1]

In preferring what he called the 'real estimate', he was preferring the estimate of the common reader who, again by definition, knows nothing of the associations which, falling to a single reader, fall to one who is uncommon. Arnold's dismissal of the personal estimate was his dismissal—perhaps a conscious one—of the theories of Pater.

Pater's use of the word 'impression' indicated that, for his part, he was moving away from Arnold and the common reader. That, at bottom, is why he invoked epistemology. By profession he was a purveyor of philosophy: his book on Plato was a printed version of lectures given at Oxford. And he was interested in philosophy more generally than a profession always guarantees: witness the use made of it in *Marius* and in his essay on Coleridge. Not that he needed these credentials—those epistemological matters were by that time common knowledge. In choosing to speak of impression along with object he was appealing to Locke and the rest. And as Locke did he thought of impression and object as both being real. For Locke the object existed to be known, and so on several occasions for Pater. It was in this domain of external fact that Pater saw the scientist as employed—the artist and writer of literature being employed in another domain, their 'sense of fact'.[2] For Pater this domain of fact had even a vigorous life of its own: even colour— that favourite quality of things for Pater—has such a life:

[1] *Essays in Criticism: Second Series*, p. 7.
[2] *Appreciations*, pp. 3 f.

the more you come to understand what imaginative colouring really is, that all colour is no mere delightful quality of natural things, but a spirit upon them by which they become expressive to the spirit, the better you will like this peculiar quality of colour [in Botticelli's 'Venus rising from the sea'].[1]

The external world, then, had its own existence, and for their knowledge of that existence men were indebted in the first place to their senses. Pater remembered the 'impression' that Locke and other psychologists had spoken of, and added it to the 'object' spoken of by Arnold. He would have forgotten epistemology as completely as Arnold had done unless it had suited his purpose to remember it. He sought the impression because, if one chose to insist, no one could deny that it existed in a private sanctum. When Locke spoke of impressions he was not concerned with the privacy of one man's as against another's. He was, like any philosopher, generalising; he was trying to show how all human beings enter into their knowledge. Pater, on the other hand, was insisting on the uniqueness of the impressions to every individual man. He spoke not of impressions but of 'one's own impressions'. And in the same paragraph of the Preface to *The Renaissance* from which I have been quoting, he even allowed himself one of his rare italics in asking

What is this song or picture, this engaging personality presented in life or in a book, to *me*? What effect does it really produce on me? Does it give me pleasure? and if so, what sort or degree of pleasure?[2]

And further, he went on to invoke a concept invoked only by those who see mankind as divided up, the concept of

[1] *The Renaissance*, p. 48.

[2] We can see this as in part a protest against the communal emotions aimed at by the Utilitarians: as F. H. Bradley was soon to say:
'The end for modern Utilitarianism is not the pleasure of one, but the pleasure of all, the maximum of pleasurable, and minimum of painful, feeling in all sentient organisms, and not in my sentient organism. . . .' (*Ethical Studies*, 1876, p. 80.)

'temperament': he concluded his brief argument with

What is important, then, is . . . that the critic should possess . . . a certain kind of temperament.

Pater could rest content now that impression and temperament were enthroned.

The word 'temperament' indicated how far and how quickly Pater had left Arnold behind. Arnold's phrase 'the object as in itself it really is' was for rescuing the object from the clutches of the individual. Pater was for clutching it closer. Arnold had sought to disencumber the object of any 'individual fancy', but here was Pater exalting temperament, the very hive of such fancies; we cannot see him trying to get himself out of the way and let humanity decide. For Arnold the object lay in the external world sharply clear for anybody who had not blinded himself with some insular or provincial zeal or other. For Pater the object as it really is lay in the privacy of the individual impression of it. Obviously, the way to see an object more for what it is in itself is not to centre attention in the impression it makes so much as to go on collecting impressions of it till they cease to show enough new differences to make further collection worth while. Then you may feel satisfied that you are being fair to the object, as fair as in you lies. But it seems that Pater had little interest in this sort of fairness. We can see him as one who got an impression quickly enough to get it more as he wanted it, to get it while it was still fluid enough to be workable and transformable. He wished it to be Paterine as much as possible, more Paterine than objective. We are left wondering why he quoted Arnold's phrase at all. And the explanation may well be more to his credit as a man than as a critic—he liked Arnold's criticism and liked it too indiscriminately, and liked also to show his liking.

We can see how disproportionate was the contribution that Pater's encouraged temperament made to his criticism if we contrast Ruskin's way of describing a picture with Pater's. Here is Ruskin's description of Botticelli's 'Crowning of the Madonna':

[The Madonna] is surrounded by a choir of twelve angels, not dancing, nor flying, but carried literally in a whorl, or vortex, whirlwind of the breath of heaven; their wings lie level, interwoven among the clouds, pale sky of intense light, yet darker than the white clouds they pass through, their arms stretched to each other, their hands clasped—it is as if the morning sky had all been changed into marble, and they into living creatures; they are led in their swift wheel by Gabriel, who is opposite to you, between the Christ and the Madonna; a close rain of golden rays falls from the hand of Christ, He placing the crown on the Virgin's head; and Gabriel is seen through it as a white bird through rain, looking up, seeing the fulfilment of his message.[1]

As well as to indicate his own evaluation of the object, Ruskin intended his description to serve as a second-best for those who lacked opportunity to see the object itself: and his editors in 1906 noted how much more satisfactory is his description even than the excellent photographic reproduction which by that date they had by them. Ruskin's description is humbly tendering us the means of seeing an object as in itself it really is. Ruskin suppressed his own rich originality—his originality, that is, at the degree at which the originality of anybody becomes noticeable—in the interests of our seeing the picture for what it really is.

There was still another limitation recommended by Pater. Not a limitation, however, taking him further into himself, but one operating on the object. The impression fondled by the temperament was to be an impression of an object that was beautiful. The 'certain kind of temperament'

---

[1] *Works*, xxiii. 273 f.

recommended for the critic was 'the power of being deeply moved by the presence of beautiful objects', and it took some authority from 'the words of a recent critic of Sainte-Beuve'[1]:

De se borner à connaître de près les belles choses, et à s'en nourrir en exquis amateurs, en humanistes accomplis.[2]

Pater's sanctum might be a private one but it was not without its window. And of necessity. Only through an inlet would the objects get at Pater to produce their impressions on him. Pater had perforce to be accessible. But if so, only to beautiful things.

The thing was as important to Pater as its beautifulness. He could not breathe among abstractions. For all his interest in philosophy he distrusted everything except the concrete. So to some extent did Arnold who, on one occasion, even went so far as to recommend that poetry should be tested touchstone-wise by means of supreme single lines. As the opening paragraph of his Preface to *The Renaissance*, Pater placed this persuasive argument against abstraction:

Many attempts have been made by writers on art and poetry to define beauty in the abstract, to express it in the most general terms, to find a universal formula for it. The value of such attempts has most often been in the suggestive and penetrating things said by the way. Such discussions help us very little to enjoy what has been well done in art or poetry, to discriminate between what is more and what is less excellent in them, or to use words like beauty, excellence, art, poetry, with more meaning than they would otherwise have. Beauty, like all other qualities presented to human experience, is relative; and the definition of it becomes unmeaning and useless in proportion to its abstractness. To define beauty not in the most abstract, but in the most concrete terms possible, not to find a universal formula for it, but the

---

[1] I have made no attempt to discover his identity.
[2] *The Renaissance*, p. ix.

formula which expresses most adequately this or that special manifestation of it, is the aim of the true student of æsthetics.[1]

Many years later he was to ask:

Who would change the colour or curve of a rose-leaf for that οὐσία ἀχρώματος, ἀσχημάτιστος, ἀναφής—that colourless, formless, intangible, being—Plato put so high?[2]

And though 'beauty' remained one of Pater's favourite words, it was often given some sort of a footing in the concrete when he provided it with 'this or that special manifestation' in his favourite adjectives: *blithe, delicate, strange, comely, fresh, sweet, quaint, grave,* and so on.

## VI

W H E N once Pater had withdrawn into the private sanctum of the impression and the temperament, a sanctum giving on to beautiful objects, he was no less busy than Arnold. He differed, therefore, from the 'aesthete' as he, or it, is conceived by the popular imagination. This, a century earlier, had been Burke's account of how men are affected in body and mind when beholding a thing sufficiently beautiful:

When we have before us such objects as excite love [i.e., 'love in the mind'] and complacency; the body is affected, so far as I could observe, much in the following manner: the head reclines something on one side; the eye-lids are more closed than usual, and the eyes roll gently with an inclination to the object; the mouth is a little opened, and the breath drawn slowly, with now and then a low sigh; the whole body is composed, and the hands fall idly to the sides. All this is accompanied with an inward sense of melting and languor. These appearances are always proportioned to the degree of beauty in the object, and of sensibility in the observer. And this gradation from the highest pitch of beauty and sensibility even to the lowest of mediocrity

---

[1] *The Renaissance*, p. vii. The wording was slightly revised in 1877 and again in 1888.

[2] *Appreciations*, p. 67.

and indifference, and their correspondent effects, ought to be kept in
view, else this description will seem exaggerated, which it certainly is
not . . . a relaxation somewhat below the natural tone seems to me to
be the cause of all positive pleasure.[1]

And, in mockery of Pater's 'Conclusion', there soon came
Mr. Rose in Mallock's *New Republic*:

'. . . the aim of culture . . . is indeed to make the soul a musical
instrument, which may yield music either to itself or to other's, at any
appulse from without; and the more elaborate a man's culture is, the
richer and more composite can this music be. The minds of some men
are like a simple pastoral reed. Only single [*sic*] melodies, and these
unaccompanied, can be played upon them—glad or sad; whilst the
minds of others, who look at things from countless points of view, and
realise, as Shakespeare did, their composite nature—their minds
become, as Shakespeare's was, like a great orchestra. Or sometimes',
said Mr. Rose dreamily, as if his talk was lapsing into a soliloquy,
'when he is a mere passive observer of things, letting impressions from
without move him as they will, I would compare a man of culture to an
Æolian harp, which the winds at will play through . . . wandering in
like a breath of air amongst the chords of his soul, touching note [*sic*]
after note into soft music, and at last gently dying away into silence'

—a reverie which is broken into, 'in a very matter-of-fact
tone,' by one of the company who

saw that Mr. Rose's dreamy manner always tended to confuse Lady
Ambrose.[2]

But though Pater's aesthetic critic might look supremely
and even morbidly idle, incapacitated, decadent, Pater saw
him as intensely occupied. The imagery in which Pater
described him is kinetic.

An interest in power was strong during the nineteenth

[1] *A Philosophical Inquiry into the Origin of our Ideas of the Sublime and the Beautiful*
(*Works*, 1845, i. 182 f).
[2] *The New Republic*, ii. 23 f. I have marked the mistaken references to music.
If they are intended as mistakes they sharpen the mockery of Pater, whose own
references to music trespass beyond his knowledge. See p. 139 below, n. 2.

century, and in claiming power for his temperament Pater stood among the many disciples of Wordsworth.[1] In the 'Essay, Supplementary to the Preface [of 1815]', Wordsworth thundered against those who gave the word 'taste' (when used in the sense of a refined liking for the arts) a denotation that was passive:

It is a metaphor, taken from a *passive* sense of the human body, and transferred to things which are in their essence *not* passive,—to intellectual *acts* and *operations*.

And he concluded:

without the exertion of a co-operating *power* in the mind of the Reader, there can be no adequate sympathy with [great poetry].[2]

In his turn, therefore, Pater came to unite passive and active in that remarkable phrase, the 'power of being deeply moved'. He also described the aesthetic critic as one

who experiences these impressions *strongly*, and *drives directly at* the discrimination of them.[3]

This is the sort of masculine temperament that overtook the tender impression. And when for one moment Pater represented the mind as harbouring an impression passively, the impression being the active force—'How is my nature modified by its presence, and under its influence?'—on that occasion, instead of thinking of Mr. Rose, we retort with 'Yes, but how is its nature modified by yours?' For Pater's power of modifying impressions was a power like that of lust.

[1] 'Power' and 'might', and words formed from them, are among those most characteristic of Wordsworth. Keats learned Wordsworth's usage. On occasions the debt is a subtle one: Keats' 'taste the sadness of her might' ('Ode on Melancholy', l. 29) is derived from such expressions as 'the might of joy' ('Resolution and Independence', ll. 22 f.).

[2] *Poetical Works*, ed. cit., ii. 427.

[3] My italics.

## VII

IT WAS perhaps because there was all this power available that the critic who proclaimed his limitation to the impression of objects that are beautiful made so many predatory raids on objects whose prime quality is not aesthetic. If Pater did not insist that 'beauty is truth', he was inclined to insist that truth—or goodness or wisdom or thinking—is beauty. In his Preface he listed the following as objects giving pleasure to the aesthetic critic:

the picture, the landscape, the engaging personality in life or in a book, La Gioconda, the hills of Carrara, Pico of Mirandula, are valuable for their virtues,[1] as we say in speaking of a herb, a wine, a gem; for the property each has of affecting one with a special, unique impression of pleasure.[2]

The predatory instincts of the aesthetic critic were to be made clearer still in a hoveringly daring sentence given to Mr. Rose:

To the eye of true taste, an Aquinas in his cell before a crucifix, or a Narcissus gazing at himself in a still fountain, are—in their own ways, you know—equally beautiful.[3]

On several other occasions Mallock quietly copied Pater's way of listing incompatibles as if they were all on the same footing. One such list I reserved on transcribing the dreamy disquisition of Mr. Rose:

a beautiful face, a rainbow, a ruined temple, a death-bed, or a line of poetry.

As satiric method it is consummate. By doing nothing more than make a list such as Pater himself might have made Mallock makes Pater's lists look silly: the only difference is that Mallock's list is compiled with the tongue in the cheek.

[1] That is, their 'powers and forces'.
[2] p. ix.
[3] *The New Republic*, ii. 129.

The attempt to absorb other categories into the aesthetic was one that Pater vividly encouraged rather than originated. In the nineteenth century attempts were often made to absorb the beautiful into whatever category was preferred. What remained constant throughout the rearrangements was the beautiful, whether absorbed or absorbing. Wordsworth had made it the victim of an absorption effected by a sort of pagan religiosity: as a human being he had been prompted to thoughts too deep for tears by a flower, by 'the meanest flower that blows'. On the other hand Keats pulled the beautiful near to man—to man who had no religion except a love of beauty—as if it were a fur coat. He showed no decided sense of the difference between a warmth supplied him by a flower (not the meanest) and that supplied him by a human being:

> . . . when the melancholy fit shall fall . . .
> Then glut thy sorrow on a morning rose,
>   Or on the rainbow of the salt sand-wave,
>   Or on the wealth of globed peonies;
> Or if thy mistress some rich anger shows,
>   Emprison her soft hand, and let her rave,
>   And feed deep, deep upon her peerless eyes.[1]

I used the word 'man' in my description of Keats. But the term was too generous: the figures of the last three lines are dolls: 'Among the objects', commented Bridges, 'on which a sensitive mind is recommended to indulge its melancholy fit, the anger of his mistress is enumerated with roses, peonies, and rainbows, as a beautiful phenomenon plainly without respect to its cause, meaning or effect.'[2] Keats's list of incompatibles was seized on and made into a formula. Then there was the famous list drawn up by one of Browning's

---

[1] 'Ode on Melancholy', ll. 11 ff.
[2] *Collected Essays, Papers &c.*, iv (1929), p. 163.

bishops, a list which scarcely had an ecclesiastical authority:

> how can we guard our unbelief,
> Make it bear fruit to us?—the problem here.
> Just when we are safest, there's a sunset-touch,
> A fancy from a flower-bell, some one's death,
> A chorus-ending from Euripides—
> And that's enough for fifty hopes and fears. . . .[1]

Here the objects of painter, poet, ordinary man, scholar are all merged as equally prompting religious enquiry. And it was from this list that Mallock took his most shockingly incongruous item. Repeated criticism of these pleasant confusions came from Newman. He pilloried a string of them in the Appendix to his *Discourses on the Scope and Nature of University Education*—the work which we now read as it ended its textual history in *The Idea of a University*.[2] In that Appendix Newman illustrated various points in his lectures by widely ranging quotations. Among them is one from a translated volume of Tieck which shows the hero beside himself with erotic ecstasy while participating in the devotions of his mistress:

It seemed to him as if, from the wounds of longing, his existence was bleeding away in ardent prayers. Every word of the priest thrilled through him; every tone of the music gushed devotion into his bosom; his lips quivered, as the fair one pressed the Crucifix of her rosary to her rosy mouth.

And so on. Newman turns from his transcript with the comment:

Which is the object of worship here—the true Incarnate Lord, or the dust and ashes?[3]

---

[1] 'Bishop Blougram's Apology'.

[2] The best brief account of the text of Newman's writings is that indispensable essay, 'On Reading Newman' which Fr. Tristram contributed to *Newman Centenary Essays*, 1945, pp. 223 ff.

[3] Op. cit., 1852, p. 438.

Pater's confusions were subtler and more fastidious than this German carnival, but confusion no less. Under the thickest bank of garden flowers Mallock's arm was long enough to find the serpent. Nor was Henry James more merciful. Mallock had substituted a clear moral line for a blur, but had left undisturbed the high level on the social and intellectual scale: his story takes place among notables in an English country house; he made the confusion look comic but kept it fashionable and English. Henry James, ignoring the moral ambiguity, enlarged the discredit by exhibiting an early convert, one of 'the children of this world'[1], in the person of his Mrs. Church. This American lady, travelling Europe, had found in the 'Conclusion' of *The Renaissance* (and in Arnold's boosting of 'the best') a gospel delightfully easy to follow:

... Mrs. Church was as gracious as I could have desired; she put her marker into her book, and folded her plump little hands on the cover ... she embarked ... upon those general considerations in which her refined intellect was so much at home.

'Always at your studies, Mrs. Church', I ventured to observe.

'Que voulez-vous? ... Do you know my secret?' she asked, with an air of brightening confidence. And she paused a moment before she imparted her secret—'To care only for the *best*! To do the best, to know the best—to have, to desire, to recognise, only the best. That's what I have always done, in my quiet little way. I have gone through Europe on my devoted little errand, seeking, seeing, heeding, only the best. ... That's the real secret—to get something everywhere. ... Sometimes it has been a little music, sometimes a little deeper insight into the history of art; every little counts you know. Sometimes it has been just a glimpse, a view, a lovely landscape, an impression. We have always been on the look-out. Sometimes it has been a valued friendship, a delightful social tie.[2]

---

[1] See p. 133 below.
[2] *Washington Square: The Pension Beaurepas* ... 1881, ii. 173 f.

I

## VIII

A N 'Appreciation' by Pater was sometimes another name for an attempt to claim territory for the aesthetic critic which belongs rightfully, or belongs in the first place, to literary criticism in general. On this head Pater's worst offence, so far as English literature goes, was the Appreciation entitled 'Wordsworth'. That Appreciation begins by announcing a concern with 'the true aesthetic value' of Wordsworth's poetry. Any one, however, who brings such a concern to Wordsworth's poetry is doomed to an early disappointment or to an early conversion; if he continues in his reading it will be to discover other things. Wordsworth was not Keats. His sense of beauty was merely a minor function, cowed by his sense of the sublime. His poetry concerned things which, even if they are beautiful, are valued first of all because they interest, interpret, console or ennoble mankind; or if not always mankind, Wordsworth. The Wordsworth that Pater built up is not the Wordsworth as (in his life and works) he really was in his own time, was in Pater's, or is in ours. He is made out as too exquisite, too tremulously sensitive, too freely passionate. Pater spoke of his 'life of much quiet delicacy', and described his imagery also as 'delicate'. Then the fellow-ship Wordsworth discovered between man and such a thing as a lichened stone is called 'weird', many of his effects called 'strange', and the 'mysticism' of 'Daffodils' and 'Two April Mornings' 'half playful'. These qualities of delicacy, weird-ness, strangeness, are not cardinal qualities of Wordsworth's poetry, even if they exist there at all. And Pater found them because he was looking for beauty. It may be noted that the Wordsworth presented here and there in the Appreciation of Coleridge is much truer both as to life and as to poems: e.g., Pater forgot himself enough to perceive Wordsworth's

'fine mountain atmosphere of mind'.[1] Truer also is the
Wordsworth occupying a page of the Preface to *The
Renaissance*. The Wordsworth of the Appreciation bearing
his name is a scented Wordsworth. In making him an
aesthete, Pater was as far astray as when he compared
'Resolution and Independence' with 'The Eve of St. Agnes'
in respect of 'fullness of imagery'.[2] And he was far astray
because he was near home: he applied to Wordsworth the
epithets denoting the qualities that delighted himself, and that
delighted himself in things that were beautiful. His Wordsworth was too much like Pater. He strikes one as a mixture
of Gissing's Henry Ryecroft and Mr. Walter de la Mare.
Here the temperament got the better of the object. After
perverting it into the beautiful, it annexed it.

## IX

PATER, then, extended the bounds of the aesthetic critic
illegitimately. But to transgress a bad law is to obey a better
one. And the beneficent result of the transgression was that
in practice Pater's limitation of his object was not so drastic as
he had advertised. And sometimes there was a cleaner emanci-
pation. Sometimes Pater took over objects not mainly, or in
the first place, beautiful, and did not degrade them by
ignoring all but their beauty. On these occasions he went out
into the object, shedding his aesthetics as he went. When he
forgot that the aesthetic bounds existed, his criticism was not
aesthetic criticism at all, except as any and every sort of
criticism is so. Pater rightly saw that beauty was a constant in
literature—classical literature exhibiting beauty with order,

[1] *Appreciations*, p. 87.
[2] Op. cit., p. 43. Pater calls Keats's poem by the title of one of Tennyson's,
'Saint Agnes' Eve'.

and romantic literature beauty with strangeness.[1] But this beauty, as Pater also saw, was not invariably fierce and claimant. It was often merely beautiful to the pitch of providing the pleasure that readers had always asked of literature—a pleasure that is usually a mild one. Every critic is aware of the need for literature to provide this degree of beauty, however vague his awareness of it, and whatever other qualities he attends to mainly or in the first place. Pater, therefore, is sometimes no more an aesthetic critic than other critics are.

To some extent, Pater's confusions may have been due to the uncertain meaning of the very term he paraded on his banner. The term 'aesthetic' has been a hard one to pin down to one meaning—witness its history as given in the *Oxford English Dictionary*. Not concerned with its use by the epistemologists, Pater considered it as pertaining to 'taste'. Even so he did not limit its application to the beautiful objects on which 'taste' is properly exercised—that is, to aspects of external nature and to the 'fine' arts. He allowed it to stray into literature. And to leave plains and mountains, pictures and music, for literature is to leave objects in which beauty may be allowed on occasions and for most men to be supreme for objects in which beauty is almost always submerged or outfaced by admixture with the human, and so with the moral, social, political and what not. Literature deals with man, and though it is beautiful, beauty is seldom its prime characteristic.

Pater had the good sense to see this, if not always squarely. From the start his objects included man. When he represented the aesthetic critic as asking 'Does [this object] give me pleasure?' he included among the possible givers of that

[1] *Appreciations*, p. 248.

pleasure objects other than objects of 'taste'. 'The objects with which aesthetic criticism deals' were made to include from the start, 'artistic and accomplished forms of human life', and 'engaging personalit[ies] presented in life or in a book'—those as well as 'music', 'poetry', 'song' and 'picture'. Of course he claimed all these things and persons as aesthetic. But his interest did not stop at the aesthetic when as always his human objects had other claims on him. When he spoke of men 'artistic', 'accomplished' and 'engaging', he was not so much limiting the interest these objects provided *qua* men, as ruling out certain sorts of men altogether—we cannot see him writing on the Borgias, Machiavelli or Henry VIII. When he put certain Renaissance figures in 'the *House Beautiful*', they included 'saints' as well as the painters of certain beautiful pictures. In the second edition of *The Renaissance*, among other passages, this was added:

> For in the *House Beautiful* the saints too have their place; and the student of the Renaissance has this advantage over the student of the emancipation of the human mind in the Reformation, or the French Revolution, that, in tracing the footsteps of humanity to higher levels, he is not beset at every turn by the inflexibilities and antagonisms of some well-recognised controversy, with rigidly defined opposites, exhausting the intelligence and limiting one's sympathies. That opposition of the professional defenders of a mere system to the more sincere and generous play of the forces of human mind and character, which I noted as the secret of Abelard's struggle, is indeed always powerful. But the incompatibility of souls really 'fair' is not essential; and within the enchanted region of the Renaissance, one needs not be for ever on one's guard; here there are no fixed parties, no exclusions; all breathes of that unity of culture in which whatsoever things are comely are reconciled, for the elevation and adornment of our spirits. And just in proportion as those who took part in the Renaissance become centrally representative of it, just so much the more is this condition realised in them. The wicked popes, and the loveless tyrants,

who from time to time become its patrons, or mere speculators in its fortunes, lend themselves easily to disputations, and, from this side or that, the spirit of controversy lays just hands on them. But the painter of the *Last Supper*, with his kindred, live in a land where controversy has no breathing-place, and refuse to be classified.[1]

Though Pater excluded from consideration certain sorts of men, he did not exclude men. And though he might often speak of such human matters as 'self-restraint', 'austerity', and 'human feeling'[2] as if they were flowers, he did not always do so. His total response was other than the aesthetic, and being other was deeper—deeper, that is, as depth is measured by mankind as a whole. Some of the works he singled out for aesthetic criticism were works that had little to offer such criticism. In so far as English literature went, they included Shakespeare's histories (which though they have no wicked popes, have loveless tyrants in plenty and in addition have Falstaff, Doll Tearsheet and Pistol) and *Measure for Measure* (a play which is squarely based on the matter and morals of sexual relationships); and he wrote on Sir Thomas Browne who wrote on vulgar errors. As Pater well knew, a critic cannot live by cake alone. And the non-aesthetic exists so plentifully in Pater's objects that we should be ready to overlook his self-elected title, and read his writings as unlabelled criticism, taking whatever they give. It was seldom that he allowed his title to restrict him. In his essay on Botticelli, he threw it over and spoke of himself as providing 'general criticism', and what was more, general criticism on 'a secondary painter'. And towards the end of his essay on Winckelmann, there was an unaesthetic blast that might have come straight from Arnold:

The aim of a right criticism is to place Winckelmann in an intel-

---

[1] 1877 edition, pp. 28 f.          [2] *Appreciations*, pp. 14, 32, 103.

lectual perspective, of which Goethe is the foreground. For, after all, he is infinitely less than Goethe; it is chiefly because at certain points he comes in contact with Goethe that criticism entertains consideration of him.[1]

Here aesthetic criticism was conveniently forgotten in a larger if less manageable interest. In that late essay on style he was to write that

the chief stimulus of good style is to possess a full, rich, complex matter to grapple with.[2]

Here was the kinetic imagery which Pater first enlisted for the aesthetic critic, but serving now other ends. Even from the start, however, Pater had had the good sense not to deny himself his share of interest in those ends. And to call those ends aesthetic would be to slight them.

---

[1] *The Renaissance*, p. 200.    [2] *Appreciations*, p. 12.

# V

## Pater, Mr. Rose, and the 'Conclusion' of 'The Renaissance'

LOOKING back over forty years on the most brilliant novel ever written by an undergraduate, William Hurrell Mallock told how and why he had written it:

from my second year of residence [at Balliol] onwards I was constantly engaged in tentative sketches of a book in which I hoped some day to give a comprehensive picture of the moral and intellectual conditions to which my Oxford experiences had by that time raised or reduced me. That book was *The New Republic* [or, to give it its full title, *The New Republic; or, Culture, Faith and Philosophy in an English Country House*]. . . .

The form of nearly every book is more or less fashioned on some model or models. My own models in the case of *The New Republic* were *The Republic* of Plato, the *Satyricon* of Petronius Arbiter, and the so-called novels of Peacock. All these books introduce us to circles of friends who discuss questions of philosophy, religion, art, or the problems of social life, each character representing some prevalent view, and their arguments being so arranged as to have, when taken together, some general and coherent meaning. Many of Peacock's characters are taken direct from life, and in this respect I made myself a disciple of Peacock. My characters in *The New Republic* were all portraits, though each was meant to be typical. . . . The principal speakers . . . were drawn without any disguise from persons so eminent and influential that a definite fidelity of portraiture was in their case essential to my plan. Mr. Storks and Mr. Stockton, the prosaic and the sentimental materialists, were meant for Professors Huxley and Tyndal [*sic*]. Mr. Luke was Matthew Arnold. Mr. Rose was Pater. Mr. Saunders, so far as his atheism was concerned, was suggested by Professor Clifford. Mrs. Sinclair was the beautiful 'Violet Fane'; and finally—more important than any others—Dr. Jenkinson was Jowett, and

Mr. Herbert was Ruskin. All these people I set talking in polite antagonism to one another, their one underlying subject being the rational aim of life, and the manner in which a definitive supernatural faith was essential, extraneous or positively prejudicial to this.

To all the arguments advanced I endeavoured to do strict justice, my own criticisms merely taking the form of pushing most of them to some consequence more extreme, but more strictly logical, than any which those who proclaimed them either realised or had the courage to avow.[1]

This is not the only account of the particular matter which is one of the concerns of the present essay, the matter of the creation of Mr. Rose. In a letter of 1904 to Thomas Wright (the author of that vulgarising but informative biography of Pater) Mallock gave another account of his aims:

The fanciful sketch of Pater introduced into *The New Republic* was meant to represent an attitude of mind rather than a man.[2]

This version, one must believe, is not so faithful as the longer version: it makes too little of the amount of Pater included in Mr. Rose.

In the more faithful account two matters may be roughly distinguished: firstly, that Mr. Rose is derived from Pater (i.e., from a particular human being) and also from the type to which Pater was thought to belong (i.e., the pre-Raphaelites, the hedonists); and, secondly, that Mr. Rose pushes Pater's views a step farther than Pater pushed them, bringing them to the test of a clearer light than that of the fallen day which, while they remained Pater's, they had about them. On the one hand physical characteristics, on the other philosophy. Both are important for Mallock's purposes because, though he is aiming at criticism, he has chosen to aim at it in a novel.

[1] *Memoirs of Life and Literature*, 1920, p. 65 f.
[2] Thomas Wright, *The Life of Walter Pater*, 1907, ii. 12.

II

IT IS immediately clear that Mr. Rose resembles Pater in appearance and in manner of talking. Mallock, so Matthew Arnold happens to tell us, had met his object.[1] It could scarcely have been otherwise: they were both resident in Oxford, and by that time Pater was famous or almost so, and the young Mallock as social as he was brilliant. But meeting can scarcely have been necessary in streets where every 'aesthete' stares hard at every other, and in rooms where vivid gossip may be picked up at pleasure. By whatever means he got his knowledge, Mallock certainly knew enough about Pater to make a telling sketch of him. Mr. Rose bears the moustache which was already the salient object, indeed the 'heavy Bismarckian' object, on Pater's 'uncomely' face.[2] Mallock also knew enough about Pater's manner of talking. In Gosse's account of the Pater of these years come this description and this explanation (the description is the more interesting because of the reluctance with which Pater is yielded up to Mallock):

With natures like his, in which the tide of physical spirits runs low, in which the vitality is lukewarm, the first idea in the presence of anything too vivacious is to retreat, and the most obvious form of social retreat is what we call 'affectation'. It is not to be denied that, in the old days, Pater, startled by strangers, was apt to seem affected: he retreated as into a fortress, and enclosed himself in a sort of solemn effeminacy. It was, at its worst, mild in comparison with what the masters of preposterous behaviour have since accustomed us to, but it reminded one too much of Mr. Rose. It was put on entirely for the benefit of strangers, and to his inner circle of friends it seemed like a joke. Perhaps in some measure it was a joke; no one could

[1] *Letters*, ii. 140.

[2] Wright, op. cit., i. 193 and 236. In his chapter 'The Story of a Moustache', Wright tells how friends of Pater encouraged its cultivation in the interest of diminishing his plainness.

ever quite tell whether Pater's strange *rictus* was closer to laughter or to tears.[1]

But, of course, the main source of the talk and general behaviour lay in the written word, in the *Studies in the History of the Renaissance*, which Pater had published four years earlier. For the detecting of this source no reader of *The New Republic* had need of any local advantage. On one occasion in the novel Mr. Rose is made to lift his eyebrows wearily, and if this was not Pater's habit, it was that of the eyelids of somebody even more widely known than himself, his Mona Lisa. And whereas Pater had written

This at least of flame-like our life has, that it is but the concurrence, renewed from moment to moment, of forces parting sooner or later on their ways,[2]

here was Mr. Rose fluting

This much at least of sea-like man's mind has, that scarcely anything so distinctly gives a tone to it as the colour of the skies he lives under.[3]

It is not surprising that the magazine reviewers readily detected the original of Mr. Rose.

Since *The Renaissance* was as famous for its style as for anything else, a word may be said of Mallock's skill as a parodist. The reviewer in *The Athenaeum* thought that skill wholly successful:[4] he found *The Renaissance* parodied so beautifully as to seem, on occasions, original Pater. But except where Mr. Rose mimics the conformation of actual bits of *The Renaissance*, the original of the parody is not more

[1] *Critical Kit-Cats*, 1896, p. 266 f.

[2] *Studies in the History of the Renaissance*, 1873, p. 208. Quotations from this book, unless it is otherwise stated, derive from this, the first edition. In the second edition, 1877, Pater changed the title to *The Renaissance: Studies in Art and Poetry*. When I refer to the book below I call it *The Renaissance*, whatever the edition referred to.

[3] *The New Republic*, ii. 124. The novel was published anonymously.

[4] 1877, p. 378.

than faintly recognisable. *The Renaissance* was written as if English were a learned language: that is how Pater recommended that English should be written.[1] Its sentences were compacted not so much out of language as out of fragments of language, fragments cherished as individually beautiful: they lend themselves, as if temporarily, to the sentence they help to fit out. Conversation in a novel, therefore, could scarcely be carried forward by their means, and Mallock is wise in giving Mr. Rose sentences as flowingly readable as those which he gives his other speakers. After all, it was not his style which had won Pater his place in *The New Republic*.

## III

M R. R O S E is introduced into *The New Republic* along with all the other guests at Otho Laurence's house-party, a house-party so intellectual as almost to have the air of a Summer School. He is pointed out to one of them by their host:

That, too, is another critic close by [Mr. Luke]—the pale creature, with large moustache, looking out of the window at the sunset. He is Mr. Rose, the pre-Raphaelite. He always speaks in an under-tone, and his two topics are self-indulgence and art.[2]

A little later we find that

Mr. Rose had taken a crimson flower from a vase on the table, and, looking at it himself with a grave regard, was pointing out its infinite and passionate beauties to the lady next him.[3]

When Mr. Rose 'almost directly' breaks into the discussion

---

[1] 'A busy age will hardly educate its writers in correctness. Let its writers make time to write English more as a learned language; and completing that correction of style which had only gone a certain way in the last century, raise the general level of language towards their own.' *Essays from 'The Guardian'*, 1901, p. 15. For an instance of this principle working to bad effect see the quotation from Pater's review of *Dorian Gray* (pp. 132 f. below).

[2] *The New Republic*, i. 24.

[3] Op. cit., i. 31.

on life which is proceeding according to Laurence's plan, it is to this effect and with this inevitable result:

'[As for] me', he said, raising his eyebrows wearily, and sending his words floating down the table in a languid monotone, ' . . . I rather look upon life as a chamber, which we decorate as we would decorate the chamber of the woman or the youth that we love, tinting the walls of it with symphonies of subdued colour, and filling it with works of fair form, and with flowers, and with strange scents, and with instruments of music. And this can be done now as well—better rather— than in any former time: since we know that so many of the old aims were false, and so cease to be distracted by them. We have learned the weariness of creeds; and know that for us the grave has no secrets. We have learned that the aim of life is life; and what does successful life consist in? Simply', said Mr. Rose, speaking very slowly, and with a soft solemnity, 'in the consciousness of exquisite living—in the making our own each highest thrill of joy that the moment offers us— be it some touch of colour on the sea or on the mountains, the early dew in the crimson shadows of a rose, the shining of a woman's limbs in clear water or—'

Here unfortunately a sound of ' 'Sh' broke softly from several mouths. Mr. Rose was slightly disconcerted. . . .[1]

And so the book proceeds, giving several speeches to Mr. Rose, but not of course making him figure very prominently: after all, the other guests include Ruskin, Arnold, and Jowett. The speeches given him are enough to earn him Lady Ambrose's summary:

'What a very odd man Mr. Rose is! . . . He always seems to talk of everybody as if they had no clothes on. . . .'[2]

And yet Lady Ambrose is spared the worst:

'I was looking before dinner', said Mr. Rose, who with Laurence was bringing up the rear, 'at the books in your Uncle's pavilion in the garden [Laurence had inherited the house from his atheist and loose-

---

[1] Op. cit., i. 40 ff.          [2] Op. cit. ii. 139.

living uncle]; and I saw there, in a closed case, a copy of the "Cultes secrets des Dames Romaines".'

'Well?' said Laurence a little stiffly. 'It has been locked up for years.'

'I conceived as much', said Mr. Rose gently. 'As you do not seem to set much store by the work, I will give you thirty pounds for it.'[1]

I V

M A L L O C K said that his portrait of Pater, like that of each of his speakers, was a portrait both individual and typical. But that double value is of a kind which a novelist cannot transmit in practice: when once the reader has spotted the individual, he makes him the helpless repository of everything said of the type. Pater had to bear the full brunt of both the individual and the typical, the reader either agreeing or not agreeing that to bear the full brunt was just. The reviewer in *The Saturday Review* was among those who did not agree, though he shows that he knew what was at stake: 'Mr. Rose', he said, 'is not the man that he is meant to be.'[2] (When reviewing *The Renaissance* four years earlier, *The Saturday Review* had begun by saying that 'Mr. Pater . . . is free from the grossness which has been laid to the charge of "the fleshly school".')[3] Mallock's crucial distinction was lost on the reviewer, who could not forget the moustache and the eyebrows. It was a pity that this was inevitably so when Mallock's aim was mainly the criticism of Pater's ideas.

Pater was bearing the brunt of Mr. Rose earlier than readers of any but the first edition of *The New Republic* have

---

[1] Op. cit., ii. 219 f.

[2] 1877, p. 554.

[3] 1873, p. 123. Robert Buchanan, writing under the name 'Thomas Maitland', had published 'The Fleshly School of Poetry: Mr. D. G. Rossetti' in *The Contemporary Review* of 1871. In 1872 he enlarged it and published it as a pamphlet bearing the title *The Fleshly School of Poetry: And other phenomena of the day*. In the enlarged form Swinburne was attacked also.

supposed. The first edition was published in March 1877. That is, the first edition in book form. For the verso of the title-page of its first volume makes this bibliographical announcement:

The New Republic was originally published in Belgravia, but in an incomplete and somewhat fragmentary condition. . . . It is now, with complete revision, restored to its original form, which differs materially from that which it had for a time to assume.[1]

This note is not as clear as it might be. I do not understand why the novel is said to be 'restored to its original form', when Mallock tells us that its original form had been long and painfully overlaid by successive re-writings: 'I wrote *The New Republic*', he says, 'six or seven times over.'[2] Presumably the version in the magazine was the fifth (if there were six versions in all) or the sixth (if there were seven). So far as Mr. Rose is concerned the changes which the 1877 version made over the version in *Belgravia* were not 'material': they were verbal changes and changes of arrangement. (The most amusing verbal change is that by which Mr. Rose's bid for the *Cultes secrets* is raised by five pounds: in the *Belgravia* version he only offered twenty-five). The version in *Belgravia* ran monthly from June to December 1876. Mr. Rose had therefore been in the public eye well and long by the time that Pater's second edition appeared in June 1877, an edition enhanced by the inclusion of a new essay but mutilated by the withdrawal of its famous 'Conclusion'. When that piece was reinserted in the third edition of 1888, Pater added an explanation:

This brief 'Conclusion' was omitted in the second edition of this book, as I conceived it might possibly mislead some of those young men

---

[1] In transcribing I simplify the typography.
[2] *Memoirs*, ed. cit., p. 66.

into whose hands it might fall. On the whole, I have thought it best to reprint it here, with some slight changes which bring it closer to my original meaning. I have dealt more fully in *Marius the Epicurean* with the thoughts suggested by it.

In drawing up this note Pater was thinking mainly of the undergraduates around and about him in Oxford: he speaks of young men, not of young people. Among the under-graduates who were misled Pater no doubt numbered Oscar Wilde. Wilde had read *The Renaissance* in 1874 during his freshman term, and, looking back, he declared what a 'strange influence [it exercised] over [his] life'.[1] Pater, we may believe, disapproved of the strangeness of this influence.[2] After all, Wilde was quite as merciless as Mallock in his zeal for developing Pater's views. It was one thing for Pater to have written

Not the fruit of experience, but experience itself is the end.[3]

and another thing for Wilde to write

One could never pay too high a price for any sensation.

So wrote Wilde in *Dorian Gray*,[4] and it was this novel that roused Pater to make, for once, a clear and comprehensive statement about his own version of epicureanism; it is a pity that when the oracle did speak unambiguously it should have been so late in the day:

Clever always, this book . . . seems intended to set forth anything but a homely philosophy of life for the middle-class—a kind of dainty Epicurean theory, rather—yet fails, to some degree, in this; and one can see why. A true Epicureanism aims at a complete though har-monious development of man's entire organism. To lose the moral sense therefore, for instance, the sense of sin and righteousness, as Mr. Wilde's hero—his heroes are bent on doing as speedily, as com-

---

[1] *De Profundis*, 1908 edition, p. 66.    [2] Wright, op. cit., ii. 125.
[3] See below p. 135.    [4] *Dorian Gray*, 1891, p. 84.

pletely as they can, is to lose, or lower, organisation, to become less complex, to pass from a higher to a lower degree of development.[1]

Pater must also have numbered Mallock among those misled; for Mr. Rose is a sensualist, at least in mind. Pater dropped his 'Conclusion', the main source and excuse for Mr. Rose, and by the time it reappeared it had been revised. Pater called it revisions 'slight'. But though they are slight in volume, they cannot be called slight in substance. Some of them change the values in sentences which use crucial terms like 'religion' and 'morality'.[2] The effect of these crucial changes is that they remove the discussion from the forum to a place apart: what was at first recommended to all as a system of life came to be recommended only to those included under the conveniently vague term 'children of this world'. The revisions tinker, therefore, rather than re-cast. Mallock could still have derived Mr. Rose from the new version but he could not have found in it the old degree of permissibility. Root and branch revision, however, was less necessary by 1888 since by then *Marius the Epicurean* was three years old. In that novel Pater, as he says, 'dealt more fully ... with the thoughts suggested by [the "Conclusion"]'. The novel makes it abundantly clear that Marius, nurtured on the same Heraclitean philosophy as the 'Conclusion', is no sensualist. What attracts him in *The Golden Ass* of Apuleius is its tale of Cupid and Psyche.[3]

[1] *The Bookman*, November 1891, p.59; reprinted in *Uncollected Essays*, 1903, p. 127.

[2] See below pp. 135 f.

[3] Pater's grasp of the dangers of his 'Conclusion' may have been strengthened by Bradley's *Ethical Studies*, which had appeared in Oxford in 1876, and which being designed to be controversial would almost certainly have been read by Pater. Bradley's third essay was entitled 'Pleasure for Pleasure's Sake', and contained the words:
  supposing it possible that Hedonism could be worked, yet common moral opinion is decided against its being, what it professes to be, a sufficient account of morals. (p. 81).

K

V

THE SOURCE for Mr. Rose's thoroughgoing philosophy is mainly in the 'Conclusion', a conclusion offering itself as a conclusion in two senses of the word. Those six laboriously exquisite pages are not so familiar as they once were, and it will be best to quote from them generously.

Pater, drawing on the discoveries of the scientists, represented man's physical being as a collocation of chemical elements, of elements cohering for a brief time during their career through universal flux. And, drawing on the discoveries of the epistemologists, he gave an account of man's mental being as 'a drift of momentary acts of sight and passion and thought'. 'At first sight', he continued,

experience seems to bury us under a flood of external objects, pressing upon us with a sharp importunate reality, calling us out of ourselves in a thousand forms of action. But when reflection begins to act upon those objects they are dissipated under its influence; the cohesive force is suspended like a trick of magic; each object is loosed into a group of impressions,—colour, odour, texture,—in the mind of the observer. And if we continue to dwell on this world, not of objects in the solidity with which language invests them, but of impressions unstable, flickering, inconsistent, which burn and are extinguished with our consciousness of them, it contracts still further; the whole scope of observation is dwarfed to the narrow chamber of the individual mind.

Pater dwells on the isolation of the individual:

Experience . . . is ringed round for each one of us by that thick wall of personality through which no real voice has ever pierced on its way to us, or from us to that which we can only conjecture to be without. Every one of those impressions is the impression of the individual in his isolation, each mind keeping as a solitary prisoner in its own dream of a world.

Analysis goes a step further still, and tells us that those impressions of the individual to which, for each one of us, experience dwindles down, are in perpetual flight; that each of them is limited by time, and that as time is infinitely divisible, each of them is infinitely divisible also; all that is actual in it being a single moment, gone while we try to apprehend it, of which it may ever be more truly said that it has ceased to be than that it is. To such a tremulous wisp constantly reforming itself on the stream, to a single sharp impression, with a sense in it, a relic more or less fleeting, of such moments gone by, what is *real* in our life fines itself down. It is with this movement, the passage and disso- lution of impressions, images, sensations, that analysis leaves off,—that continual vanishing away, that strange perpetual weaving and un- weaving of ourselves.

It seems that Pater cannot wholly believe in the completeness of the isolation since he proceeds to offer advice (the acts of writing and of publishing are themselves proofs that in practice he ignores at least the rigours of his philosophy). That advice is as follows:

The service of philosophy, and of religion and culture as well, to the human spirit, is to startle it into a sharp and eager observation.[1] Every moment some form grows perfect in hand or face; some tone on the hills or sea is choicer than the rest; some mood of passion or insight or intellectual excitement is irresistibly real and attractive for us, —for that moment only. Not the fruit of experience, but experience itself is the end. A counted number of pulses only is given to us of a variegated, dramatic life. How may we see in them all that is to be seen in them by the finest senses? How can we pass most swiftly from point to point, and be present always at the focus where the greatest number of vital forces unite in their purest energy?

To burn always with this hard gemlike flame, to maintain this ecstasy, is success in life. Failure is to form habits; for habit is relative to a stereotyped world; meantime it is only the roughness of the eye that makes any two persons, things, situations, seem alike. While all melts under our feet, we may well catch at any exquisite passion, or any contribution to knowledge that seems, by a lifted horizon, to set the spirit free for a moment, or any stirring of the senses, strange dyes,

[1] In the edition of 1888 this sentence became: 'The service of philosophy, of speculative culture, towards the human spirit, is to rouse, to startle it into sharp and eager observation.'

strange flowers, and curious odours, or work of the artist's hands, or the face of one's friend. Not to discriminate every moment some passionate attitude in those about us, and in the brilliance of their gifts some tragic dividing of forces on their ways is, on this short day of frost and sun, to sleep before evening. With this sense of the splendour of our experience and of its awful brevity, gathering all we are into one desperate effort to see and touch, we shall hardly have time to make theories about the things we see and touch. What we have to do is to be for ever curiously testing new opinions and courting new impressions, never acquiescing in a facile orthodoxy of Comte, or of Hegel, or of our own. Theories, or religious or philosophical ideas, as points of view, instruments of criticism, may help us to gather up what might otherwise pass unregarded by us.[1] *La philosophie, c'est la microscope de la pensée.* The theory, or idea, or system, which requires of us the sacrifice of any part of this experience, in consideration of some interest into which we cannot enter, or some abstract morality we have not identified with ourselves, or what is only conventional, has no real claim upon us.[2]

And so to the last words, the conclusion of the 'Conclusion'.

Well, we are all *condamnés*, as Victor Hugo says: *les hommes sont tous condamnés à morte avec des sursis indéfinis*: we have an interval, and then our place knows us no more. Some spend this interval in listlessness, some in high passions, the wisest[3] in art and song. For our one chance is in expanding that interval, in getting as many pulsations as possible into the given time. High passions give one this quickened sense of life, ecstasy and sorrow of love, political or religious enthusiasm, or the 'enthusiasm of humanity'.[4] Only, be sure it is passion, that it does yield you this fruit of a quickened, multiplied consciousness. Of this wisdom, the poetic passion, the desire of beauty, the love of art for art's sake has most; for art comes to you professing frankly to give nothing but the

[1] In the edition of 1888 the opening of this sentence became: 'Philosophical theories or ideas. . . .'

[2] In the edition of 1888 'some abstract morality' became 'some abstract theory'.

[3] In the edition of 1888 'the wisest' became 'the wisest, at least among "the children of this world".'

[4] In the edition of 1888 this sentence read: 'Great passions may give us this quickened sense of life, ecstasy and sorrow of love, the various forms of enthusiastic activity, disinterested or otherwise, which come naturally to many of us.'

highest quality to your moments as they pass, and simply for those moments' sake.

It is easy to pick a score of holes in these famous paragraphs: indeed holes are in them before we start. How, for instance, can we live 'a life of constant and eager observation' if 'experience seems to . . . call . . . us out of ourselves in a thousand forms of action', and not only seems but does? Pater left holes gaping, and they still gape in the final form of 1888.

Two holes, in particular, attract the point of the pen. Pater gives it out that 'Not the fruit of experience, but experience itself is the end'. But is it not clear that experience grows its fruit in us whether we will or no, and that, however we rank experience and its fruit, the fruit may be of such a kind as to make further experience of the same aesthetic kind impossible? When Oscar Wilde spoke of 'that book which has had such strange influence over my life', he spoke of it so in *De Profundis*, at a time when the old sort of aesthetic experience could never be the same again. And, for a second hole, Pater gives us no advice as to how we are to deal with that sort of aesthetic experience which takes it on itself to become action (that is one way of wording it). We can look at the tones of the sea and the hills, and, however long we look, they do not respond. But this is not so when we look at the face of a friend. Then, even if our observation produces no action in us of itself and directly, it may well produce some reaction: a friend looked at for a second too long acts, and willy-nilly we must act too. And if observation turns or leads to action, it is observation taking place in the world of men, and in that world some of the men who ignore the thickness of the walls which isolate individuals are lawyers, registrars, chemists, doctors, policemen. It was this particular hole that Mallock picked, and Pater looked foolish accordingly.

And yet there are certain other things to say about Pater and his 'Conclusion'. For it is a private as well as a public document, and even as a public document it could, and did, produce other effects than those seized on by Mallock.

## VI

THE ISOLATION of the individual is a concept that haunted nineteenth-century writers, but it was a concept that had more home-truth for Pater than for most. When a poem of Matthew Arnold invoked it as explanation of the frustrated passion of a young man, we have the comfort of knowing that, as he grew older, the young man was more readily able to ignore his isolation, and to believe that, however neatly the epistemologists managed to prove that 'no real voice has ever pierced [the walls] on its way to us', it was still possible to say with Newman that 'voices melt us, looks subdue us, deeds inflame us'.[1] Matthew Arnold came to forget about isolation. When he did think about it later on it was to deny it: 'men are solidary, or co-partners; and not isolated'.[2] But for Pater there was never very much inducement to forget. Gosse was to speak of his luke-warm vitality, and what was warmest in it—it aspired to the forbidden—was kept to itself by a moral constraint, a constraint operating with great completeness in life, if not with a firm-minded completeness in the writings. The prose-poem of the 'Conclusion', therefore, may be partly seen as the sort of lyric poem that exists to make a personal confession. For all

[1] Newman, 'Tamworth Reading Room' (1841), *Discussions and Arguments*, 1872, p. 293.
[2] *Last Essays on Church and Religion*, 1877, p. 115.

its happy vividness and intensity, and partly of course because of them, the confession is a poignant one. We must read it partly in the light of such a mixed passage as this:

One notable friendship, the fortune of which we may trace through [Winckelmann's] letters, begins with an antique, chivalrous letter in French, and ends noisily in a burst of angry fire. Far from reaching the quietism, the bland indifference of art, such attachments are nevertheless more susceptible than any others of equal strength of a purely intellectual culture. Of passion, of physical stir, they contain just so much as stimulates the eye to the last lurking delicacies of colour and form;[1]

or this from the 'imaginary' but virtually autobiographical 'portrait' 'The Child in the House':

he could trace two predominant processes of mental change in him— the growth of an almost diseased sensibility to the spectacle of suffering, and, parallel with this, the rapid growth of a certain capacity of fascination by bright colour and choice form—the sweet curvings, for instance, of the lips of those who seemed to him comely persons, modulated in such delicate unison to the things they said or sang,— marking early the activity in him of a more than customary sensuousness, 'the lust of the eye', as the Preacher says, which might lead him one day, how far! Could he have foreseen the weariness of the way![2]

Discreet self-revelation could scarcely go further, and to passages like these we can only listen with humility and submission. After such listening, the 'Conclusion' loses some of its extravagance, and Mr. Rose almost vanishes away.

## VII

AND at the same time the 'Conclusion' should be read in its

---

[1] *The Renaissance*, p. 163. As revised for the second edition, 1877, 'stir' became 'excitement', and 'last lurking' became 'finest'.

[2] *Miscellaneous Studies*, 1895, p. 181. The image from music, 'modulated in such delicate unison', is nonsense; cf. 'that modulated unison of landscape and persons' in 'The School of Giorgione' (*The Renaissance*, 1888, p. 160).

wide Victorian context. Four years earlier than Pater had published his *Renaissance* Arnold had published *Culture and Anarchy*, and that book owed its existence to his hope that the British middle-class might even yet take on some of the sweetness and light which he admired in the Greeks. Pater used the term 'culture' as confidently as Arnold. He even spoke of rendering a 'service to culture' (once in the 'Conclusion' and once in the essay on Winckelmann). He, too, was aiming at making the middle-class mind more lovely. The additions which Pater wanted to make to that mind differed, of course, from those Arnold wanted to make, though in differing Pater's wording of them seems to cling to Arnold's words, even to his syntax, perhaps even to his italics. Pater admired Arnold: he deferred to him as a master in the preface to his *Renaissance*. And if *Culture and Anarchy* was made of sterner stuff than anything Pater had it in him to make, Arnold to some extent had sanctioned a good deal of Pater's 'Conclusion' elsewhere. In his essay on Maurice de Guérin we read:

In few natures . . . is there really such essential consistency as in Guérin's . . . Poetry, the poetical instinct, was indeed the basis of his nature; but to say so thus absolutely is not quite enough. One aspect of poetry fascinated Guérin's imagination and held it prisoner. Poetry is the interpretress of the natural world, and she is the interpretress of the moral world; it was as the interpretress of the natural world that she had Guérin for her mouthpiece. To make magically near and real the life of Nature, and man's life only so far as it is a part of that Nature, was his faculty; a faculty of naturalistic, not of moral interpretation. This faculty always has for its basis a peculiar temperament, an extraordinary delicacy of organisation and susceptibility to impressions; in exercising it the poet is in a great degree passive (Wordsworth thus speaks of a *wise passiveness*), he aspires to be a sort of human Æolian-harp, catching and rendering every rustle of Nature. To assist at the evolution of the whole life of the world is his craving, and

intimately to feel it all:
> 'the glow, the thrill of life,
> Where, where do these abound?'

is what he asks: he resists being riveted and held stationary by any single impression, but would be borne on for ever down an enchanted stream. He goes into religion and out of religion, into society and out of society, not from the motives which impel men in general, but to feel what it is all like; he is thus hardly a moral agent. . . . He hovers over the tumult of life, but does not really put his hand to it.[1]

Arnold overrated Maurice de Guérin to this extent because, though he admitted that he found him a little morbid, Maurice de Guérin had the merit of making a salutary addition to the Philistine mind. And when Pater came to speak of rendering a service to culture, his service was intended to be none the less practical because some worthy people would find its hazing-over of the distinction between the beautiful and the good disturbing and even sickening. Pater confused the two categories because he was half in love with confusion *as* confusion (many of the aesthetic and historical effects he responded to were mingled effects). He confused them also because he was faced with more items of aesthetic pleasure than he knew what to do with. But there was an additional reason and sanction for confusion: the confusion of the beautiful and the good could be counted on to startle the British middle-class. If Pater was faced with too many items of aesthetic pleasure, they were faced with too few. And in order to clear away the confusion of the categories, the middle-class, after how long an abstinence, would have to attend, for however brief a space, to the beautiful.

Some members of the middle-class were so well convinced of the sincerity and timeliness of Pater's philanthropy that

[1] *Essays in Criticism*, pp. 104 f. The verses quoted are adapted from Arnold's own poem 'Obermann', ll. 97 f.

they saw the confusion as less important than, before the publication of *Marius*, it actually was.[1] Mallock and Wilde were misled, but not John Morley. As editor of *The Fortnightly Review* Morley had already published four of the chapters of *The Renaissance*, and on the appearance of the book he not only took the opportunity to review it himself but made his review an article. This is his comment on the 'Conclusion':

Of course this neither is, nor is meant to be, a complete scheme for wise living and wise dying. The Hedonist, and this is what Mr. Pater must be called by those who like to affix labels, holds just the same maxims with reference to the bulk of human conduct, the homespun substance of our days, as are held by other people in their senses. He knows perfectly well that the commonplace virtues of honesty, industry, punctuality, and the like, are the conditions of material prosperity, and moral integrity. Here he stands on the same ground as the rest of the world. He takes all that for granted, with or without regret that these limitations should be imposed by inexorable circumstances upon the capacity of human nature for fine delight in the passing moments. He has no design of interfering with the minor or major morals of the world, but only of dealing with what we may perhaps call the accentuating portion of life. In the majority of their daily actions a Catholic, a Protestant, a Positivist, are indistinguishable from one another, just as they are indistinguishable in the clothes they wear. It is the accentuating parts of conduct and belief that reveal their differences, and this is obviously of the most extreme importance,— less in its effect upon commonplace external morality which can take care of itself on independent grounds, than in its influence over the spiritual drift of the believer's life. It is what remains for a man seriously

---

[1] A testimony to the pleasant effect Pater had on a youth brought up strictly as a Non-conformist came recently from Mr. Eric Bligh: 'I found sentences and paragraphs I could not leave, [which caused me] profound mental excitement.' These sentences came from Pater's *Miscellaneous Studies* (1895) and were of the sort Pater could longest remain pleased with: '. . . a basket of yellow crab-apples left in the cool, old parlour . . .'; or:

Life in modern London even, in the heavy glow of summer, is stuff sufficient for the fresh imagination of a youth to build its 'palace of art' of.

(Eric Bligh, *Tooting Corner*, 1946, pp. 332 ff.)

to do or feel, over and above earning his living and respecting the laws. What is to give significance and worth to his life, after complying with the conditions essential to its maintenance and outward order? A great many people in all times, perhaps the most, give a practical answer to the question by ignoring it, and living unaccented lives of dulness or frivolity. A great many others find an answer in devotion to divine mysteries, which round the purpose of their lives and light the weariness of mechanical days. The writer of the essays before us answers it as we have seen, and there is now a numerous sect among cultivated people who accept his answer and act upon it.[1]

Of course Morley gave Pater the benefit of several doubts— 'pray pardon my light dealing with his transgressions', he begged of Frederic Harrison.[2] But to deal lightly with Pater merely showed that he understood Pater better than Pater yet understood himself. He saw excesses as excesses:

In all this, notwithstanding its exaggeration, there is something to be glad of. It is the excess of a reaction, in itself very wholesome.[3]

Pater himself expressed his gratitude to Morley

for your explanation of my ethical point of view to which I fancy some readers have given a prominence I do not mean it to have.[4]

William James read Morley's 'big little article' with all its quotations from *The Renaissance*, and saw it as just the book for Henry to review if he had not unfortunately lost the chance by being abroad. His sister Alice had already read the book itself, and had pronounced it exquisite.[5] The 'better' Pater could have wished for no worthier testimonial.

---

[1] *The Fortnightly Review*, 1873, pp. 474 ff.
[2] F. W. Knickerbocker, *Free Minds: John Morley and His Friends*, Cambridge, Mass., 1943, p. 193.
[3] *The Fortnightly Review*, p. 475.
[4] F. W. Knickerbocker, *Free Minds: John Morley and His Friends*, Cambridge, Mass., 1943, p. 193.
[5] R. B. Perry, *The Thought and Character of William James*, [1936], i. 344.

VII

FINALLY, Pater's 'Conclusion' should not be read apart from the splendid essay on Winckelmann which, when the 'Conclusion' was held back from the second edition, took up its stand as itself the conclusion.

Pater believed that the 'secret' of Winckelmann's response to ancient art lay in his being able to respond to its 'breadth, centrality . . . blitheness and repose' as if he himself were a pagan.[1] But that was an achievement far away in the eighteenth century before men became distracted by 'the gaudy, perplexed light of modern life . . . with its conflicting claims, its entangled interests'.[2] 'Certainly for us of the modern world', he knew, 'the problem of unity with ourselves in blitheness and repose, is far harder than it was for the Greek within the simple terms of antique life.'[3] The question for Goethe, who learned so much from Winckelmann, and the problem for Goethe's successors is this: 'Can [the completeness and serenity] of the antique be communicated to artistic productions which contain the fulness of the experience of the modern world? . . . Can art represent men and women in these bewildering toils so as to give the spirit at least an equivalent for the sense of freedom?'[4] for 'What modern art has to do in the service of culture is so to rearrange the details of modern life, so to reflect it, that it may satisfy the spirit.'[5] And the answer to Pater's questions is an affirmative answer because of the great novels of the modern world:

Goethe's *Wahlverwandtschaften* [i.e. his novel *Elective Affinities*] is a high instance of modern art dealing thus with modern life; it regards that life as the modern mind must regard it, but reflects upon it

---

[1] *The Renaissance*, p. 201.     [2] Ibid.
[3] Op. cit., p. 201 f.     [4] Op. cit., p. 204 ff.
[5] Ibid.

blitheness and repose. Natural laws we shall never modify, embarrass us as they may; but there is still something in the nobler or less noble attitude with which we watch their fatal combinations. In *Wahlverwandtschaften* this entanglement, this network of law, becomes a tragic situation, in which a group of noble men and women work out a supreme *dénouement*. Who, if he foresaw all, would fret against circumstances which endow one at the end with so high an experience?[1]

In the second edition, and in all later ones, Victor Hugo's name is coupled with Goethe's, and with their 'romances' are coupled 'some excellent work done *after* them', and 'so high an experience' becomes with even more gratitude 'those great experiences' (which are the last three words of *The Renaissance* of 1877).

The conclusion of 'Winckelmann' presents a very different account of the contemporary human lot, and offers a very different remedy for its troubles than those presented and offered by the 'Conclusion'. Instead of the exquisite pulsations of the becalmed spectator Pater offers us work (our predicament is 'far harder' to solve than the Greeks found theirs); instead of 'a drift of momentary acts of sight and passion and thought', Pater promises 'fulness' of experience, 'great' experience; instead of an impenetrable isolation Pater offers, for 'the service of culture', 'certain groups of noble men and women'. In other words Pater is here content to deal with his fellows as he finds them, as people who, if they turn to literature at all for an interpretation of their daily lives, turn not to Greek literature but to novels. For all his love of the Greeks, of aged Rome and infantine Christianity, of Renaissance pictures, we should not be far wrong if we saw Pater, throughout his career as a critic, 'aspiring' towards and finally achieving the content of the last paragraph of his late essay 'On Style':

[1] Op. cit., p. 206 f.

the distinction between great art and good art depend[s] immediately, as regards literature at all events, not on its form, but on the matter. Thackeray's *Esmond*, surely, is greater art than *Vanity Fair*, by the greater dignity of its interests. It is in the quality of the matter it informs or controls, its compass, its variety, its alliance to great ends, or the depth of the note of revolt, or the largeness of hope in it, that the greatness of literary art depends, as *The Divine Comedy, Paradise Lost, Les Misérables, The English Bible,* are great art. Given the conditions I have tried to explain as constituting good art;—then, if it be devoted further to the increase of men's happiness, to the redemption of the oppressed, or the enlargement of our sympathies with each other, or to such presentment of new or old truth about ourselves and our relation to the world as may ennoble and fortify us in our sojourn here, or immediately, as with Dante, to the glory of God, it will also be great art; if, over and above those qualities I summed up as mind and soul— that colour and mystic perfume, and that reasonable structure, it has something of the soul of humanity in it, and finds its logical, its architectural place, in the great structure of human life.[1]

In this declaration the nineteenth-century novel is calmly named along with instances of literature at its greatest. Nor does this paragraph stand alone. The praise of great nineteenth-century novels rises to full volume in the 'Postscript' to *Appreciations*. For Pater as for the ordinary run of his fellows the nineteenth century was the age of the great novelists (one notes that Thomas Hardy lifted the title of *A Group of Noble Dames* from a phrase I have just quoted). Arnold had used words like Pater's, but had limited them to readers of the classics, men who have 'commerce with the ancients': such readers he likened to

persons who have had a very weighty and impressive experience.[2]

Pater's remedy was more practical. To the last Arnold expected a little too much of the Greeks and not enough of George Eliot.

[1] *Appreciations*, p. 35 f.      [2] In the Preface to the Poems of 1853.

# VI

## Newman's Essay on Poetry: An Exposition and Comment

THE intellectual range and powers of Newman as a young don are nowhere concentrated more splendidly than in his essay on poetry.[1] 'Poetry with Reference to Aristotle's Poetics' was furnished in response to a request of the strangely versatile Blanco White,[2] who had been asked to edit a new magazine, and who looked to his friend Newman for a secular contribution to it: 'Give me an article on any subject you like', he pleaded, 'Divinity excepted for the present, for of that I expect a flood.'[3] Blanco White had known the young Newman for the few years during which his 'reputation as a thinker pure and simple—though confined to a comparatively small circle—was [perhaps] at its highest, [the days] when the bent of his mind was towards liberalism',[4] and he knew him well enough to know 'how difficult it is to persuade a mind like [his] to write without preparation.'[5] Fearing a refusal because of short notice, he offered anxious advice: 'I should strongly advise you to venture upon the strength of your *household stuff*—on the reading and reflection of many years. Write without much concern';[6] advice not unmixed with flattery: 'you are sure to write well . . . imagine yourself in our Common-Room [at Oriel], myself in the corner, Dornford passing the wine, &c., and tell us your mind on paper.'[7]

---

[1] *Essays Critical and Historical*, i. 1-26, to which is appended a Note, pp. 27-29.
[2] See Ward's *Life*, i. 38.  [3] *Letters*, i. 193.
[4] Ward's *Life*, i. 38.  [5] *Letters*, i. 194.
[6] Ibid.  [7] Ibid.

Newman responded with enthusiasm: he promised the essay requested and another besides. The first, on poetry, is that now under discussion; but the one on music never reached manuscript, or if manuscript, not print, the reason being, presumably, that the *London Review* ceased publication with its second number.[1] (So that Newman on music has to be pieced together from scattered sources, of which there happen to be two minor ones in the course of the essay on poetry.)

Newman took about two months to write his 11,000 words: Blanco White's letter asking for the essay bears the date 11 September 1828, and his letter rejoicing over its receipt the date 8 November. But though Newman could on occasion produce literature at as fast a rate as anybody—witness the race won against the clock in the composition of the *Apologia* and of some of the *Tracts for the Times*—it is unlikely that he found much leisure during those two autumn months. By 1828 he was not habituated to writing for print: the only things he had published so far (apart from the undergraduate poem, *St. Bartholomew's Eve*, of which he was part author only, and the few pages he had contributed to the *Logic* of his 'gentle and encouraging instructor',[2] Whately) were three articles in the *Encyclopaedia Metropolitana* on Cicero, Apollonius Tyanaeus, and the miracles of Scripture. Moreover, the public that would read a new London magazine was a more numerous and worldly public than that

[1] Newman's reasons for the failure of the magazine, in so far as it was due to editor and contributors, are given in the note he appended to the reprint of his essay in 1871, and could scarcely be more telling:
> the new publication required an editor of more vigorous health and enterprising mind, of more cheerful spirits, and greater power of working, and with larger knowledge of the English public, than Mr. White possessed; and writers, less bookish and academical than those, able as they were, on whom its fate depended. . . . As a whole, the Review was dull.
(*Essays Critical and Historical*, i. 27 f.)
[2] *Apologia*, p. 114.

which read anonymous minor poetry and books on logic, or encyclopaedia articles, or even than that which he was already drawing round his pulpit in St. Mary's: the public proposed was the whole 'liberal' reading public of England.

In its original form, the essay started off with a review of a contemporary work on Greek drama ('Take up any book you like',[1] Blanco White had cajoled, advised, commanded), and, after criticising Aristotle's remarks on the same subject, proceeded to its main business, a discussion of poetry in general in the threefold form of stating Aristotle's theory, explaining it, and modifying it,[2] with the help of 'illustrations'[3].

The essay appeared in the first number of the *London Review* in January 1829.[4] When Newman reprinted it among the *Essays* in 1871, he cut out the review section,[5] replaced it by one sentence as introduction, and, according to his Note, had the rest set up from his original manuscript, Blanco White having altered 'several sentences' by virtue of what his victim generously conceded as an 'editor's just prerogative'.

---

[1] *Letters*, i. 194.

[2] These are Newman's own terms (*Essays Critical and Historical*, i. 20).

[3] Unless otherwise stated, words and passages in quotation marks come from the essay under discussion. If any reader wishes to trace these quotations to their immediate context, he has only twenty-six pages to search: meanwhile other readers are spared the tedium of finding a flock of numerals related only to further numerals.

[4] See *Essays Critical and Historical*, i. 26, and 27f.

[5] In doing so, he sacrificed a Johnsonian paragraph of which the following is the latter half:

It is an officious aid which renders the acquisition of a language mechanical. Commentators are of service to stimulate the mind, and suggest thought; and though, when we view the wide field of criticism, it is impossible they should do more, yet, when that field is narrowed to the limit of academical success, there is a danger of their indulging indolence, or confirming the contracted views of dullness. These remarks are not so much directed against a valuable work like the [book under review], the very perusal of which may be made an exercise for the mind, as against an especial fault of the age. . .

(Text from *English Critical Essays* (*Nineteenth Century*), ed. Edmund D. Jones, 1916, pp. 224 f.)

L

II

NEWMAN's essay dives into its subject, and its subject, to begin with, is not so much Aristotle's *Poetics* as Newman's personal preference for a great number of other Greek tragedies over the tragedy which Aristotle 'is constantly thinking of... as he writes his Poetic',[1] the *Oedipus Tyrannus* of an author whom the young Newman had elsewhere described as 'dry, stiff, formal, affected, cold, prolix, dignified'.[2] What it comes to is that Newman cannot accept the primacy Aristotle accords to action, to plot, in a play. Aristotle's scheme he summarises as follows:

> Aristotle considers the excellence of a tragedy to depend upon its plot—and, since a tragedy, as such, is obviously the exhibition of an action, no one can deny his statement to be abstractedly true. Accordingly, he directs his principal attention to the economy of the fable; determines its range of subjects, delineates its proportions, traces its progress from a complication of incidents to their just and satisfactory settlement, investigates the means of making a train of events striking or affecting, and shows how the exhibition of character may be made subservient to the purpose of the action.

Aristotle finds great satisfaction in the dovetailed plot of the *Oedipus Tyrannus*, but Newman sees the plot of that play as something too obviously produced by an ingenious application of 'workmanship'. That word is crucial: Newman dislikes any evidence of skill.[3] And, leaving Aristotle to his

---

[1] J. T. Sheppard, *The Oedipus Tyrannus of Sophocles, translated and explained*, 1920, p. xii. Since I do not read Greek, I can only know the works of Aristotle and the Greek dramatists in translation, and my criticism of Newman's views on the literature translated is prompted mainly by S. H. Butcher's *Aristotle's Theory of Poetry and the Fine Arts*, 1895.

[2] Henry Tristram, 'The Classics', *A Tribute to Newman*, ed. M. Tierney, 1945, p. 256.

[3] Cf. 'Literature' (*The Idea of a University*, p. 279): '*Poeta nascitur, non fit*, says the proverb; and this is in numerous instances true of his poems, as well as of himself. They are born, not framed; they are a strain rather than a composition; and their perfection is the monument, not so much of his skill as of his power'.

preference, he turns to the many plays of Aeschylus, Sophocles, and Euripides that are 'beautiful', 'exquisite', endowed with 'grace and interest', and all this when at the same time they are plainly defective by the standards which centre in the *Tyrannus*: one play is found to provide little 'interest', one to be 'stationary', one 'irregular', one 'inartificial' (that is, constructed without art), one to exist merely as a pretext for 'the introduction of matter more important than itself', and 'sometimes [a plot] either wants or outlives the catastrophe'. Newman takes pleasure in listing these defects because he believes all such defects to be nugatory. 'Gods, heroes, kings, and dames, enter and retire: they may have a good reason for appearing,—they may have a very poor one; whatever it is, still we have no right to ask for it; the question is impertinent.' What he wants from a tragedy is not so much its tragic course as its moments of poetic greatness. And he departs from Aristotle because he sees that 'the inferior poem may, on his principle, be the better tragedy'. His point is clinched, to his own liking, by reference to the 'sudden inspiration . . . of the blind Oedipus, in the second play bearing his name, by which he is enabled, "without a guide", to lead the way to his place of death', an incident which in Newman's judgment 'produces more poetical effect than all the skilful intricacy of the plot of the Tyrannus. The latter excites an interest which scarcely lasts beyond the first reading—the former *decies repetita placebit*'.[1]

Unfortunately Newman simplifies Aristotle's conception of plot, crediting a critic he otherwise finds almost entirely sound and subtle with the belief that plot is at external

---

[1] Matthew Arnold took up the cause of plot in the preface to his *Poems* (1853), but the position he adopted does not wholly contradict Newman's. Both saw the importance of the 'primary human' emotions and differed only about how they wanted them presented.

contrivance. His simplication is almost that of Miss Dorothy
Sayers, who has amusingly adopted Aristotle as the patron
saint of detective novelists. And though he missed seeing his
low estimate of the *Tyrannus* reduced to the absurd by the
thousand masterpieces of twentieth-century detective fiction,
he had a ready means of restraining himself from error in his
own experience of the play of Sophocles, an experience
which, on his own showing, was complete enough to have
saved him: these are his words introducing a comparison of
the play with the *Agamemnon* of Aeschylus and the *Bacchae*
of Euripides:

the action of the Oedipus Tyrannus is frequently instanced by [Aristotle]
as a specimen of judgment and skill in the selection and combination of
the incidents; and in this point of view it is truly a masterly composition.
The clearness, precision, certainty, and vigour with which the line of the
action moves on to its termination is admirable. The character of
Oedipus, too, is finely drawn, and identified with the development of
the action.

And later we get this further testimonial—a surprising one
in view of the rest of the essay: 'The sweet composure, the
melodious fulness, the majesty and grace of Sophocles.' Now
if these are qualities of the *Tyrannus*, what becomes of the
remark that the play 'excites an interest which scarcely lasts
beyond the first reading'?

Is it true that a play well constructed and nothing more
can only 'interest' us once? Even if the *Tyrannus* offered
nothing worth our attention but its plot (which, as plot,
Newman admits to be very good), we should still be able to
read and see it a second time, if only because we do not
trouble to remember the particular moves by which the
parts of the action slide into place, and are quite happy to sit
back and watch them happen afresh: after an interval, people

can even re-read a detective novel. But Newman would not have allowed any play that showed 'sweet composure . . . melodious fulness . . . majesty and grace' to herd with the detective novels. And yet the greatness of the *Tyrannus*, and its characteristic greatness as a play, brings it nearer to the detective novel than to the lyric poem: for the first reason that it is a great play is because it is a detective novel and something more. It is a question of the end for which materials are used. No one goes to a detective novel for a reading of the nature of man and the universe. Novels in that form exist, it is true, in a relationship with those august matters, but in a relationship that is perfunctory. They base themselves on the law that requires a sin against society to be punished by society; but all their effort goes in constructing something with that law as foundation accepted and then forgotten. They exist to build a superstructure and to stock it with surprises.

The *Tyrannus*, however, works to a different end. It gives us the free run of the building in order to make us remember the foundation. Oedipus has killed his father and married his mother in ignorance of their identity, and the play consists of the series of jolts by which his guilt is uncovered as piece by piece his ignorance is removed. The word 'guilt' if not also the word 'ignorance' serves to show the distance separating the *Tyrannus* from the detective novel with its plot-for-plot's-sake. The plot of the *Tyrannus* is a vehicle, the vehicle of a criticism of the nature of man and the universe. The plot is the criticism. And not only that: the criticism consists in the very elaboration of the plot. The play exists to protest against a 'scheme of things', and the protest would have been strong even if the plot had been simpler, even if knowledge of the horrid facts had come on Oedipus like a bolt from the blue. But the strong protest made by a plot that was simple would merely have repeated the strong protest made by the prime facts of the tale themselves, the initial killing and marriage, facts which, already known to the audience, had already pointed the audience to the conclusion that fate was cruel. Sophocles writes his play because he can take his audience farther than they have gone of themselves. And his means of taking them farther is the construction of the plot, his making Oedipus learn the facts of his history one by one.

It is this process that embodies the dramatist's addition to the criticism already made by the audience: a fate already known as cruel is seen as more cruel still because it craftily arranges that Oedipus' enlightenment shall be a crescendo of torture.

> I play the torturer, by small and small
> To lengthen out the worst that must be spoken.[1]

Moreover, this course of torture is the more painful both for Oedipus and for the audience because it is his own goodness as a man and a king that has put him in its way—he has decreed that the offence which has brought the plague on his city shall receive punishment, not knowing that he himself is its perpetrator. The elaboration of the plot is therefore an elaboration of the suffering of a man who is doing his duty.

Newman allows that 'The character of Oedipus . . . is finely drawn, and identified with the development of the action', but he does not see how this identification excites more emotion and thought in the audience because the action develops ingeniously.

[1] Shakespeare, *Richard II*, III. ii. 198 f.

## III

THE critic who discusses Newman's conception of the role of the plot goes to great lengths to put him right, only to find his criticism virtually acknowledged in certain judgments scattered over the essay. What can we make of the following sentences but a confession that elements which Newman professes to admire most can defeat the ends of elements he confesses, on this occasion, to admire even more, elements that are in the keeping of the plot? Caught off his guard, he well sees the dilemma to which the lauded 'carelessness' of Euripides may lead:

Moral excellence in some characters may become even a fault. The Clytemnestra of Euripides is so interesting, that the divine vengeance, which is the main subject of the drama, seems almost unjust.

And why, if Newman believes that 'poetry' is more necessary than plot, should he look to plot, if not to save poetry, at least to improve it:

The original conception of a weak or guilty mind may have its intrinsic beauty; and much more so, when it is connected with a tale which finally adjusts whatever is reprehensible in the personages themselves. Richard [III] and Iago are subservient to the plot.

And finally, why this on Byron?

[The] bearing of character and plot on each other is not often found in Byron's poems. The Corsair is intended for a remarkable personage. We pass by the inconsistencies of his character, considered by itself. The grand fault is, that whether it be natural or not, we are obliged to accept the author's word for the fidelity of his portrait. We are told, not shown, what the hero was. There is nothing in the plot which results from his peculiar formation of mind. An everyday bravo might equally well have satisfied the requirements of the action.

And so on to some remarkable sentences about *Childe Harold*, which I shall quote in another connection.

If Newman is talking sense in these passages, his objections to the *Tyrannus* are nonsense. And nonsense, whether or not he might have invoked in defence the distinction between plots simple and plots complex. The plots of *Richard III* and *The Corsair* are less complicated than those of *Othello* and the *Tyrannus*, but the degree of complication, while it may make the identifying of plot and character a harder task for the dramatist, does not affect the status accorded that identity. In any play or poem concerning human beings, that status is primary. And though the capacity to identify plot and character may not be a poetical capacity, it is a crucial one for any poet setting up to write narrative, whether in play or poem. If, writing in those forms, he fails to achieve that identification, any poetry he supplies in his capacity as lyric poet is a mockery, flowers without roots. For it is the plot and the characters who embody the plot, creating it and being created by it, that convey the very meaning of the work. How can we attend to what goes on, if we think the pains and pleasures of the action fall on dummies, even if on dummies endowed with poetry—with a poetry which, being beside the point, can never be more than pretty? Many poets, in every age from the Elizabethan to our own, have neglected this consideration, and in consequence a thousand poetic dramas are, if they are anything at all, poems to feed the anthologist rather than plays to be played.

But even if Newman had gained a surer grasp of the *Poetics* in the way Butcher[1] did, it is unlikely that he would have fully accepted its doctrines about 'action': his simplification merely made him fly further away from a critic he was bound to detach himself from in any event: he would have been less rebellious if he had written on Longinus. When

[1] See Appendix, pp. 185 ff. below.

all is allowed for, there existed the estranging incompatibility of temperament implied in the remark that 'we may be allowed to suspect [Aristotle] of entertaining too cold and formal conceptions of the nature of poetical composition, as if its beauties were less subtle and delicate than they really are'. Moreover, diverse as were their temperaments, Newman and Aristotle also differed in their assumptions as psychologists dealing with the mind of poets. Neither saw that mind as abnormal: Aristotle treated it as he treated the mind of any man; and Newman found so much poetry abroad in the world that not all its possessors could be madmen. Newman believed that Aristotle expected work from a poet's mind which no poet's mind can do. The difference appears at its widest when it is a question of composition, of composition in general, not only of the composition of anything with a plot. For Aristotle the datum was that the poetry exists written down (or uttered by actors): the poet for him is by definition a maker, and his poem a thing made. But for Newman in the nineteenth century there was 'an ambiguity in the [very] word "poetry", which is taken to signify both the gift itself, and the written composition which is the result of it'. For Newman poetry exists apart from pen and paper, and, moreover, only exists at its most characteristic and pure when so existing, since 'the poet's habits of mind lead to contemplation rather than to communication with others'.

Newman almost begrudges the putting of the poem on paper, as if 'the spirit of poetry' suffers when an attempt is made to fit it with a body. He sees composition as the mere consequence of the poet's decision to communicate his poetry, and he sees that decision almost as dependent on accident. A poem is an 'accessory', 'no essential part of poetry, though [obviously] indispensable to its exhibition', 'the artificial part', 'dexterity', 'accomplishment';[1] and the 'talent for composition' is compared to those of dancing, of elocution, and even of typesetting:

poetical composition requires that command of language which is the mere effect of practice. The poet is a compositor; words are his types; he must have them within reach, and in unlimited abundance.

Newman considers that Aristotle's insistence on a 'laboured and complicated plot' deflects the poet's mind away from its proper function when composing, 'tend[ing] to withdraw [it] from the spontaneous exhibition of pathos or imagination to a minute diligence in the formation of a plot'; and whereas Aristotle sees a play as 'an exhibition of ingenious workmanship', Newman sees it, if it is poetical, as 'a free and unfettered effusion of genius'. He leaves us in no doubt on the point, even going so far as to see plot itself as a by-product, as happening of itself, as something 'breathed' out of the mind, 'effused' along with the characters and their voices of joy and sorrow: Aristotle's sort of counsel, it is held, 'leads to negative, more than to positive excellence; [plot, "the artificial part",] should rather be the natural and, so to say, unintentional result of the poet's feeling and imagination, than be separated from them as the direct object of his care'.

[1] I have not attempted to relate Newman's essay to the criticism of the time. The influence of Wordsworth on it would be worth tracing and is particularly noticeable at this point. In the *Excursion* (i. 77ff.), Wordsworth had written:

> Oh! many are the Poets that are sown
> By Nature; men endowed with highest gifts,
> The vision and the faculty divine;
> Yet wanting the accomplishment of verse;

with which, of course, compare the 'mute inglorious Miltons' of Gray's 'Elegy'. The American scholar, A. S. Cook, editing Newman's essay for a school edition (1891), gave many cross references to Shelley's *Defence of Poetry*. Similarities, however, between the views of Shelley and Newman cannot be due to borrowing, since Shelley's *Defence*, though written in 1821, was not published until 1840. Keble's essay, 'Sacred Poetry', had appeared in 1825 and had related 'inspiration' and composition in the way Newman does. Keble's essay, like Newman's, is a 'liberal' attempt to enfold poetry in religion.

If the poet does write a poem, then it is bound to be obscure for one reason or another, and to one degree or another. The degree will depend on the several counts: for example, on the kind of poem he is writing (he will be 'less [obscure] in epic, or narrative and dramatic representation,—more so in odes and choruses'), and on the 'depth of his feelings' and their 'acuteness', both these poetical qualities causing him to shrink 'from any formal accuracy in [their] expression'.

Newman, who himself strove so hard to write simply, always disliked what, in the sermon on 'The Danger of Accomplishments', he called 'unreal words';[1] and in the essay on poetry we find him deprecating a technical care lavished in excess of what the initial inspiration warrants. He scorns

the power of throwing off harmonious verses, which, while they have a respectable portion of meaning, yet are especially intended to charm the ear. In popular poems, common ideas are unfolded with copiousness, and set off in polished verse—and this is called poetry.

His view may be put in something like this way. The poet is inspired like an Old Testament prophet and may write the inspired poem down. He is inspired with his poem complete, and, as far as the poem is concerned, inspired once for all. There is no opportunity, therefore, for further inspiration while composition is proceeding. (Newman would have countered Dryden's remark that the act of riming often helped him to a thought with 'So much less poetical the thought'.) The poet ought to write his poem down (if write he must) simply; he should not require the given inspiration

---

[1] Sentences of this sermon might have found a place in the essay: '[Dangerous] too is the abuse of poetical talent, that sacred gift. Nothing is more common than to fall into the practice of uttering fine sentiments, particularly in letter writing, as a matter of course, or a kind of elegant display' (*Parochial and Plain Sermons*, ii. 376).

to sponsor more than its own direct expression; this held for small things, as it clearly held for great:

When a deed or incident is striking in itself, a judicious writer is led to describe it in the most simple and colourless terms, his own being unnecessary; for instance, if the greatness of the action itself excites the imagination, or the depth of the suffering interests the feelings. In the usual phrase, the circumstances are left 'to speak for themselves'.

Newman considers Pope an offender under this head: he sees him as elaborating his couplets too independently of the poetry that originally prompted their existence. They are beautiful as couplets, but beautiful only as Chippendale's furniture is beautiful; Chippendale made his furniture by reference to a pattern laid up in his head, which was how Pope made his couplets. If you must have elaborate art, then let your poems be like those of Virgil and Milton:

though Virgil is celebrated as a master of composition, yet his style is so identified with his conceptions, as their outward development, as to preclude the possibility of our viewing the one apart from the other. In Milton, again, the harmony of the verse is but the echo of the inward music which the thoughts of the poet breathe.

## V

NEWMAN'S theory, then, may be called Protestant, or better, Evangelical. Like Protestants, the poet is justified rather by faith than by works; like Evangelicals, rather by 'spiritual-mindedness'[1] than by faith. Newman is unconsciously applying to poetry his religious discoveries up to date. In 1828 he was still much of an Evangelical. Until 1825 he had '[taken] for granted, if not intelligently held, the opinions called Evangelical',[2] and nine years later he could still 'go on ... a great way with [them]'.[3] When he left them behind in

---

[1] *Lectures on Justification*, p. 324.    [2] Letters, i. 119.
[3] Ibid., ii. 66.

the *Lectures on Justification* of 1838, he did so mainly because, like the poets he thought most poetical, they were people exclusively concerned with their 'spiritual-mindedness', their 'experiences', their 'sensations'.[1] Much later, in the *Idea of a University*, he was to describe their religion in words all of which he might, and some of which he did, apply to poetry; describing it as consisting 'in the affections, in the imagination, in inward persuasions and consolations, in pleasurable sensations, sudden changes, and sublime fancies'.[2] When Newman threw off his Evangelical views, he only threw off what he came to see as wrong in them. After all, spiritual-mindedness was not wrong in itself, but only being stuck fast in it: the better Christian was spiritual-minded and something more. Newman went so far as to exclaim that it was to an Evangelical, to Thomas Scott, that '(humanly speaking) I almost owe my soul',[3] and no 'development' in doctrine could call on him to discard that. But Newman as literary critic is too much for keeping the poet where the Evangelicals kept the Christian. In 1832 after showing Luther as a reformer who 'found Christians in bondage to their works and observances', he went on to show the Evangelicals as having landed Protestants in another bondage, that to 'their feelings'.[4] His many attacks on the Evangelical system were attempts to rescue Evangelicals from a bondage in which, so far as his essay went, he was willing to keep the poets.

## VI

IN THE same way that Newman's evaluation of the *Oedipus Tyrannus* looks different after the advent of the detective story, his view that plot grows (so to speak) independently of the

[1] *Lectures on Justification*, pp. 324-330.    [2] p. 28.
[3] *Apologia*, p. 108.    [4] *Lectures on Justification*, p. 340.

poet looks different after Mr. Max Beerbohm's 'Savonarola' Brown:

'I've hit on an initial idea', [Brown] said, 'and that's enough to start with. I gave up my notion of inventing a plot in advance. I thought it would be a mistake. I don't want puppets on wires. I want Savonarola to work out his destiny in his own way.'[1]

The production of literature is surely more of a dialectic than Newman allows, and of a compromise which takes account of elements Newman will not frankly acknowledge. We have only to think of the many different requirements which Shakespeare, for instance, had to satisfy, when, as most often, he was writing a play—requirements imposed from several quarters including the groundlings and his own need to create something solidly and intricately balanced out of chaotic materials. Newman's views apply best to certain kinds of short lyric poems, the kind which Wordsworth called 'effusions', and of which his voluminous poetical works contain only ten instances;[2] and after all, if an extempore lyric comes right first time, it comes right because the hand, like Giotto's hand making the circle, is a practised one. The upshot is that Newman's eloquent statement of a romantic and unworldly position is useful mainly as a corrective against an explanation that makes the writing of poetry too much a mechanical thing. But one would have thought his own experience of composition would have led him to a more balanced view: we know how thoroughly his prose drafts were disciplined into sense and grace, and may suspect that the drafts of his poems had a similar evolution—a similar evolution up to a point: they seldom end by achieving the grace of the prose works.

[1] *Seven Men*, 1920 edition, p. 180.

[2] See J. C. Smith, *A Study of Wordsworth*, 1944, p. 16. Mr. Smith adds pointedly: 'I doubt if even these were all what he calls one of them, "extempore to the letter".'

That more balanced view had to wait till those excellent pages of his *Lectures . . . on University Subjects* which are devoted to the great writer who subjects his work to severe correction.[1] But even here Newman assigns the need for such correcting to initial clumsiness and inadequacy: the battle of pen strokes is seen as nothing more than improving attempts to say what from the start had been seen. He does not make enough allowance for the poet whose 'wheels', to use the words of Pope and Coleridge, 'take fire' while driving.[2] When he praises Virgil and Milton, he forgets that he never saw their eyes glittering with inspiration, but can only infer their glitter from the printed page, and therefore cannot be sure at what point the inspiration, which it is agreed the verses embody, became available. On the evidence of Milton's manuscripts, some of it happened very charily and had only finished happening with the last of the many corrections: it seems that there were some things which Milton won his way through to seeing for the first time in the process of winning his way through to saying what he may have thought he had seen clearly from the start.

## VII

SOMETHING of the nature of poetry as Newman saw it may be gathered from his word *breathe*, a word used several times in the course of the essay. When he used it in the sentence on Milton (quoted above), he was adapting Gray's line which attributed to Dryden

Thoughts that breathe, and words that burn.[3]

---

[1] *The Idea of a University*, pp. 282 ff.

[2] See Preface to Homer, third paragraph, and *Biographia Literaria*, ii. 56.

[3] 'Progress of Poesy', III. iii. 4. Newman, too, thought highly of Dryden: see, in particular, *The Idea of a University*, p. 279, where he is set beside Homer, Pindar, Shakespeare, and Scott.

The metaphor, however, had had a long history before Gray used it. And perhaps as varied a one as any in poetry. When Virgil spoke of *aera* as *spirantia*,[1] it was a way of saying that the statues were life-like, successful instances of art as *mimesis*.[2] This simple metaphorical use was often copied: until a late edition 'breathing statues' appeared in Pope's *Temple of Fame*,[3] and Joseph Warton spoke of 'breathing Forms' sculpted 'By fair *Italia*'s skilful Hand'.[4] Not far from Virgil's use was Pope's in his epistle 'To Mr. Jervas':

> Yet still her [the Muse's] charms in breathing paint engage.

Jervas was a portrait painter, and so his paint could seem to breathe; and there was also the close presence of the muse, a 'person' we can think of as even nearer to literal breathing than statues are. But already we are sliding into subtleties which may become tedious when analysed. And the subtleties grow subtler still when the noun to which 'breathing' is affixed is itself a metaphor. When that happens, 'breathing' becomes doubly metaphorical or mixed metaphorical and literal, or it reverts to the literal. In 'Hero and Leander' Marlowe wrote

> every street like to a firmament
> Glistered with breathing stars,[5]

where 'breathing' is metaphorical as stars are stars and literal as they are women. But when Milton called nymphs 'the breathing roses of the wood',[6] 'breathing' is literal as roses are nymphs and metaphorical as they are roses, but not so boldly metaphorical since roses, unlike stars, emit a scent as (sweet) breath does. After uses such as this it is less surprising to

---

[1] *Aeneid*, vi. 847.
[2] See p. 102 f. above.
[3] See Pope, Twickenham ed., ii. 249.
[4] 'The Enthusiast', ll. 131 f.
[5] i. 97 f.
[6] 'Arcades', l. 32.

find Joseph Warton's 'ambrosial Hair Breathing rich Odours'.[1] The method here is metaphor but metaphor explained. Collins took advantage of the explanation and of the comparative lucidity of Milton's 'breathing roses' and Warton's 'breathing Mead'[2] to bestow on his Evening 'breathing tresses'. He could count on 'breathing tresses' to mean hair emitting a scent. That was in 1747, and from then onward the word figured so often in poetical writing that it aroused the protest of that excellent small critic, Sir Henry Taylor, the author of *Philip van Artevelde*. Taylor saw Byron as the chief offender, and we know how much Newman read Byron's poems, and, with reservations, how much he admired them. In a passage from his essay on Wordsworth, which cogently criticised the romantic poetry of the time, Taylor wrote:

'The mind, the music *breathing* from her face',[3] is suggestive of as much false metaphor as could well be concentrated in a single line; but it conveyed some vague impressions of beauty and fervour, and was associated with the feelings with which Lord Byron's writings were usually read; and 'to breathe' became thenceforth, amongst the followers of Lord Byron, a verb poetical which meant anything but respiration. Indeed the abuse seems to have spread to a circle which might be supposed to be remote from Lord Byron's influence; for a book was published two or three years ago with the title of '*Holy Breathings*'.[4]

[1] 'The Enthusiast', ll. 231 f.
[2] 'The Enthusiast', l. 56. A powerful instance had been provided by Dryden: whereas Ovid, speaking of men who eat animal flesh, had written 'tristia mandere saevo/vulnera dente,' Dryden gave as translation 'And chaw with bloody Teeth the breathing Bread' ('Of the Pythagorean Philosophy. From Ovid's Metamorphoses Book XV', l. 132).
[3] Byron, *The Bride of Abydos*, i. 179. The expression had been attacked before Taylor attacked it, and Byron defended it in a note in the second edition.
[4] Henry Taylor, *Notes from Books. In Four Essays*, 1849, pp. 5 f. It is amusing to find Taylor himself writing: 'one [sonnet] entitled "Sorrow", breathing a very full and noble strain of moral exhortation' (p. 215). The offending volume of

M

Newman, however, had an unusual right to make use of this fashionable verb since, like Keble, he placed most value on those manifestations of life which are gentlest, most intimate and commonplace: the Abbé Brémond has drawn attention to the quiet stroke 'blushing for joy' in *Callista*.[1] We can allow a critic to use *breathe* when his essay on poetry exists to effect a dematerialisation of poetry—breath is an appropriate symbol: like breath, poetry exists whether or not it voices words. Newman found poetry in the pages of, say, Shakespeare, and equally in the wordless minds of children ('Alas! what are we doing all through life, both as a necessity and as a duty, but unlearning the world's poetry, and attaining to its prose!'),[2] and in the often wordless minds of young people, especially in the season of spring (see chapter iii of *Loss and Gain*), and in the ritual of the church.[3] When Newman visited the Keble household, he thought 'Keble's verses are written (as it were) on all their faces',[4] the only difference being that John had the capacity and took the trouble to seize the beautiful poetry that fell to his share and

devotions was Lady Charlotte S. M. Bury's *Suspirium Sanctorum, or Holy Breathings* (1826). Later in the century appeared *Heart Breathings* by Agnes M'Neile Malden. Newman himself serves to bridge the use of the word by Byron and its use by devotional writers. The word was discredited by the time that a New York publisher, W. B. Ketcham, published two dictionaries in 1895-96. He called one a *Dictionary of Burning Words*, but avoided 'breathing' by calling the other a *Dictionary of Living Thoughts*.

[1] *The Mystery of Newman*, tr. H. C. Corrance, 1907, p. 247. See *Callista*, p. 221.

[2] *The Idea of a University*, pp. 331 f. Newman here is consciously indebted to Wordsworth, who 'has asserted that a child is the only true poet, and has pictured in one of his poems . . . a child with all the poetry of childhood thrown around him, yet gradually losing these associations as he grew older, until when he arrived at manhood, he became a mere ordinary mortal' ('On the Characteristics of True Poetry', a reported lecture by Newman, *The Tablet*, July 21, 1849, reprinted by F. Tardivel, *La personnalité littéraire de Newman*, Paris, 1937, pp. 388-89; cf. *The Sayings of Cardinal Newman*, 1890, p. 2).

[3] For an early reference to this idea, see *Letters*, i. 338.

[4] *Letters*, i. 190.

extend its manifestation to paper. The world has its poets, as it has its saints, without knowing it has them. But it is only in the estimation of men that the mute Miltons are inglorious Miltons: in the estimation of God, who looketh on the heart, the mute Miltons are as glorious as the Milton who, instead of being mute, wrote *Paradise Lost*. For Newman the thing is to be a poet: the rest is a question of showing or not showing, and so a question ultimately beside the point for one who, like Newman, 'rest[ed] in the thought of two and two only supreme and luminously self-evident beings, myself and my Creator';[1] for one who, like Newman, saw the Christian as 'the greater part of his time by himself, and when he is in solitude, that is his real state';[2] and for one who, like Newman, saw the poet as a person whose 'habits of mind lead to contemplation rather than to communication with others'.

## VIII

SO FAR I have drawn mainly on the opening and closing sections of Newman's essay, and in these sections one of the virtues of his argument is, despite lapses, its clarity. It does not take account of enough material; it says nothing about Aristotle's doctrine of catharsis;[3] nor has it any sense of the historical—after all, certain allowances are due imperatively to literature surviving out of the past, especially the distant past. Newman tells us in the *Apologia* that Whately was much 'dissatisfied' with the essay.[4] But the clarity of the essay so far is delightful. When we proceed to investigate the remaining middle sections, however, we meet a fullness which is embarrassing because obscure. It could scarcely be other than obscure being so full: how much surer is the argument of the

[1] *Apologia*, p. 108.     [2] *Parochial and Plain Sermons*, v. 69.
[3] See Appendix, pp. 185 ff. below.     [4] *Apologia*, p. 114.

lecture on literature,[1] its sureness being the result of the same maturity which prompted Newman to confine himself to a sparer argument. Part of the trouble with the essay on poetry is that it attempts to cover too much ground—in his dedication of the collected *Essays* to William Froude, he confessed that 'portions of their contents . . . are not always in agreement with each other'. In the middle sections of the present essay, he has no line of argument, but instead a great tidied-up heap of odds and ends of thought. Some of the bits are tidied up with a brilliant show of confidence: the spiritedness of the whole procedure is delightful to watch; in these middle sections Newman is indeed the talker in the Oriel common room, 'Dornford passing the wine'. And so it is one of those essays that can only receive adequate treatment by critics willing to pay it the disproportionate honour of a thorough analysis and a thorough reconstruction: and critics equal to this task prefer to construct their systems *ab initio*. I propose to make only a few comments on these teasing middle sections.

Their concern is to state, to illustrate and to modify Aristotle's 'general doctrine of the nature of poetry', a doctrine which Newman holds to be 'most true and philosophical'. Here are the most ambitious of the paragraphs:

Poetry, according to Aristotle, is a representation of the ideal. Biography and history represent individual characters and actual facts; poetry, on the contrary, generalizing from the phenomenon of nature and life, supplies us with pictures drawn, not after an existing pattern, but after a creation of the mind. Fidelity is the primary merit of biography and history; the essence of poetry is fiction. 'Poesis nihil aliud est', says Bacon, 'quam historiae imitatio ad placitum'. It delineates that perfection which the imagination suggests, and to which

[1] *The Idea of a University*, pp. 268 ff.

as a limit the present system of Divine Providence actually tends. Moreover, by confining the attention to one series of events and scene of action, it bounds and finishes off the confused luxuriance of real nature; while, by a skilful adjustment of circumstances, it brings into sight the connexion of cause and effect, completes the dependence of the parts one on another, and harmonizes the proportions of the whole. It is then but the type and model of history or biography, if we may be allowed the comparison, bearing some resemblance to the abstract mathematical formulae of physics, before they are modified by the contingencies of atmosphere and friction. Hence, while it recreates the imagination by the superhuman loveliness of its views, it provides a solace for the mind broken by the disappointments and sufferings of actual life; and becomes, moreover, the utterance of the inward emotions of a right moral feeling, seeking a purity and a truth which this world will not give.

It follows that the poetical mind is one full of the eternal forms of beauty and perfection; these are its material of thought, its instrument and medium of observation,—these colour each object to which it directs its view. It is called imaginative or creative, from the originality and independence of its modes of thinking, compared with the commonplace and matter-of-fact conceptions of ordinary minds, which are fettered down to the particular and individual. At the same time it feels a natural sympathy with everything great and splendid in the physical and moral world; and selecting such from the mass of common phenomena, incorporates them, as it were, into the substance of its own creations. From living thus in a world of its own, it speaks the language of dignity, emotion, and refinement.

In all this Newman is certainly taking full advantage of his programme of modifying the views of Aristotle, for whom the poet was a man gifted to discover, and gifted to write down for the good of others, an aspect of the actual otherwise overlooked, the general in the particular. That was all the base in the *Poetics* for Newman's dazzling superstructure, though he was also indebted to another view drawn from Aristotle indirectly, the view that 'in general art partly completes what

Nature is unable to elaborate, and partly imitates her'.[1] What else exists in Newman's paragraphs belongs to Plato and to what intervening critics have dreamed over their Aristotle and Plato.

There is only the narrowest basis in Aristotle for what Newman managed to work into his essay about revealed religion. Blanco White had expressly forbidden theology, but could not object when theology was softened into religion, and religion, however strongly emphasised, emphasised in the midst of the secular. Newman writes:

According to the above theory, Revealed Religion should be especially poetical[2]—and it is so in fact. While its disclosures have an originality in them to engage the intellect, they have a beauty to satisfy the moral nature. It presents us with those ideal forms of excellence in which a poetical mind delights, and with which all grace and harmony are associated. It brings us into a new world—a world of overpowering interest, of the sublimest views, and the tenderest and purest feelings. The peculiar grace of mind of the New Testament writers is as striking as the actual effect produced upon the hearts of those who have imbibed their spirit. At present we are not concerned with the practical, but the poetical nature of revealed truth. With Christians, a poetical view of things is a duty,—we are bid to colour all things with hues of faith,[3] to see a Divine meaning in every event, and a superhuman tendency. Even our friends around are invested with unearthly brightness—no longer imperfect men, but beings taken into Divine favour, stamped with His seal, and in training for future happiness. It may be added, that the virtues peculiarly Christian are especially poetical—meekness, gentleness, compassion, contentment, modesty, not to mention the devotional virtues; whereas the

---

[1] *Physics*, bk. II (B), chap. 8.

[2] The word 'poetical' is used here to mean the qualities Newman has remarked in the poet.

[3] See p. 169 above: the poet's 'mind is . . . full of the eternal forms of beauty and perfection', and 'these colour each object to which it directs its view'. In 1874 we find Blackie's *Self-Culture* recommending that 'To live poetry, . . . is always better than to write it' (see *O.E.D.*, s.v. 'poetry' §5). Would Blackie have allowed that it is better to live *Don Juan* or *Les Fleurs du Mal* than to write *Paradise Lost?*

ruder and more ordinary feelings are the instruments of rhetoric more justly than of poetry—anger, indignation, emulation, martial spirit, and love of independence.

In this passage the link with Aristotle is discernible, but only just. According to Aristotle, the poet sees something in the world which men who are not poets cannot see: the Christian, says Newman, sees a brightness in his friends invisible to non-Christians. But he calls the brightness 'unearthly', whereas for Aristotle the general which poets see in the particular is a part of the actual. And for Newman not only is the brightness 'unearthly', but it is partly bestowed by the Christian as well as discerned: 'we are bid to colour all things with hues of faith'. Newman is modifying Aristotle to some purpose.

Newman ascribes to revealed religion the quality of being 'poetical'. The poet accordingly is free to write about it. But if revealed religion is a suitable subject for a poet, then the poet surrenders some of the qualities which, following Aristotle, Newman had fixed on him. How can revealed religion be a proper object of poetry if the poet's business is to 'generalise', to imitate for the sake of pleasure (*ad placitum*), to bound and finish off, to improve? The best comment on this absurdity is Dr. Johnson's: in his Life of Waller he takes occasion to argue his dislike of pious poetry, his argument providing this weighty logic:

Poetry pleases by exhibiting an idea more grateful to the mind than things themselves afford . . . but religion must be shewn as it is; suppression and addition equally corrupt it, and such as it is, it is known already.

Or we can confute early Newman by later Newman:

[In theology] the simple question is, What is revealed? . . . If we are able to enlarge our view and multiply our propositions, it must be merely by the comparison and adjustment of the original truths; if we would solve new questions, it must be by consulting old answers. The notion of doctrinal knowledge absolutely novel, and of simple addition from without, is intolerable to Catholic ears . . . Revelation is all in all in doctrine; the Apostles its sole depository, the inferential method its sole instrument, and ecclesiastical authority its sole sanction. The Divine Voice has spoken once for all, and the only question is about its meaning.[1]

## IX

NEWMAN's essay culminates in his paragraph on revealed religion, but despite this he is still 'liberal' enough in 1828 to ascribe not only virtue but religion and holiness to authors of poetry which he thinks good poetry, and even to speak of religion without insisting on the distinction between religion and Christianity. He gladly joins all those Renaissance critics who see the good poet as a good man. He is indeed quite unembarrassed by the ease with which the formula applies itself. Here are his sentences on Burns:

Burns was a man of inconsistent life; still, it is known, of much really sound principle at bottom. Thus his acknowledged poetical talent is in nowise inconsistent with the truth of our doctrine, which will refer the beauty which exists in his compositions to the remains of a virtuous and diviner nature within him.

And then more generally:

Nay, further than this, our theory holds good, even though it be shown that a depraved man may write a poem. As motives short of the purest lead to actions intrinsically good, so frames of mind short of virtuous will produce a partial and limited poetry. But even where this is instanced, the poetry of a vicious mind will be inconsistent and debased; that is, so far only poetry as the traces and shadows of holy truth still remain upon it. On the other hand, a right moral feeling places the mind in the very centre of that circle from which all the rays have their origin and range; whereas minds otherwise placed command but a portion of the whole circuit of poetry. Allowing for human

[1] *The Idea of a University*, p. 223.

infirmity and the varieties of opinion, Milton, Spenser, Cowper, Wordsworth, and Southey, may be considered, as far as their writings go, to approximate to this moral centre. The following are added as further illustrations of our meaning. Walter Scott's centre is chivalrous honour; Shakespeare exhibits the characteristics of an unlearned and undisciplined piety; Homer the religion of nature and conscience, at times debased by polytheism. All these poets are religious. The occasional irreligion of Virgil's poetry is painful to the admirers of his general taste and delicacy. Dryden's Alexander's Feast is a magnificent composition, and has high poetical beauties; but to a refined judgment there is something intrinsically unpoetical in the end to which it is devoted, the praises of revel and sensuality. It corresponds to a process of clever reasoning erected on an untrue foundation—the one is a fallacy, the other is out of taste. Lord Byron's Manfred is in parts intensely poetical; yet the delicate mind naturally shrinks from the spirit which here and there reveals itself, and the basis on which the drama is built. From a perusal of it we should infer, according to the above theory, that there was right and fine feeling in the poet's mind, but that the central and consistent character was wanting. From the history of his life we know this to be the fact.[1] The connexion between

[1] By 1833, when Newman wrote the essay, the 'Conversion of Augustine', he was more severe on Byron:

> We have seen in our own day, in the case of a popular poet, an impressive instance of a great genius throwing off the fear of God, seeking for happiness in the creature, roaming unsatisfied from one object to another, breaking his soul upon itself, and bitterly confessing and imparting his wretchedness to all around him. I have no wish at all to compare him to St. Augustine; indeed, if we may say it without presumption, the very different termination of their trial seems to indicate some great difference in their respective modes of encountering it. The one dies of premature decay, to all appearance, a hardened infidel; and if he is still to have a name, will live in the mouths of men by writings at once blasphemous and immoral: the other is a Saint and Doctor of the Church. Each makes confessions, the one to the saints, the other to the powers of evil. And does not the difference of the two discover itself in some measure, even to our eyes, in the very history of their wanderings and pinings? At least, there is no appearance in St. Augustine's case of that dreadful haughtiness, sullenness, love of singularity, vanity, irritability, and misanthropy, which were too certainly the characteristics of our own countryman. Augustine was, as his early history shows, a man of affectionate and tender feelings, and open and amiable temper; and, above all, he sought for some excellence external to his own mind, instead of concentrating all his contemplations on himself.'
(*Historical Sketches*, ii. 144-45.)

want of the religious principle and want of poetical feeling, is seen in the instances of Hume and Gibbon, who had radically unpoetical minds. Rousseau, it may be supposed, is an exception to our doctrine. Lucretius, too, had great poetical genius; but his work evinces that his miserable philosophy was rather the result of a bewildered judgment than a corrupt heart.

In later years Newman was to apply to poets, and to authors generally, a more crucial religious test. As, for instance, in the sermon 'Nature and Grace',[1] preached soon after he became a Catholic:

many are the tales and poems written now-a-days, expressing high and beautiful sentiments; I dare say some of you, my brethren, have fallen in with them, and perhaps you have thought to yourselves, that he must be a man of deep religious feeling and high religious profession who could write so well. Is it so in fact, my brethren? it is not so; why? because after all it is *but* poetry, not religion. . . .

And so to a definition of poetry drawn up by Newman the theologian:

[Poetry] is human nature exerting the powers of imagination and reason, which it has, till it seems also to have powers which it has not. There are, you know, in the animal world various creatures, which are able to imitate the voice of man; nature in like manner is often a mockery of grace.

And in conclusion:

The truth is, the natural man sees this or that principle to be good or true from the light of conscience; and then, since he has the power of reasoning, he knows that, if this be true, many other things are true likewise; and then, having the power of imagination, he pictures to himself those other things as true, though he does not really understand them. And then he brings to his aid what he has read and gained from others who *have* had grace, and thus he completes his sketch; and then he throws his feelings and his heart into it, and meditates on it, and

---

[1] *Discourses Addressed to Mixed Congregations*, p. 156. I am indebted for this reference to Mr. Alvan S. Ryan's thoughtful essay, 'Newman's Conception of Literature', *University of Iowa Humanistic Studies*, vi (1942), 119 ff.

kindles in himself a sort of enthusiasm, and thus he is able to write beautifully and touchingly about what to others indeed may be a reality, but to him is nothing more than a fiction.

The most telling statements of this later position are those made in *The Idea of a University*—in 'Discourse ix' and in the lecture on English Catholic literature. Here is the latter of them. Newman has been speaking of the indecency of French and Italian literature, and concludes:

These are but specimens of the general character of secular literature, whatever be the people to whom it belongs. One literature may be better than another, but bad will be the best, when weighed in the balance of truth and morality. It cannot be otherwise; human nature is in all ages and in all countries the same; and its literature, therefore, will ever and everywhere be one and the same also. Man's work will savour of man; in his elements and powers excellent and admirable, but prone to disorder and excess, to error and to sin. Such too will be his literature; it will have the beauty and the fierceness, the sweetness and the rankness, of the natural man, and, with all its richness and greatness, will necessarily offend the senses of those who, in the Apostle's words, are really 'exercised to discern between good and evil'.

It is a pity that Newman did not stop at this point. Instead he proceeds with:

'It is said of the holy Sturme', says an Oxford writer, 'that, in passing a horde of unconverted Germans, as they were bathing and gambolling in the stream, he was so overpowered by the intolerable scent which arose from them that he nearly fainted away'. National Literature is, in a parallel way, the untutored movements of the reason, imagination, passions, and affections of the natural man, the leapings and the friskings, the plungings and the snortings, the sportings and the buffoonings, the clumsy play and the aimless toil, of the noble, lawless savage of God's intellectual creation.[1]

This is Newman off the rails. On his own showing, these savages are no fit symbol for the natural man. They are merely disgusting, only more faintly so that Swift's Yahoos,

[1] *The Idea of a University*, pp. 316 f.

and they have no right to the epithet 'noble' which Newman perfunctorily attaches to them. They have nothing but fierceness and rankness, whereas the natural man and his product, literature, have beauty as well as fierceness, sweetness as well as rankness.

Another modification of Aristotle is worth noting. In the passage on revealed religion, Newman uses the words 'especially poetical'. Those words leave Aristotle for philosophers such as Plotinus who see poetry as choosing its material, or as preferring to choose it, from what is already beautiful. There are a score of straws, and bigger things, in the essay to show which way the gentle wind is blowing: such a phrase as 'the loveliness of its views' could only be used of poetry by one for whom the poet's mind was a pristine garden of Eden. Further, Newman speaks of the imagination, 'refined and delicate' in its enjoyment, as preferring to 'have the elements of beauty abstracted out of the confused multitude of ordinary actions and habits', and as neglecting not only their 'improbabilities [and] wanderings', but their 'coarsenesses'. And in the discussion on originality, Newman marks off the originality of the poet from originality in general by discriminating the field of their operation. He had already said

the poetical mind . . . is called imaginative or creative, from the originality and independence of its modes of thinking, compared with the commonplace and matter-of-fact conceptions of ordinary minds, which are fettered down to the particular and individual;

and he returns to discriminate the term originality, beginning with the question, 'How does originality differ from the poetical talent?' and proceeding,

Without affecting the accuracy of a definition, we may call [poetical talent] the originality of right moral feeling.

Originality may perhaps be defined [as] the power of abstracting for one's self, and is in thought what strength of mind is in action. Our opinions are commonly derived from education and society. Common minds transmit as they receive, good and bad, true and false; minds of original talent feel a continual propensity to investigate subjects, and strike out views for themselves;—so that even old and established truths do not escape modification and accidental change when subjected to this process of mental digestion. Even the style of original writers is stamped with the peculiarities of their minds. When originality is found apart from good sense, which more or less is frequently the case, it shows itself in paradox and rashness of sentiment, and eccentricity of outward conduct. Poetry, on the other hand, cannot be separated from its good sense, or taste, as it is called; which is one of its elements. It is originality energizing in the world of beauty; the originality of grace, purity, refinement, and good feeling.

Poetry, that is, concerns itself not with the world in general (the world in general is the concern of originality in general), but with that part of the world which is capable of matching the 'eternal forms of beauty and perfection' that exist in the poetic mind, and which is therefore capable of responding to grace, purity, refinement, and good feeling.

This is to show too much favouritism. Newman divides matters into poetical and unpoetical, and the poetical itself into poetical and 'especially poetical'. And his favouritism spreads more widely still: the unpoetical is made to include whatever does not square with Newman's scheme of morality. 'Sometimes', he writes,

and not unfrequently in Shakspeare, the introduction of unpoetical matter may be necessary for the sake of relief, or as a vivid expression of recondite conceptions, and, as it were, to make friends with the reader's imagination.

Matter that Newman considers unpoetical in this way is matter offending his sense of poetic justice:

Romeo and Juliet are too good for the termination to which the plot leads; so are Ophelia and the Bride of Lammermoor. In these cases there is something inconsistent with correct beauty, and therefore unpoetical.

We can assign this delicate favouritism to Newman's native fastidiousness of mind, and also to his habit, at this time, of dividing sheep from goats. For all his liberalism, the essay on poetry is part of the movement which later became the Tractarian. It was noticeable that when he spoke of the Christian's vision of an 'unearthly brightness', he made it invest not men in general, as for Wordsworth brightness invested children in general, but only 'our friends'. Newman was not yet equal to the humane sentence, which I shall quote later, about the people of Birmingham. Already the Tractarians are taking on each other's feelings: Hurrell Froude refused to Wordsworth the title of true poet on the score of his unchristian egotism.[1] For Aristotle there were none of these subdivisions of poetry: matter, of whatever sort, was fit for poetry if seen by a poet.

It is already clear that no one but Newman could have written this essay on poetry. Not even Keble, whose exquisite critical essays and lectures lack Newman's range of ancient and modern example (if the *London Review* failed because its writers were too 'bookish and academical', not enough 'attractive' and versed in 'current literature',[2] Newman was not among those responsible). And if we weigh some of the subsidiary argument, Newman stands out as himself more clearly still.

Take, to begin with, his reference to Thomson as an instance of a modern writer who puts into verse material which, because it has not been seen with poetical originality, belongs rightfully to prose:

[1] William Knight, *Principal Shairp and His Friends*, 1888, pp. 370 f.
[2] See the Note appended by Newman in the edition of 1871.

Empedocles wrote his physics in verse, and Oppian his history of animals. Neither were poets—the one was an historian of nature, the other a sort of biographer of brutes. Yet a poet may make natural history or philosophy the material of his composition. But under his hands they are no longer a bare collection of facts or principles, but are painted with a meaning, beauty, and harmonious order not their own. Thomson has sometimes been commended for the novelty and minuteness of his remarks upon nature. This is not the praise of a poet; whose office rather is to represent known phenomena in a new connection or medium. In L'Allegro and Il Penseroso the poetical magician invests the commonest scenes of a country life with the hues, first of a cheerful, then of a pensive imagination.

Perhaps the reference to Thomson ought not to be taken too seriously: Newman may be concerned only with what was sometimes said about *The Seasons*, not with the justice of what was said. But, even so, he does not remove the implication that Thomson is justly represented by the critics he is attacking. Whereas, of course, part of Thomson's praise as a poet—as the author, for example, of lines like

> The yellow wall-flower, stained with iron brown
> . . . auriculas, enriched
> With shining meal o'er all their velvet leaves—[1]

is precisely that he did paint facts with a meaning, beauty, and harmonious order not their own, and that he did represent known phenomena in a new connection or medium (by 'medium' Newman means the intervening substance through which an object is seen).[2] The facts and phenomena drawn on by Thomson were known merely in the sense that they were perfunctorily and, so to speak, theoretically agreed to exist; and as it happens both Dr. Johnson and Hazlitt expressly state that Thomson added to them a meaning,

[1] 'Spring', ll. 533 ff.
[2] Cf. Johnson's 'medium' and Hazlitt's 'vapour of his brain' in the quotation on p. 180 below, n. 1.

beauty, and order of his own.[1] The poet whom Newman
does take as his instance of a descriptive poet to be commended is the author of 'L'Allegro' and 'Il Penseroso'. But
since *The Seasons* would have served his purpose equally
well, the instance and the implication are at variance. And
the explanation of this discrepancy is, I think, that Newman
has little interest in descriptive poetry. If he likes 'L'Allegro'
and 'Il Penseroso', that is because they are short, and because
Milton, in the person of his cheerful or pensive deputy, is
solidly present throughout either poem. Newman does not
care for *The Seasons* because, in the main, they concern
external nature rather than man. If his essay tells us anything
at all about himself, it is that, much as he prized solitude, he
did not go to poetry to escape from man into fantasy or into
scenery either earthly or heavenly. There is corroboration of
this inference in what follows. Newman quickly leaves the
poet who deals in 'natural history or philosophy' (material
for poetry to which he pays only lip service) for the poet who
uses description as an element in a poem otherwise realistically
about man: 'Ordinary writers . . . compare aged men to
trees in autumn—a gifted poet will in the fading trees
discern the fading men'; and the quatrain from *The Christian
Year* follows in a footnote. Later, there is this on Byron:

Childe Harold . . . if he is anything, is a being professedly isolated from
the world, and uninfluenced by it. One might as well draw Tityrus's
stags grazing in the air,[2] as a character of this kind; which yet, with

---

[1] G. Birkbeck Hill (Johnson's *Lives*, iii. 298) has this note: 'Johnson. Thomson,
I think, had as much of the poet about him as most writers. Everything appeared
to him through the medium of his favourite pursuit. He could not have viewed
those two candles burning but with a poetical eye [Boswell's *Johnson*, edited by
G. B. Hill, 1887, i. 453]. Hazlitt, in a criticism of Crabbe, says:—"Even Thomson
describes not so much the naked object as what he sees in his mind's eye,
surrounded and glowing with the mild, bland, genial vapours of his brain" [*The
Spirit of the Age*, 1825, pp. 199 f.]'

[2] The reference is to Virgil, *Eclogues*, i. 60.

more or less alteration, passes through successive editions in his other poems. Byron . . . did not know how to make poetry out of existing materials. He declaims in his own way, and has the upperhand as long as he is allowed to go on; but, if interrogated on principles of nature and good sense, he is at once put out and brought to a stand.

Byron offers an escape from the humdrum human lot, an invitation which Newman will not accept.

Then again, in Newman's paragraph on lyric poetry, none of the poems instanced there consist mainly of description. In other words, Newman preferred lyrics of a very different content from that, say, of Collins's 'Ode to Evening' or of Keats's 'To Autumn' (which he may not have read): the poets represented in those odes would have seemed to Newman like the poet of *Childe Harold* 'a being professedly isolated from the world, and uninfluenced by it'. The paragraph he devotes to the lyric deals with lyric poets very different from Collins and Keats:

Opinions, feelings, manners, and customs, are made poetical by the delicacy or splendour with which they are expressed. This is seen in the *ode, elegy, sonnet,* and *ballad*; in which a single idea, perhaps, or familiar occurrence, is invested by the poet with pathos or dignity. The ballad of Old Robin Gray will serve for an instance, out of a multitude; again, Lord Byron's Hebrew Melody, beginning, 'Were my bosom as false', etc.; or Cowper's Lines on his Mother's Picture; or Milman's Funeral Hymn in the Martyr of Antioch; or Milton's Sonnet on his Blindness; or Bernard Barton's Dream. As picturesque specimens, we may name Campbell's Battle of the Baltic; or Joanna Baillie's Chough and Crow; and for the more exalted and splendid style, Gray's Bard; or Milton's Hymn on the Nativity; in which facts, with which every one is familiar, are made new by the colouring of a poetical imagination.

The list contains two instances of the picturesque and two of the splendid, but as many as six of the kind we can call quietly personal, religious, popular, homely. It is a list

N

compiled by the same person who preferred the less exciting dramas of the Greeks to the *Oedipus Tyrannus*, who exhorted us to go to those plays, whether well- or ill-constructed, in order to 'listen to [the] harmonious and majestic language [of the characters], to the voices of sorrow, joy, compassion, or religious emotion,—to the animated odes of the chorus'; to listen and to find that 'A word[1] has power to convey a world of information to the imagination, and to act as a spell upon the feelings; there is no need of sustained fiction,— often no room for it'; by the same person who looked to pastorals to provide more shepherd-like personages than those of Virgil's and Pope's; by the same person who here speaks of 'the conciseness and simplicity of the poet' and who in his lecture on literature went so far as to speak of 'that simplicity which is the attribute of genius'[2] Newman preferred the lyrical in plays, and, among lyrics, homely lyrics.

It was this quiet kind of poetry which Keble had written his essay on sacred poetry to commend. I have mentioned that Newman quoted a quatrain from *The Christian Year*, the only verses, except for a passage of three lines translated from a play of Euripides, included in the 1871 text:

> How quiet shows the woodland scene!
> Each flower and tree, its duty done,
> Reposing in decay serene,
> Like weary men when age is won.[3]

Newman honours Keble. He does not honour Blanco White,

---

[1] Ryan, op. cit., pp. 129 f, notes this interest in the single word as 'a characteristic note of romantic criticism'. Hurd had said that 'A lucky word in a verse, which sounds well and every body gets by heart, goes farther than a volume of just criticism': his instance is *clinquant*, applied by Boileau to Tasso, and which destroyed his fame (Hurd, *Letters on Chivalry and Romance*, ed. Edith J. Morley, 1911, p. 133).

[2] *The Idea of a University*, p. 283.

[3] *The Christian Year*, xciv: 'All Saints' Day', ll. 9 ff.

who in the previous year had published a sonnet which
Coleridge, to whom it was dedicated, hailed as 'the finest and
and most grandly conceived . . . in our language'.[1] That
sonnet, entitled 'Night and Death', reads as follows:

> Mysterious night, when the first man but knew
> Thee by report, unseen, and heard thy name,
> Did he not tremble for this lovely frame,
>   This glorious canopy of light and blue?
> Yet 'neath a curtain of translucent dew
> Bathed in the rays of the great setting flame,
> Hesperus, with the host of heaven, came,
>   And, lo! creation widened on his view!
> Who could have thought what darkness lay concealed
>   Within thy beams, oh Sun? Or who could find,
> Whilst fly, and leaf, and insect stood revealed,
>   That to such endless orbs thou mad'st us blind?
> Weak man! Why to shun death, this anxious strife?
> If *light* can thus deceive, wherefore not *life*?[2]

Though Newman's essay belongs to the period of his
academic brilliance, his quoting Keble and not Blanco White
(who, though editor of the magazine, could have been
quoted, as Keble was quoted, anonymously) is a further
indication that his essay belongs as securely to the Oxford
Movement as do his parochial sermons and tracts, and as
Keble's essay on sacred poetry. On the other hand, Blanco
White's sonnet belongs to the grand deistic utterances of the
eighteenth century: its aim was to enlarge and ennoble the
human mind and to calm it, to calm it into a marmoreal
repose. The human mind, as Newman and Keble saw it,
needed rather to be humbled and refined.

To his list of lyrics Newman appends this caveat:

It must all along be observed, that we are not adducing instances

---

[1] See *D.N.B.*, s.v. Blanco White.       [2] *The Bijou*, 1828, i. 16.

for their own sake; but in order to illustrate our general doctrine, and to show its applicability to those compositions which are, by universal consent, acknowledged to be poetical.

By 'universal consent' Newman means nothing more august than 'the consent of everybody in 1828 who reads English poems'. It was Shelley, not Newman, who had the right to invoke a universal consent. In comparison with the grand and momentous instances of the *Defence of Poetry*, Newman's list of the poetical that is universally allowed is a very high-ways-and-byways affair. And this is a constant characteristic of his essay, which draws on the great, of course, for some of its instances—the Greek dramatists, Virgil, Spenser, Shake-speare, Pope, Scott, Byron—but also draws on Maria Edgeworth,[1] Southey, *Brambletye House*,[2] and contemporary writers of tracts ('which we must not be thought to approve, because we use them for our purpose'). We feel, accordingly, that we are in the presence of the essential Newman, of the Newman whose famous reply to the offer of an educated congregation in Rome has for its cornerstone 'Birmingham people have souls'.[3]

A final point. Newman's essay is not written as an in-direct puff of the virtues of its author. This is clear from the basic assumption that 'genius' is always of the romantic kind. Euripides is 'careless'; we hear of the 'wantonness of exuberant genius' and of the poet's 'indolence of inward enjoyment'. Newman himself is also a genius (to retain his term). And yet what could be more different from Newman's con-ception of genius than the form which genius took in himself?

[1] For Whately on Maria Edgeworth, see *Thoughts and Apothegms*, 1856, pp. 190 f.

[2] *Brambletye House*, or *Cavaliers and Roundheads*, by Horatio (or Horace) Smith (who collaborated with his brother in *Rejected Addresses*), was a best seller. Published in 1826, it had run through three editions in that year (see *Cambridge Bibliography of English Literature*, iii. 417).

[3] Ward, *Life*, ii. 539.

As a writer and thinker, his genius is summed up in his subtle saying: 'every thought I think is thought, and every word I write is writing'.[1] Nothing could be further from careless wantonness, exuberance, indolence: instead, Newman is viligant, exact, thorough; he is free from all idleness, and he has what he saw to be lacking in Blanco White, 'power of working'.

## APPENDIX

IN THE Note appended to the essay in the collected edition of 1871, Newman recalls that

Blanco White good-humouredly only called [the essay] 'Platonic';[2] and, indeed, it certainly omits one of the essential conditions of the idea of Poetry, its relation to the affections,—and that, in consequence, as it would seem, of confusing the function and aim of Poetry with its formal object. As the aim of civil government is the well-being of the governed, and its object is expediency; as the aim of oratory is to persuade, and its object is the probable; as the function of philosophy is to view all things in their mutual relations, and its object is truth; and as virtue consists in the observance of the moral law, and its object is the right; so Poetry may be considered to be the gift of moving the affections through the imagination, and its object to be the beautiful.

The omission may be at its worst in the opening sections on the drama: for example, Newman makes the ridiculous statement that the Greek dramatists revelled 'without object or meaning beyond [the] exhibition [of the imagination]'. He need not, however, have accepted Blanco White's criticism completely. His essay does establish a connection between poetry and the 'affections'; it discriminates some of the effects poetry produces on human minds and lives. If he did not say in so many words how poetry affected the reader

---

[1] *Letters*, i. 254.        [2] *Apologia*, p. 114.

practically, his telling him to be himself a poet was practical enough, since what affects being also affects doing. The practical effect which finds place in Newman's essay is not so much the effect of somebody else's poetry as the effect of your own. In his essay on Keble, Newman made ample amends for any omission on this score:

[Keble] did that for the Church of England which none but a poet could do: he made it poetical. It is sometimes asked whether poets are not more commonly found external to the Church than among her children; and it would not surprise us to find the question answered in the affirmative. Poetry is the refuge of those who have not the Catholic Church to flee to and repose upon, for the Church herself is the most sacred and august of poets. Poetry, as Mr. Keble lays it down in his University Lectures on the subject, is a method of relieving the overburdened mind; it is a channel through which emotion finds expression, and that a safe, regulated expression. Now what is the Catholic Church, viewed in her human aspect, but a discipline of the affections and passions? What are her ordinances and practices but the regulated expression of keen, or deep, or turbid feeling, and thus a 'cleansing', as Aristotle would word it, of the sick soul? She is the poet of her children; full of music to soothe the sad and control the wayward,—wonderful in story for the imagination of the romantic; rich in symbol and imagery, so that gentle and delicate feelings, which will not bear words, may in silence intimate their presence or commune with themselves. Her very being is poetry; every psalm, every petition, every collect, every versicle, the cross, the mitre, the thurible, is a fulfilment of some dream of childhood, or aspiration of youth.[1]

But, if Blanco White's criticism is to be accepted because Newman in fact accepts it, then the omission he is charged with is an omission on the grand scale. Aristotle's doctrine of purgation being one of the main matters of the *Poetics*. And the leaving of so large a loophole for criticism is another indication that Newman was attempting too much in this

[1] *Essays Critical and Historical*, ii. 442 f.

essay in too short a time and at too immature an age. Butcher was forty-five when, shortly after Newman's death, he published his masterly *Aristotle's Theory of Poetry and the Fine Arts*, a work that makes only one reference to Newman's essay, and that merely to one of his 'illustrations'. Newman is not numbered among the few friends of the *Poetics* who were intent on trying to discover what Aristotle had originally meant. The value of Newman's essay lies in other departments.

# VII
## English Poetry in the Nineteenth Century

BIRKBECK COLLEGE, alone of all the Colleges of London University, stands in the City, and the craft of business is in its blood. As instances of it there are those two strokes of advertising on the handbill that announced this lecture. First, the name of Mr. G. M. Young, a name of power wherever the Victorian age is mentioned. Certain of his writings typify that age for us, whether we are historians, sociologists, or literary critics. So that it is almost like having for chairman Queen Victoria herself. And then the sub-title of my lecture: 'The Figure in the Carpet'. If the name of Mr. Young has lent power to the handbill, that sub-title has lent mystery. Speculation has been rife, and even Professors of English have failed to catch the allusion. 'The Figure in the Carpet' is the title of a story written in the 1890's by Henry James, a story which concerns a curious but, alas, blunt-minded critic and his imperceptive search for the pattern hidden in the work of a novelist who died without helping him to perceive it. The curious critic was, as I have said, blunt of mind. And, in my case, there is another reason for inconclusiveness. For him the carpet did exist: it existed in the twenty volumes of the novelist's works. But the carpet of nineteenth-century poetry exists only in the fictitious mind of the Muse of History. It does not exist in the mind of any human being now, and it never did. Not even in Tennyson's, who as poet laureate received innumerable presentation copies of new poetry. Even he did not know the whole carpet. For instance, he had no knowledge of the poetry of Gerard Manley Hopkins (whose poetry, by the way, constitutes for a certain Cambridge critic pretty well all the carpet that matters). If Tennyson was ignorant, I am ignorant indeed. What I have been able to recover of a carpet which, unlike Tennyson, I have never had my feet on, is merely a square yard here and there; and what I have seen in those few lighted patches has been at the mercy of my powers of vision; and what I have had the power to perceive suffers a further diminution now that it is at the mercy of my power to communicate, and to communicate in the remaining minutes of my 'hour upon the stage'. In addition to all this, there is the imperfect knowledge of my audience: your knowledge of the carpet is, like mine, imperfect, and into the bargain you know patches different from those I know. While I am talking I shall be hearing those silent shrieks of dissent which are the lot of anyone attempting to run up ramshackle generalisations on the scale I am now attempting to.

II

T H E nineteenth century certainly went in for quantity. The previous century had been greatly impressed by plenitude, but what did the eighteenth century know of plenitude beside the nineteenth? The spreading multitudinousness of that later age I can recall by naming the two big volumes on Early Victorian England to which our chairman, besides his silent contributions as editor, supplied a piece of all-in criticism that must for long, perhaps for ever, remain the best imaginable. Or I could name the third volume of the *Cambridge Bibliography of English Literature*; in that bibliography our literature up to 1660 gets nine hundred pages, 1660-1800 gets a thousand; whereas the nineteenth century by itself gets eleven hundred. These two publications, coming from the other two great

English universities, serve to indicate much of the literary work accomplished by the nineteenth century. And we ourselves, mature samples of the twentieth, we who have long outgrown the ribald need to mock at our grandfathers, we of the now fully sobered twentieth century, can admit our envy. We have our masterpieces, but they are more thinly spaced and smaller than those of a hundred years ago. I need not go over the roll-call. Instead, I will adapt the amusing statistics of Swift, who, in his *Tale of a Tub*, casually mentioned the hundred and thirty-six first-rate poets then writing; if we extend the term 'first-rate poets' to include all first-rate writers, his figure is less ludicrous at any point in the mid-nineteenth century than at any point in any other century. When Dryden looked back and up at the Elizabethans, he exclaimed:

Theirs was the Giant Race before the Flood;[1]

but the giant race of the nineteenth century was much more numerous, and most of its members lived longer, and as far as writing went were more industrious; finally, giant for giant, most of them were more gigantic. 'No writer' wrote John Morley,

can now expect to attain the widest popularity as a man of letters unless he gives to the world *multa* as well as *multum*. Sainte-Beuve, the most eminent man of letters in France in our generation, wrote no less than twenty-seven volumes of his incomparable *Causeries*. Mr. Carlyle, the most eminent man of letters in England in our generation, has taught us that silence is golden in thirty volumes.[2]

In all the multitudinousness of the nineteenth century, what part was played by poetry? As we should expect, it was a big part, the nineteenth century, like Shakespeare's *Troilus and Cressida*, being a collection of big parts.

[1] 'To my Dear Friend, Mr. Congreve', l. 5.
[2] *Critical Miscellanies. Second Series*, 1877, p. 381.

### III

TALKING in this way of 'centuries' and 'poetry' has little to commend it. A century is a series of a hundred years, each year of which for the people alive in it lasted as long as the current year is lasting for ourselves. Those historians who speak of centuries should mark the lines which the appreciative Jacques overheard one morning in the forest of Arden:

> 'Tis but an hour ago since it was nine,
> And after one hour more 'twill be eleven.

That indicates the pace at which time was moving, the pace at which life was being lived, in 1600. Most historians do not allow this 'petty pace' to trouble their imaginations. It troubles mine, as I am also troubled by that other term in my title, the term 'poetry'.

What do we mean by 'poetry'? The word has many senses, and had more of them in the nineteenth century than previously—see, for instance what the word meant to Newman on p. 157 above. Do we mean by it 'poems written'? 'poems published'? 'metrical pieces that to their authors seemed poetry, at least until after the moment of publication'? 'great poems' (for instance, the 'Ode to Autumn' or *The Prelude* or 'The Bishop orders his Tomb at St. Praxed's')? Or do we mean by it, 'poeticalness'—which I might curtly define as the result of image-making, as the result of saying 'a stitch in time saves nine' instead of 'however irksome one finds it to put a thing to rights at the first moment it is seen to be wrong, one often saves a great deal of labour later on by doing so'? If we mean any or some of these in their nineteenth-century totality, then, I repeat, no one knows enough to have authority to speak. And if we limit 'poetry' to 'great poems', even that is too vast a matter since the nineteenth century produced very many of them, more than the eighteenth, and of a wide variety. Even if I settle for a moment on 'great' poems, I am still speaking unprofitably since I have no time to air what I fancy to be the standards by which I promote this poem and not that.

Furthermore, in the nineteenth century poetry existed plentifully outside metre. In the former half of the previous century there was sometimes a cleavage between poetry and prose, between what things and aspects of things were spoken of in metre and what out of it. In many of the writings of the great poet of the time this was so, and in those of several minor poets. Pope wrote 'great' prose—he was a classic of our prose, remarked W. P. Ker (winking at Arnold), *when he wrote prose*. But his prose is not so noticeably that of a poet, is not so noticeably 'poetical', as Dryden's is or Arnold's. In his prose, to put it roughly, he deliberately sought to speak like an *honnête homme*, and in his poems to speak like a poet. I said the former half of the eighteenth century advisedly: in the later half—it is one of the reasons why the 'nineteenth century' may be said to begin about 1750—there was as much 'poeticalness' in the prose as in the poetry: Gray's prose, I should say, is the perfect prose for an Englishman—clear and exploratory in thought but with more play of imagery than a Frenchman would care to allow himself. And in this half of the century fell the thoroughly poetical prose of Johnson, Sterne, Goldsmith, and Burke. In the nineteenth century much prose belonged to poetry as certainly as it belonged to what I shall call 'prose of thinking'—this was the time when Carlyle, Newman, Ruskin, Arnold, George Eliot and Pater were writing. In all, so much poetry existed outside metre that though Arnold promised that 'The future of poetry [would be] immense',[1] Pater saw that poetry was at least beginning its immense future as poetry in prose form.[2]

In the nineteenth century, then, poetry in metre, which is the only sort I shall proceed to talk about, flourished. We have only to think of the mountainous bibliography of Tennyson to see how thoroughly. But poetry is seldom in any age what people most like to read. They have to be won to read it—blandishments of pretty type, pretty bindings, the unusual 'slimness' of the volumes, all lend their aid. Sometimes the inducements of the poetry itself are meretricious, and, having got itself read, it fades overnight. Sometimes as well as the needful temporary attractiveness there is an attractiveness that persists, because of which the poetry goes on being read after the first bloom has gone off. In the nineteenth century the usual reluctance to read poetry could find any number of excuses. It was not easy to dispute the superior claims of a whole army of splendid novels and a hundred splendid instances of the prose of thinking.

First the novel. I propose to take two remarks made in the 1850's. The first is this from an article in *Fraser's*, which may well be the work of James Anthony Froude:[3]

[poetry] has ceased to be the natural expression of the deepest currents of man's thought.[4]

It was not the remark of one who had the last right to speak of poetry. Talking of depth it could not see the depth reached by the recent poems of Tennyson (*In Memoriam* had appeared four years earlier) or of Arnold. And talking of deepest currents of man's thought, it could not see how deep ran the currents of new thought in Clough's poems as well as in *In*

[1] *Essays in Criticism: Second Series*, p. 1.
[2] *Appreciations*, pp. 7 f.
[3] See *The Review of English Studies*, xvii, 1941, p. 317.
[4] 1854, p. 140.

*Memoriam.* I quote the remark because though ill informed it at least shows what the men of that time were looking for. Looking for, and finding as far as 'literature' went—literature as distinct from the prose of thinking—in the novel. And so to my second small exhibit. Writing a year earlier than the previous writer, Clough had noted that

poems after classical models, poems from Oriental sources, and the like, have undoubtedly a great literary value. Yet there is no question, it is plain and patent enough, that people much prefer Vanity Fair and Bleak House.[1]

For the sake of poetry, he wished it were otherwise. But in the meantime 'The modern novel is preferred to the modern poem'. This names explicitly the first great rival of poetry in the nineteenth century. Having nothing to fear from poetic drama it had much to fear from the novel. Since that form had got going—I am being vague deliberately—say with Defoe, it had always been the staple diet of those readers who, if there had been no novels to turn to, would have turned to poetry. In the nineteenth century the novels were so magnificent as literature that even unlikely men like Shelley, Macaulay, Darwin,[2] Newman, Tennyson, Matthew Arnold, and Hort were readers of them. I am not proposing to try to say whether or not the novel of the nineteenth century was greater than its poetry—it would take too long to try to establish the basis on which such a comparison could work. But at the time it

[1] *North American Review*, lxxvii, 1853, pp. 2 f.

[2] Though Darwin lost his taste for poetry, music and painting, coming to find even Shakespeare 'so intolerably dull that it nauseated me', he found in novels 'a wonderful relief and pleasure ... and ... often bless[ed] all novelists.' (The 'Autobiography' in Francis Darwin's *Life and Letters of Charles Darwin*, 1887, i. 101). Darwin read novels (or had them read to him) purely for recreation: accordingly he did not see the great novels of his time for what they were, and never questioned the belief that they belonged to an inferior order of literature—the popular half-ethical belief touched by what Henry James recalled as the 'old Evangelical hostility to the novel' ('The Art of Fiction', *Longman's Magazine*, Sept. 1884, p. 503).

was seen, and seen truly, that the *form* of the novel at least had taken over all that had been so well done in the Elizabethan age by the form of verse drama. I named Tennyson in my list of unlikely novel-readers. He attempted a comparison of the two forms, and was in no doubt as to which in the nineteenth century was the 'greater':

The form of prose fiction is a vastly greater one, indeed it may be termed all-comprehensive, and admits of the introduction of lyric or epic verse, in all varieties, as well as the profoundest analysis of character and motive, and is susceptible of the highest range of eloquence and unrhythmical poetry, and whatever it may lose in metrical melody (which, however, is not greatly regarded in dramatic dialogue) it gains immeasurably in its other elements. All things considered, I am of opinion that if a man were endowed with such faculties as Shakespeare's, they would be more freely and effectively exercised in prose fiction with its wider capabilities than when 'cribbed, cabined, and confined' in the trammels of verse.[1]

Perhaps we need not take Tennyson's remarks as necessarily clear: they come in a letter written at the age of seventy-eight.[2] Their interest is that the greatest poet of the time and one of the greatest metrists of all time asserted the contemporary supremacy of the novel form, even in his own despite. In doing so he invoked Shakespeare. We cannot say what a second Shakespeare could and would have done: to

[1] *Tennyson and His Friends*, p. 53.

[2] Tennyson was trying to speak accurately. When Henry James about this date 'protest[ed that] the novel seems to me the most magnificent form of art' ('The Art of Fiction', *Longman's Magazine*, Sept. 1884, p. 517), we know where we are: after *Middlemarch* he was not claiming too much, and his claim was sounder for being left vaguely reposing on 'magnificence'. But Tennyson volunteered analysis of the novel form, down to the warp and woof of its expression, and excitedly or generously went too far, allowing that the novel can admit not only 'unrhythmical poetry' but verse 'in all varieties'. Not all, of course, and not usually any except where a line of verse is accidentally and so unfortunately introduced. Tennyson may have have had in mind Dickens's practice of writing pathetic paragraphs of blank verse of the sort that from the time of Beaumont and Fletcher had been sacred to verse drama.

discuss the 'ifs' of history is merely to play a pundit's parlour game. But there was Dickens, who in the lavishness of his creative force was not unshakespearean, and who into the bargain had, like Shakespeare, a passion for the theatre. Living in the nineteenth century, however, he chose to be a novelist—all his passion for acting and playwriting left the theatre as simple-minded as it found it. And to add another novelist to Dickens, so as to make Shakespeare's fancied transmigration less incomplete, there was George Eliot, who to some of Shakespeare's lavishness added an intellectual range and force which Shakespeare in his own age had not needed to work so hard and so deliberately. It was said in the late nineteenth century that

what Shakespeare did for the Drama, George Eliot has done for its modern substitute the Novel;[1]

—a saying best interpreted in the sense that, like Shakespeare, she poured around her prime strong meaning a wealth of related meaning of great subtlety, intensity and originality— meaning poetic and intellectual in one. Reading the poetic-intellectual *Middlemarch*, we do not hanker after verse, not even after verse by Shakespeare. As I have said, poetry did not depend on metre in the nineteenth century as it had tended to do in the earlier part of the eighteenth.

And now for the other formidable rival of nineteenth-century poetry. There was no better spokesman for the prose

[1] Alexander Main in his Introduction to *Wise, Witty and Tender Sayings . . . of George Eliot*, eighth ed., 1889, p. ix. In at least the first four editions, published while George Eliot was alive, the reading stood 'has been, and still is, doing for the Novel'. Main notes as the first of her virtues that George Eliot provides 'the grandest and most uncompromising moral truth', but does not omit other equally Shakespearean virtues: 'there is to be found, on almost every page of her writings, some wise thought finely expressed, some beautiful sentiment tenderly clothed, some pointed witticism exquisitely turned, or some little bit of humour genially exhibited' (pp. x f).

of thinking than Mark Pattison. His masculine writings, so much less voluminous than the writings of most of his fellows, demonstrate and argue the necessity for a wide range of enquiry into the thought of the past and of the present. Discussing the reform of studies in Oxford, two years after the remark of Clough's about *Bleak House* and *Vanity Fair*, he asserted that

When literature and art are the highest intellectual objects cultivated by a people, it argues a great weakness in the mental power of the nation. . . . The classics [he was thinking of those of Greece and Rome, but would have included our own] must always have a subordinate part: they never can have an exclusive occupation of any institution professing to give a culture adequate to our existing knowledge of the universe, and its material and spiritual laws.[1]

No one knew better than Pattison that this remark could have been made at any time during the preceding two centuries at least. Reserved for the nineteenth, it was more over-whelmingly true than ever before. Fortunately—I may pause to note—most of the prose of thinking could at that time still be called literature as literature means matter of any sort written so as to give the generally cultivated reader not only instruction but immediate pleasure—a pleasure that is notable, however much milder and less sensuous than the immediate pleasure given by poetry. No more than in the two earlier centuries was there any cleavage on the score of readability (to put it at its lowest) between the writings of, say, Huxley and Ruskin. Nor, I may add, of Ruskin and the many 'journalists' who wrote those long articles that roar like trains through the great periodicals of the time: in 1862, in an early number of the *Cornhill*, Fitzjames Stephen went so far as to declare that

Journalism will, no doubt, occupy the first place or one of the first

[1] 'Oxford Studies' (1855) in *Essays*, ed. Henry Nettleship, 1889, i. 447 f.

o

places in the literary history of the present times, for it is the most characteristic of all their productions.[1]

In no age, as I have said, do people resort readily to poetry. Still, in the nineteenth a great deal of the begrudged thing, of good and better poetry, was produced. What, then, was the nature of the product? Can we discern some of the ways in which it was distinctive?

## IV

THERE is a certain quality of metrical poetry that we could denote by the term 'Miltonic perfection'. We open a copy of Milton's poems at random, and find a poetry evenly solid in substance and evenly exquisite in the words which may be thought of as the tangible surface of that solid substance. It is poetry which, at every line, elicits into our fullest conscious-ness precisely those mental possessions, if we have them there at all, which the poet requires just then for his poem. And what the poet requires for his poem is solid, proportioned with an eye to compactness and harmony, 'no tittle gone astray' (as Yeats said of his 'phoenix'), smooth, closed: like a gold ring. This being so, it was just here that the axe fell. If this is poetry of a Miltonic perfection, we should not expect to find it in the nineteenth century. Despite everything in the turbulent seventeenth, despite Donne's lines that placed Truth on 'a huge hill, Cragged, and steep',[2] Milton could speak of

beholding the bright countenance of truth in the quiet and still air of delightful studies.[3]

But not in the nineteenth century. Then, there was small

---

[1] Quoted by M. M. Bevington, *The Saturday Review, 1855-68*, New York, 1941, p. vii.

[2] *Satyres*, III. 79 ff.

[3] *The Reason of Church Government, Prose Works*, ed. J. A. St. John (Bohn's Library, n.d.), ii, 481.

chance of a vision so blessed. Matthew Arnold was speaking
for most of his contemporaries when he said:

To try and approach Truth on one side after another, not to strive or
cry, not to persist in pressing forward, on any one side, with violence
and self-will,—it is only thus, it seems to me, that mortals may hope to
gain any vision of the mysterious Goddess, whom we shall never see
except in outline, but only thus even in outline. He who will do nothing
but fight impetuously towards her on his own, one, favourite, particular line, is inevitably destined to run his head into the folds of the
black robe in which she is wrapped.[1]

And since men are born with a propensity for driving forward
on their own, one, favourite, particular line, the prospect was
not hopeful. Always hard to contrive, Milton's quiet and still
air may well have been very hard to contrive in the nineteenth
century. 'Nothing is more rare at this day', sighed Newman in
1834, 'than *quiet* thought.'[2] Its rarity was inevitable when
materials for new thinking were distractingly pouring in from
all sides. What chance could there be, after your quiet thought,
of remaining satisfied for long with whatever had imposed
on you for truth? To seek quiet seemed premature, cowardly
and foolish. And even criminal—on p. 57 above Matthew
Arnold quotes Joubert's belief that 'ignorance in intellectual
matters is a crime of the first order'; and Joubert was repeating
Dr. Johnson. Most men, busy over their urgent problems,
were content, where quiet was concerned, to hanker after it.
Accepting the new opportunities they found them painful,
but inspiritingly so. Quiet faded in movement, a sense of
progress. It was the rousing time when the growth of knowledge carried Lyell to the point of seeing that the forces which
have moulded the earth were forces still in action, forces still
moving. It was the century in which the evolution of scientific

[1] *Essays in Criticism,* p. vii.          [2] *Tracts for the Times,* No. 41.

researches over at least two centuries carried Darwin to the point of seeing that there was such a thing as the evolution of species. Movement seemed to be taking place everywhere, and caught men's imaginations. In the earlier years of the nineteenth century the image favoured was that of military advance: we hear a great deal about 'the march of intellect', 'the march of mind'. Even Keats heard of that goose-stepping advance, and quite early: by 1818 he was agreeing that 'there is really a grand march of intellect.'[1] And, as the *Oxford English Dictionary* tells us, the phrases became very common after the founding in 1825 of the Society for the Diffusion of Useful Knowledge (a society in which our Dr. Birkbeck was an outstanding figure). But the concept of the 'march' and the earlier concept of the 'progress' were more mechanical and less biological concepts than the later concepts of development and evolution. A march is not a growth, and a progress can, like those of Queen Elizabeth, be merely a string of stages. In the eighteenth century no one spoke of marching, and after the time of Keats, no one except, like Peacock, to laugh at it.[2] By that time Hegel's substitution of the category of 'becoming' for that of 'being' was having its effect, which, on the testimony of Mark Pattison, Newman had supplemented effectively:

Is it not a remarkable thing that you should have first started the idea —and the word—Development, as the key to the history of church doctrine, and since then it has gradually become the dominant idea of all history, biology, physics, and in short has metamorphosed our view of every science, and of all knowledge?[3]

[1] *Letters*, p. 144.
[2] e.g., ch. ii of *Crotchet Castle* (1831) is entitled 'The March of Mind'.
[3] Letter to Newman of 5th April, 1878, thanking him for the gift of a new edition of the *Essay on Development*, which would join, he said, the copy of the second that had been on his shelves for thirty-two years. The letter is preserved at the Oratory, Birmingham, and I print it with their permission.

There was even a perceptible change in the way man's three-score-years-and-ten were regarded. This is a subtle matter to which I cannot claim to have given enough thought. I offer the following points, supplied by English poetry, for what they are worth.[1]

In the eighteenth century a fairly common 'kind' of poem was the 'progress poem', of which Gray's ode 'The Progress of Poesy' is the best-known example.[2] The concept of progress had long been familiar but it seems that only slowly did it come to be understood as proceeding by a single imperceptible and sliding progression rather than by stages. Shakespeare divided man's life into seven periods, and Pope into four.[3] But though these stages can never have been seen as separate like flags in a pavement, they were not usually, before the nineteenth century, seen as phases of a continuous growth. That term 'growth', it seems, had to wait for Wordsworth. Beattie's *Minstrel* had borne the subtitle 'The Progress of Genius' but *The Prelude* bore the subtitle 'The Growth of a Poet's Mind.' Both concepts, that of progress by stages and that of a single growth, seem to have been allowed for in Coleridge's remark that

The poetic PSYCHE, in its process to full development, undergoes as many changes as its Greek name-sake, the butterfly;[4]

and also in Browning's remark in the 1863 dedication of *Sordello* that his 'stress lay on the incidents in the development of a soul'. But by then people had gained a clearer view of the process of evolution, and so had lost interest in the older

[1] I have said more on the subject in 'The Manner of Proceeding in Certain Eighteenth- and Early Nineteenth-Century Poems' (Warton Lecture of the British Academy, 1948).
[2] This 'kind' has been discerned and discussed by Professor R. H. Griffith in *The Texas Review*, v, 1920.
[3] *An Essay on Man*, ii. 275 ff.
[4] *Biographia Literaria*, i. 57.

concept. Newman's *Essay* had argued for the new idea, and there was his minor essay on development ten years before the *Essay* proper, that poem of which the refrain is 'Lead Thou me on!' Like Newman, Browning gave the word prominence in a title: he called an autobiographical poem 'Development'. He also coined the compound 'soul-development'[1].

By whatever steps we are to trace the change, it is clear that during the nineteenth century men ceased to think of the life of man as a thing 'put'. Pope had described man as a being

Plac'd on this isthmus of a middle state,[2]

that is, as a being created to fill a fixed position on the great fixed 'scale of being', a position intermediary between those of beast and angel. But in the nineteenth century, instead of a fixed scale, there was, so to speak, an assembly belt; movement instead of fixity, time instead of space; and the belt was trembling and agitated with struggle and change. Sometimes the age was aware of change for the worse:

Change and decay in all around I see.[3]

Often of change for the better. As far back as the first half of the eighteenth century the word *perfectibility* had been invented,[4] and it was given a great deal to do in the nineteenth. Leslie Stephen saw that the battle of the future was being fought out by John Stuart Mill and Newman, Mill believing in human progress as in a law of Nature, Newman believing

---

[1] Late in the eighteenth century one poet-historian had taken a firm step towards the new idea. In his *History of English Poetry*, Thomas Warton had traced 'the progress of the mind, not merely as exemplified in the confined exertions of an individual, but in a succession of ages, and in the pursuits and acquirements of a people'—a claim made for him by his biographer, Richard Mant, in 1802 and endorsed by W. P. Ker (*Cambridge History of English Literature*, x, 1913, p. 240).

[2] *An Essay on Man*, ii, 3.

[3] Line 7 of the hymn 'Abide with me...' by H. F. Lyte (1793-1847).

[4] Arthur O. Lovejoy's preface to Lois Whitney's *Primitivism and the Idea of Progress*, Baltimore, 1934, p. xvii.

that the nature of man 'is evil, not good, and produces evil things, not good things', and that 'Our race's progress and perfectibility . . . is a dream. . . .'[1]

Whether lugubriously or jubilantly, then, the nineteenth century was the first age which habitually peered into the future in a grand, impersonal way, as if from a peak in Darien:

> . . . were it not a pleasant thing
>   To fall asleep . . .
> And every hundred years to rise
>   And learn the world, and sleep again;
> To sleep thro' terms of mighty wars,
>   And wake on science grown to more,
> On secrets of the brain, the stars,
>   As wild as aught of fairy lore;
> And all that else the years will show,
>   The Poet-forms of stronger hours,
> The vast Republics that may grow,
>   The Federations and the Powers;
> Titanic forces taking birth
>   In divers seasons, divers climes;
> For we are Ancients of the earth,
>   And in the morning of the times.[2]

'Terms of mighty wars' might lie ahead, but science seemed to most people to be entering on a future of beneficient advance. 'Pure' science altogether so: as when in 1833 the sober Lyell felt obliged to expect great things:

When we compare the result of observations in the last thirty years with those of the three preceding centuries, we cannot but look forward with the most sanguine expectations to the degree of excellence to which geology may be carried, even by the labours of the present generation;[3]

[1] *An Agnostic's Apology,* 1893, pp. 171 ff.
[2] Tennyson, 'The Day Dream', L'Envoi, ll. 3 ff.
[3] *Principles of Geology,* i (1830), 73.

and in 1859 the sober Darwin:

In the distant future I see open fields for far more important researches.[1]

And 'applied' science too—the way it could make mighty wars mightier a hundredfold was greatly disregarded in the welcome given to its pacific benefits.

V

THIS forward peering had some effect on the way the nineteenth century regarded those things which had been considered perfect in earlier times. In those times, if men had been aware of change they had also been aware of perfection at points on the line of progress or variation. The theme of Keats's *Hyperion* is the change which overtakes even what is perfect:

So on our heels a fresh perfection treads.[2]

But when development is accepted as a law, the concept of perfection suffers by being infinitely deferred. Perfection, a concept to delight earlier ages, was a concept which for the nineteenth century came to lose its savour. Hazlitt recoiled from the useless perfection of the Indian jugglers. For the Miltonic perfection poets and critics in general felt a distaste. Swinburne, for example, preferred the imperfect *Faithful Shepherdess* of the decadent Fletcher to the perfect *Comus* of Milton;[3] he also preferred the imperfect odes of Collins to the Miltonically perfect odes of Gray.[4] But two great poets of the nineteenth century bore in mind the ideal of the Miltonic perfection: Keats, who died before the great intellectual winds of the century had become tempestuous, though even

[1] *On the Origin of Species*, 1859, p. 488.
[2] ii. 212.
[3] *Contemporaries of Shakespeare*, 1919, p. 151.
[4] *Miscellanies*, 1886, pp. 56 ff.

he lived long enough to see that party politics were on the wane now that the contest between the aristocracy and the people was becoming one 'between right and wrong';[1] and Tennyson, who stood like Lear in the midst of the gales, however often he ducked for cover. Milton's soul, said Wordsworth, was like a star and dwelt apart, and when Keats and Tennyson do write poetry of the Miltonic perfection we can think of them as writing it by an act of stellar abstraction. Keats, as I have said, did not suffer the full force of the winds, and so enjoyed a stiller and quieter air without much effort: Tennyson, contriving his abstraction, had a harder task. We remember how dumb he would sit at meetings of the Metaphysical Society. We remember how the hero of 'Locksley Hall' longed for

Summer isles of Eden lying in dark-purple spheres of sea.

There methinks would be enjoyment more than in this march of mind,
In the steamship, in the railway, in the thoughts that shake mankind.[2]

But even after their withdrawal, neither Keats nor Tennyson achieved the Miltonic perfection on the Miltonic scale. Milton's poems are perfect, open the book where we like. But the perfection of the page subserves a larger perfection, the perfection of great wholes. Keats and Tennyson wrote several perfect small poems, many perfect paragraphs, many more perfect phrases. But Keats's most Miltonic thing is a fragment because it could never have been anything else. And Tennyson's great elegy is a series of lyrics, his epic a series of idylls. When the nineteenth century did produce big works that can be called perfect as Milton's poems can, they were not poems but novels, the novels of Jane Austen and the novels and nouvelles of Henry James.

---

[1] *Letters,* p. 407.        [2] 'Locksley Hall', ll. 164 ff.

VI

THE other nineteenth-century poets turned away from the Miltonic ideal. Except the comic poets. No age has been so amply blessed with superb small comic poets: the Smith brothers, Hood, Praed, Lear, Calverley, Lewis Carroll, Gilbert, Hilton, Dobson, Godley and J. K. Stephen. We may imagine them as arguing in this way : 'The perfection of *Comus* is a dead perfection, as all perfection is. But perfection comes alive again when a practical joke is played on it. Let us steal the singing-robes of Milton, which Keats and Tennyson have so studiously kept fresh, and snip comic figures out of them. Part of the force of our comedy will lie in the discrepancy within the poem, that between the Miltonic perfection and the use to which we put it.' These poets therefore, when they wrote at their best, wrote as perfectly as Milton; but their world was not his, nor was it the 'strenuous', 'earnest' world of Keats and Tennyson.

VII

SOME of the nineteenth-century poets, then, provided this Miltonic perfection. It is no use looking for it in the poems of the others. Mr. T. S. Eliot has looked for it in Matthew Arnold's, and lamented its almost total absence: he has found in them 'little technical interest'.[1] But the reason for the absence of Miltonic perfection is simply this: that what Arnold had got to say could not be said with the Miltonic perfection without becoming something else: without becoming something false. In the gales of that age it was sometimes as much as you could do to stand up and speak. In one of his greatest poems Arnold saw the onrush of knowledge as like incoming waves:

[1] *The Use of Poetry and the Use of Criticism,* 1943 edition, p. 105.

Like children bathing on the shore,
Buried a wave beneath,
The second wave succeeds, before
We have had time to breathe.[1]

So said Arnold in verse which is as execrable in metre as it is irregular in syntax. But the syntax breaks the rules appropriately. And if the metre is execrable, it is execrable to some purpose. A smooth metre would have failed to express the untidy spontaneity of their sudden despair. The stanza makes you shudder with sympathy. Since this was its object, it is written with art, with art decisive rather than lingering and loving. Arnold's suffering seems more poignant because his sincerity in speaking it is not shared with any insincere belated homage to the Miltonic perfection. Pater was to say that

the most characteristic verse of the nineteenth century has been lawless verse.[2]

But if we are thinking of the greatest poetry of the time it would be better to say that where it seems lawless it is often obeying the one and only law that has authority, the old law that matter must express itself appropriately: if the matter is turbulent, the expression cannot but be turbulent also. Milton himself obeyed the one law that Pater saw as absence of law, and obeyed it both in his poetry and in his prose. In his poetry the result of obedience is calmness, in the prose turbulence. Only when matter is calm is the Miltonic perfection the right sort of perfection for its expression.

## VIII

THE quality of most nineteenth-century poems, then, is the quality of things purposefully on the move. Wordsworth's

[1] 'Stanzas in Memory of the Author of "Obermann",' ll. 73 ff.
[2] *Appreciations,* p. 7.

*Prelude* is more like a growing tree than a ring of gold, and Browning's great epic more like a renaissance town on market day (or more like *Middlemarch*): it has the imperfection we associate with plenitude.

The characteristic poetry of the nineteenth century was written *currente calamo*, with a fountain pen or a pencil. The young Arnold, taught by Goethe and perhaps also by Coleridge and Macaulay,[1] saw that if he were to be a great poet, that is, one who had 'attain[ed] perfection in the region of thought and feeling, and . . . unite[d] this with perfection of form', he would have to face tearing himself to pieces, a process as long as it would be painful, and which he decided to shirk.[2] But the less acutely painful profession of school inspecting, and the less painful hobby of writing magazine articles did not prevent him from becoming a great poet. They did, of course, prevent him from becoming the sort of great poet he had imagined as the only sort possible: he became not a great finished poet, torn to pieces and then exquisitely rebuilt, but a great faulty poet, almost a slapdash one, sometimes more a Walt Whitman than a Milton. In one of his early letters he noted that

More and more I feel bent against the modern English habit (too

---

[1] It had been Goethe's opinion that 'the young poet should do some sort of violence to himself to get out of the mere general idea' (quoted by Butcher, *Aristotle's Theory of Poetry and Fine Art*, 1895, p. 181.). Coleridge had said that 'There is no profession on earth, which requires an attention so early, so long, or so unintermitting as that of poetry' (*Biographia Literaria*, i. 32). And in his essay on Milton came this from Macaulay:

> He who, in an enlightened and literary society, aspires to be a great poet, must first become a little child. He must take to pieces the whole web of his mind. He must unlearn much of that knowledge which has perhaps constituted hitherto his chief title to superiority . . .

This follows on from the proposition that as civilisation advances, poetry declines (see p. 216 below).

[2] *Letters*, i. 63.

much encouraged by Wordsworth) of using poetry as a channel for thinking aloud, instead of making anything.[1]

These words express a noble and classic concern. But Arnold, proud of his nose for the *Zeitgeist*, should have sensed that 'thinking aloud' was to be expected of anyone properly alive in the nineteenth century. Newman had noted the rarity of quiet thought. True, there was little quiet. I have already quoted Morley's remark that though Carlyle was a quietist, preaching that silence is golden, his sermon was as endless as it was deliberately noisy. And Newman's own predicament was as ironic: he said that the *Grammar of Assent* was almost the only book of his shelf-ful that he had written to please himself, each of the rest having been written 'from some especial call, or invitation, or necessity, or emergency'.[2] And if there was little quiet there was little 'thought', in the sense of pieces of truth vouched for on every hand. But for all the dearth of agreed 'thought' there was 'thinking' constant and often intrepid. The nineteenth century did a greater quantity of thinking than any other, not forgetting the seventeenth; and so more thinking aloud. The additional pressure of thought even changed men's looks. Thomas Hardy met so many living instances of Rodin's *Penseur* that he noted the supersession of the classical face by the face scarred with thought.[3]

There is enough evidence to show that in the later eighteenth century a considerable number of men had come to regard the act of thinking as a duty rather than a game. Gray remarked that his 'chief amusement', in the graver sense, was to think even 'though to little purpose'[4] —a modest disclaimer which,

[1] *Unpublished Letters of Matthew Arnold*, ed. Arnold Whitridge, 1923, p. 17.
[2] Ward's *Life*, ii. 400.
[3] *The Return of the Native*, 1878, Book iii, ch. 1.
[4] *Correspondence*, ed. Toynbee and Whibley, 1935, ii. 565 f.

both Johnson and Arnold would agree,[1] his letters belie. For Johnson, the need of all men for thinking was a sort of King Charles's head. He might be said to have preferred Descartes' 'Cogito, ergo sum' in the sense of 'I cerebrate. . . .' His power that way was perhaps what most struck Boswell; and Reynolds, for whom 'thinking' was the 'real labour',[2] praised him as the friend and master who 'qualified my mind to think justly.'[3] Even Lord Chesterfield had seen the need to counsel it:

> Of all the troubles do not decline, as many do, that of thinking.[4]

In any age of expanding interests much thinking is inevitable. But in the eighteenth century not all the new matter for thinking laid open by science, industry, slow and quick political revolution was immediately seen as likely to touch foundations. The new matter for thinking flung up by the industrial revolution did not for a long time much disturb the belief that trade was glorious, nor did ethnological discoveries yet greatly affect men's views of European religion and manners. Only in the field of politics was the new matter loudly explosive. And so in the later eighteenth century, as in the earlier, the thinking done was often a means of mastering the old conclusions rather than of arriving at new. 'Doctor' Johnson remains its most typical philosopher (in the general sense) as well as its best. As Arnold put it, he was rather

a strong force of conservatism and concentration, in an epoch which by its natural tendencies seemed to be moving towards expansion and freedom.[5]

---

[1] Life of Gray (Lives, iii. 431 f.); Essays in Criticism: Second Series, pp. 75 ff.
[2] Works, ed. Malone, 1797, ii. 247 (Discourse xii).
[3] op. cit., i. xx. Reynolds goes on: 'No man had, like him, the faculty of teaching inferior minds the art of thinking.'
[4] Letter of 7th February, 1749.
[5] The Six Chief Lives from Johnson's 'Lives of the Poets', 1879, p. xxiv.

In the next century the choice was sharper. It lay then between ignoring and facing damage visibly done, damage great and wide. The assumptions on which beliefs, conduct, professions had rested had been removed or shaken. Those men who tried to master the new materials often got no further than dipping into what Reynolds, and Newman after him, called the 'floating opinions' of the time[1]. Adapting a current term Newman called them 'viewy men'.[2] And yet it was plain not only that 'views' were numerous but, to the youthful John Stuart Mill at least, that many men could pick their own way among them in the course of thinking through to views of their own. In his essays on the spirit of the age, written about 1830, he declared that

Men may not reason, better, concerning the great questions in which human nature is interested, but they reason more. Large subjects are discussed more, and longer, and by more minds.[3]

And also that

The persons who are [able to arrive at] sound opinions by their own light form . . . a constantly increasing number.[4]

Thinking aloud rather than making something. Wordsworth knew well what he was doing. In 1833 we find him saying proudly that he

had given twelve hours' thought to the conditions and prospects of society for one to poetry.[5]

He had great hopes of thinking when at its best:

The mind often does not think, when it thinks that it is thinking. If we were to give our whole soul to anything, as the bee does to the

[1] Reynolds, *Works*, ed. cit., i. 131 (Discourse vii); Newman, *Parochial Sermons*, i (1844 edition), 66.
[2] Newman, *Loss and Gain*, Part i, ch. 3.
[3] *The Spirit of the Age*, ed. F. A. von Hayek, Chicago, 1942, p. 13.
[4] op. cit., p. 10.
[5] *Poems in Two Volumes, 1807*, ed. Helen Darbishire, 1942 edition, p. xxvii.

flower, I conceive there would be little difficulty in any intellectual employment.[1]

His clearest perceptions were not made in the social field, but he saw clearly enough how the world was going: even the horse ridden by the idiot boy was, you remember, 'a horse that thinks.'[2] Arnold ought to have allowed that Wordsworth's thinking was a portion of his being alive, no longer a state of bliss for him as in his revolutionary days, but vivid still. Nevertheless, his remark pointed to a difference between Wordsworth's poems and those, say, of Pope and Gray. The poems of these earlier poets belonged, as I have already suggested, to a past in which poetry was seen as giving not so much new thinking as old thought. And it is when drawing on old thought that poetry is most happily itself. In the most lasting and deep sense poetry draws on our old experience as it is that of men endowed with a 'pleasing anxious being'—that was how Gray summed it up—of men greatly concerned with keeping warm in winter, with eating and sleeping, moved by many obscure or sharp emotions every hour, acting blindly or with sight little better than dim, and thrown back constantly on their courage or their cowardice by all that they do not like or understand. Poetry at its best still remains the expression of the nature of man in his mainly primitive state. With less time in the nineteenth century to be his old self, man had less time and chance to write the older sort of poetry. If poetry is made out of old thought, then we should expect less of it in the nineteenth than in the eighteenth. 'Man thinks too much, nowadays, for poetry', it was said,[3] and so not only had less use for vapid verse on pretty subjects but less hope of achieving

[1] *Wordsworth's Literary Criticism*, ed. N. C. Smith, 1925 edition, p. 256: 'Hence [he concludes] there is no excuse for obscurity in writing'.
[2] 'The Idiot Boy', l. 112.
[3] *Fraser's*, 1854, p. 140.

the calm intellectual poetry of poets who felt themselves to be speaking for the cloud of past witnesses as much as for that of present, the poetry of which a late instance had been Gray's 'Elegy'. In the nineteenth century poetry had less chance of being 'a gum which oozes'.[1] Some sort of poetry, however, could still be hoped for, and that, of necessity, an intellectual sort—only poetry that was 'intellectual' was 'adequate to modern demands', said Pater, repeating a current commonplace that was still sharp.[2] But if intellectual, not intellectual with collected calmness. The intellectual poetry written in the nineteenth century was poetry expressing not thought so much as the sort of thinking that is inspired from day to day, poetry nearer the 'spasmodic' than the collected. Some of the Victorian poets—Alexander Smith, Bailey, Dobell—were given 'spasmodics' as a nickname. But, as Tennyson saw, 'Spasms . . . is the order of the day',[3] and many who kept clear of the nickname were nevertheless the thing. Arnold tried hard to 'make something'—for example, in *Sohrab and Rustum*, in *Balder Dead*, in *Merope*. In the first of these poems he was successful, but successful mainly as a poet for boys. It is not every poet who can make something which is admired by Form IV, and the nineteenth century scored other juvenile successes in Macaulay's 'Horatius', Browning's 'Pied Piper' Morris's *Sigurd the Volsung*, and Dobson's 'Ballad of Beau Brocade'. But Arnold's lyrics are instances of thinking aloud rather than of something made. Known by heart in their own day by men fully grown,[4] they have been read over and over again ever since.

Thinking possessed much of the best poetry of the century.

[1] *Timon of Athens*, I. i. 23.
[2] *Essays from 'The Guardian'*, 1901, p. 47.
[3] *Tennyson and His Friends*, p. 52.
[4] Walter Bagehot, *Physics and Politics*, 1872, p. 58.

P

The technical interest which Mr. Eliot missed from Arnold's poems was the less verbal technical interest of a poet's thinking.

And when the critic in *Fraser's* dispensed with poetry he overlooked one great advantage it offered the thinkers of the time. Nineteenth-century thinkers did not work at the formation of systems. The encyclopaedic range and concatenation which Mill admired in Auguste Comte and Herbert Spencer were not often attempted, and the age dropped the terms 'philosopher' and 'metaphysician' for the humbler Saxon 'thinker'. Systems are the product of men who rearrange 'what oft was thought', not the product of men faced suddenly with a multitude of facts that are new. Thomas Huxley spoke of his setting out as a young man without rudder or compass.[1] It was a common image for a new dilemma. And even if rudder and compass had been fixed on to start with, you often lost them: Dr. Arnold tied them on to Clough's boat very tightly, but they soon worked loose and came off. These men were not in the mood for systems. They thought, instead, in flights which were numerous, shorter and more baffled. They thought up to the point at which thinking became exhausted, or afraid, or (if they were men of smaller minds, or of minds requiring comfort at all costs) self-satisfied. They thought until they needed to turn aside to something 'soothing', something 'consoling' (I am using favourite words of the time). They thought until they gave up thinking for hoping, for trusting, for praying, for mystic visions, for patriotism, for action, and so on. Now such panicking from thinking is intolerable in prose because prose exists to allow men to think on and on. This is why so many were disturbed by the prose of Newman; it worked like a beautiful machine—Newman

[1] *Life and Letters of Thomas Henry Huxley*, ed. Leonard Huxley, 2nd ed., 1900, ii. 34.

has been called a logician of genius—but it worked only to make a present of itself to what most Englishmen thought to be superstitition. In poetry, however, which has always sheltered man as he is—man as a bundle of contradictions—a deflection into hoping and trusting was allowable, and indeed expected. And so we get the many poems of Tennyson that put a stop to life-and-death inquiry and realism with a smile, with a smile which is meant to be reassured and reassuring, but which is, of course, weaker than it need have been. The latter of Matthew Arnold's magnificent 'Obermann' poems ends in the relief of

> I saw the morning break,

just as Tennyson's 'Two Voices' had ended with a vision of a family going to church, and Browning's *Easter Day* with the breaking of that day. We know too well what those flattering mornings turned into: the poets should have looked longer and seen that their dawns were false. Some poets kept on thinking with more consistency, or for longer without collapsing: Clough, Fitzgerald, Meredith and Hardy, for instance. But even in the thoughtful poems of these stalwarts, there is still present that consoling ambiguity of poetry. Thinking, we feel, is not quite so binding when it has chosen for its medium verse instead of prose. Poetry, in the nineteenth century as always, was a refuge for thinkers. The poets think as long as they can, then they

> fasten
> Their hands upon their hearts.[1]

In thinking as hard as they could the poets of this century were in the thick of their times. It is characteristic of them that they did not plead their being poets as a ground for exemption

[1] A. E. Housman, *Last Poems*, X ('Could man be drunk for ever . . .').

from the common lot. They did not accept the version of the poet sanctioned by Gray in the 'Elegy' (where the solitary unhappy poet pores upon the brook that babbles by), the version puffed out by Beattie in his much-read poem *The Minstrel*. Beattie's Edwin certainly fascinated them. In her youthful William, Dorothy Wordsworth saw another Edwin.[1] Keats stood tiptoe upon a little hill. There was Shelley's poet who

> Will watch from dawn to gloom
> The lake-reflected sun illume
> The yellow bees in the ivy-bloom.[2]

Edwin fascinated them; but they rejected him for the painful world of men.

## IX

THEY acquiesced, therefore, in the view that poetry stands second or worse to certain other things. In the nineteenth century poetry was often made to know its place. Certain writers in the late eighteenth century, primed with new facts about far-off and primitive countries, and taught by Montesquieu how to interpret those facts, had manufactured many accounts of the growth of civilisation, instances of what one of them (with more frankness than his successors showed) called '*Theoretical* or *Conjectural History*'.[3] The instance that most concerns nineteenth-century poetry is *The Four Ages of Poetry*, in which Peacock enjoyed himself demonstrating that as civilisation advances—and most people agreed that it was then advancing rapidly—poetry declines (a view which

---

[1] *The Early Letters of William and Dorothy Wordsworth 1787-1805*, ed. E. de Selincourt, 1935, p. 98.

[2] *Prometheus Unbound*, I. i. 743 ff.

[3] Dugald Stewart in 1793: see *E. L. H., A Journal of English Literary History*, Baltimore, XII. iii. 204.

Macaulay was to repeat in his essay on Milton five years later). Poetry, explained Peacock, had passed through four ages: the age of iron when rude bards celebrated the exploits of their chief, the age of gold when Homer recalled past exploits, the age of silver (stretching from Virgil to Pope) when poets copied Homer, and, finally, the age of lead, reserved for Wordsworth and the rest. In the earliest historical times the poet was honoured as the only learned member of the tribe. But, later on, the branches of his knowledge fell, one by one, to specialists; till the poet was left with nothing for himself except, say, the sextons and old women Wordsworth was always interviewing:

modern rhymsters, and their olympic judges, the magazine critics . . . continue to debate and promulgate oracles about poetry, as if it were still what it was in the Homeric age, the all-in-all of intellectual progression, and as if there were no such things in existence as mathematicians, astronomers, chemists, moralists, metaphysicians, historians, politicians, and political economists, who have built into the upper air of intelligence a pyramid, from the summit of which they see the modern Parnassus far beneath them.[1]

Auguste Comte with more precision told the same story. Men, he said, had first seen external nature theologically (trees had their dryads), then metaphysically (trees had their 'Vegetative Souls'), then, at long last, positively, or scientifically (the tree is seen as 'governed by invariable laws, with which no volitions, either natural or supernatural, interfere').[2] And this, Comte believed, was the stage destined to endure.

Poetry was also being attacked from other sides than that of the theoretical or conjectural historians. The Utilitarians (in theory at least) found little utility in it, and what little they

[1] *Peacock's Four Ages of Poetry* [ &c], ed. H. F. B. Brett-Smith, Oxford, 1921, p. 19.
[2] J. S. Mill, *Auguste Comte and Positivism*, 1865, pp. 11 f.

did find, they insulted. Bentham, whom Newman declared not to have a spark of poetry in him,[1] went out of his way to compare the pleasure afforded by poetry to the pleasure afforded by a children's game called push-pin.[2] The advice usually given to poets by Carlyle was that their writing of poetry should stop, though he did allow the stuff some value when it existed on the scale and at the pitch of Shakespeare's. Newman, the theologian, attacked it as a pastime making no hard demands of its devotees. The very *ethos* of the age seemed against it, and Matthew Arnold complained (though not so blindly as to be unfair)

how deeply *unpoetical* the age and all one's surroundings are. Not unprofound, not ungrand, not unmoving:—but *unpoetical*.[3]

## X

IF poetry declined as civilisation advanced then the real enemy was science—the science to which in a famous footnote Wordsworth had opposed it,[4] the science which, after being applied, was the main source of the unpoeticalness that Arnold had noted in his surroundings. In 1894 when Huxley was asked what name an impartial posterity would bestow on the nineteenth century—would they call it the century of Comte, of Darwin, of Renan, of Edison, of Pasteur, of Gladstone?—he refused to bet on a name, but was clear that if named or nameable the man would be a scientist:

I conceive that the leading characteristic of the nineteenth century has been the rapid growth of the scientific spirit, the consequent

---

[1] 'The Tamworth Reading Room' (*Discussions and Arguments on Various Subjects*, 1872, p. 263).

[2] *The Rationale of Reward*, 1825, p. 206. Cf. Cowper's *Table Talk* (*Works*, ed. Southey, 1836, viii. 138).          [3] *Arnold to Clough*, p. 99.

[4] In the 1800 Preface to *The Lyrical Ballads*, where he opposed 'poetry' to 'matter of fact' rather than to 'prose.'

application of scientific methods of investigation to all the problems with which the human mind is occupied, and the correlative rejection of traditional beliefs which have proved their incompetence to bear such investigation.

The activity of the scientific spirit has been manifested in every region of speculation and of practice.[1]

Huxley found the question an easy one.

I can remind you of what was happening by making the sort of contribution appropriate for an English Department and noting what was happening to certain words. When Gray said of the poet in the 'Elegy' that

> Fair Science frown'd not on his humble birth,

he meant that the poet, unlike the rustics of the poem, was learned, was 'lettered', as they used to say, had acquired some knowledge by reading. The word *science*, that is, meant for Gray what it meant for Chaucer.[2] But during the nineteenth century the meaning of the word shrank to its modern sense of what concerns 'those branches of study that relate to the phenomena of the material universe and their laws.'[3] This was only one of the meanings of the word for Gray (who, by the way, besides knowing a great deal about history, knew a great deal about natural history). It is a concise demonstration of the power of science in the nineteenth century that it was able to capture the word for itself. Human knowledge as it had existed for Gray seemed trivial beside what was still a part of it, but, as it turned out, so great and new and expanding a part that the rest of the old meaning quickly withered away. And at a dramatic moment in the century the word *science* produced

---

[1] *Life and Letters*, ed. cit., ii. 374.

[2] Its use by Johnson in *Rambler* 180 well illustrates the meaning of the word up to the nineteenth century: 'A man of science is expected to excel the unlettered and unenlightened, even on occasions where literature is of no use.'

[3] *O.E.D.*, s.v. 'science' §5 b.

an offspring we have all adopted: in 1840 Whewell, the Cambridge philosopher, hazarded that

We need very much a name to describe a cultivator of science in general. I should incline to call him a Scientist.[1]

## XI

M O S T of the great poets saw the value of science, saw that it was the great thing in their time. And, seeing this, they readily surrendered their vested interests in poetry. Shelley wrote his *Defence of Poetry*, refusing to yield to Peacock; but he agreed with him in private that there was a lot of poor poetry about, endorsing his view that the 'higher class of minds' neglected the poetry of people like 'Barry Cornwall' for 'moral, political, and physical science';[2] 'I had much rather', Shelley agreed, 'for my own private reading, receive political, geological, and moral treatises, than this stuff'.[3] Nevertheless Shelley defended poetry when it was great poetry. And when Newman as an undergraduate attended the geological lectures of Buckland, it was as a prospective poet that he responded to them: geology, he cried,

opens an amazing field to imagination and to poetry.[4]

But when the time came for Tennyson to have a mature opinion, he made no defence. Even great poetry was yielded up to science. It is all there in his poem 'Parnassus', a poem which opens with a vision of the crowned poets assembled on the awful mountain and the prayer of the poet to join them. If the prayer is answered then

Lightning may shrivel the laurel of Caesar, but mine would not wither;

that is, poetry would procure for the poet an immortality

[1] *O.E.D.*, s.v. 'scientist'.    [2] Peacock, op. cit., p. xi.
[3] id., p. xv.    [4] *Letters*, ed. Anne Mozley, 1891, i. 61.

more deathless than that procured by great action. Then Tennyson, looking again, finds the vision changed:

What be those two shapes high over the sacred fountain,
Taller than all the Muses, and huger than all the mountain?
On those two known peaks they stand ever spreading and heightening;
Poet, that evergreen laurel is blasted by more than lightning!
Look, in their deep double shadow the crown'd ones all disappearing!
Sing like a bird and be happy, nor hope for a deathless hearing!
"Sounding for ever and ever?" pass on! the sight confuses—
These are Astronomy and Geology, terrible Muses!

Man, that is, and the poetry he had so often claimed as immortal, was as nothing beside the immensities of time and space, immensities to which only the scientist held the key.

## XII

IN his *Four Ages* Peacock allowed the condemned poet alternative courses of reprieve. He could justify his continued existence either by striking out on new lines or by being content to provide ornament.[1]

Some poets of the nineteenth century chose to provide ornament. They chose to provide it when they wrote of things that only existed in the fancy, or when they wrote about people and things that belonged to earlier periods of history. But even there they often tried to be 'useful' to their times. Tennyson added some of the intellectual interests of the nineteenth century to Keats's 'Eve of St. Agnes' and gave his age *The Idylls of the King*. But the comment of the best minds of the age was that of Leslie Stephen: 'We were going through an intellectual crisis', and 'disliked a philosophy which required to be insinuated through an allegorical clothing'.[2] They therefore preferred *In Memoriam* and the poems of Clough: that is, poems

---

[1] op. cit., pp. 16 f.  [2] *Studies of a Biographer*, 1907, ii. 194.

speaking directly, and on subjects of the day, which included, of course, such age-old themes as they had time to attend to.

### XIII

O F the poets who tried to be 'useful' in the way the nineteenth century found most acceptable, I shall speak of two.

First Wordsworth. What made it possible for a dour utilitarian like John Stuart Mill to respond to Wordsworth with something like a religious[1] love was the basis of Wordsworth's respect for fact. Wordsworth's thinking, for all its perceptiveness, is not so important as the material he gathers to feed it, the facts, and his reliance on them. His material is his experience, his experience of himself, of man at his simplest, or if not that at least at his most unworldly, a human being in a house or out of doors amid external nature as it exists at its quietest around lakes and at its bleakest up in the mountains. When he read the early poems of Tennyson, Wordsworth saw that what he valued most in his own poems was 'the spirituality with which I have endeavoured to invest the material universe'.[2] But that is not their power. Their power lies in their humility before the material fact. Wordsworth is like the scientist, as he is like the saint. Anything can start, or participate in, the perceiving, thinking and feeling which becomes his poetry. Those who laugh at his idiot boy (if any still do), at Wilkinson's spade, at the painstaking exactitude of his titles ought to laugh also at

> The single sheep, and the one blasted tree,
> And the bleak music from that old stone wall.[3]

For there is no more break for Wordsworth—nor should

---

[1] Coleridge noted that 'while others are read with delight, [Wordsworth's] works are a *religion*' (quoted Shawcross, *Biographia Literaria*, ii. 289).

[2] [R. H. Shepherd's] *Tennysoniana*, 1879, pp. 95 f.

[3] *The Prelude*, xii. 319 f.

there be for us—between a spade and the 'morning [that] rose, in memorable pomp'[1] than there is a break for Dante in the glory of God which penetrates the universe, glowing in one region more and less in another.[2] Those who laugh at the spade—unless they laugh at Wordsworth's way of speaking of it through not seeing that the way was right at the time the poem was written—do not see that poetry began for Wordsworth where holiness began for St. Francis, or where science began for Darwin. Whether or not we can accept his mystic visions, he leads us so ploddingly to them that we must respect them. He presents them merely as further rungs of a ladder we have climbed with him from the very bottom. He starts like his own Peter Bell to whom a primrose was but a primrose, and he ends with thoughts about it that lie too deep for tears. Though he sheds and takes on readers at every point on the long road, we can all go some part of the way with him. You cannot say that of Swinburne.

And a technical point. In the *Lyrical Ballads* Wordsworth did a great service to the nineteenth-century poets by showing them how they could think in metre, especially in ballad metre.[3]

Then Tennyson. From the start he was marked out to be the poet of science: as a youth he loved sensuous impressions

[1] id., iv. 324.
[2] *Il Paradiso*, i. 1 ff.
[3] His influence here was supplemented for some poets by the influence of Heine. Arnold grew lyrical in praise of Heine's usual metre: 'The magic of Heine's poetical form is incomparable; he chiefly uses a form of old German popular poetry, a ballad-form which has more rapidity and grace than any ballad-form of ours; he employs this form with the most exquisite lightness and ease, and yet it has at the same time the inborn fulness, pathos, and old-world charm of all true forms of popular poetry.' (*Essays in Criticism*, p. 174). It is difficult to see, by the way, how any stanza can be more rapid than the English ballad stanza. Arnold himself chose the form he considered inferior for his two fine 'Obermann' poems. For poems of thinking the form that Wordsworth had found good enough for some of the *Lyrical Ballads* remained good enough for Arnold.

as Keats had done, but, unlike Keats, he also loved books on science. With Tennyson poetry stood up to Peacock: if in its first age it had celebrated the exploits of martial chiefs, it was now celebrating the exploits of intellectual chiefs, the exploits of Lyell and Darwin. Tennyson put into his poems all the new things that men had just learned to see and to make, and his greatness as a poet is that he put in with them his grasp of their distance, their age, their size (immense or infinitesimal), their appearance, their sudden power to stretch the mind, their meaning for mankind. The geologists had taught Tennyson that where London stands had once stood sea. Tennyson responded to that fact as a scientist, and also as a poet:

> There where the long street roars, hath been
> The stillness of the central sea.[1]

He states a fact so as to start a sublime emotion. In the minds of scientists and ordinary men scientific facts prompt an emotion which may be sublime but which they can express, if by words at all, only by words that are inadequate. Darwin, for instance, felt a strong emotion. That is clear from his visible attempts at expressing it. But the strength of his emotion is clear by implication, which is not a witness counting for much in literature. We take its strength on trust from the inadequate words, and take it rather as human beings than as readers. The expression of his emotion rises as high as it can in the paragraph which closes *On the Origin of Species*:

It is interesting to contemplate an entangled bank, clothed with many plants of many kinds, with birds singing on the bushes, with various insects flitting about, and with worms crawling through the damp earth, and to reflect that these elaborately constructed forms, so different from each other, and dependent on each other in so complex

[1] *In Memoriam*, cxxiii. 3 f.

a manner, have all been produced by laws acting around us. These laws, taken in the largest sense, being Growth with Reproduction; Inheritance which is almost implied by reproduction; Variability from the indirect and direct action of the external conditions of life, and from use and disuse; a Ratio of Increase so high as to lead to a Struggle for Life, and as a consequence to Natural Selection, entailing Divergence of Character and the Extinction of less-improved forms. Thus, from the war of nature, from famine and death, the most exalted object which we are capable of conceiving, namely, the production of the higher animals, directly follows. There is grandeur in this view of life, with its several powers, having been originally breathed into a few forms or into one; and that, whilst this planet has gone cycling on according to the fixed law of gravity, from so simple a beginning endless forms most beautiful and most wonderful have been, and are being, evolved.

'It is interesting . . .' says Darwin. It is indeed. And for the scientist the interestingness of it must come first. Only when that interestingness is fully worked out in words, can the scientist stand back and attend to his emotion. That is, if he wants to attend to it. He is not obliged to: the most we ask of him, all we have a right to ask of him, is that he communicate interestingness. Darwin elected to supply something more— the emotion he felt as a man who was deeply interested. His emotion is shown in the words 'grandeur' 'beautiful' and 'wonderful', but they are inadequate both to express his emotion for himself and to express ours for ourselves. He and ourselves have strong emotions: the facts he has recorded and passed on to us are sublime in what we can grasp of their implications. But only a poet can express the emotions at all adequately. And among poets, Tennyson in particular. Being a poet speaking of a scientific object, he was sometimes not interesting enough. He was sometimes pulled up in that knowledgeable time for stating facts wrongly: on the famous occasion, for instance, when in 'The Vision of Sin' he wrote:

> Every moment dies a man,
> Every moment one is born.

On this occasion, Tennyson failed to give a fact accurately: he merely hinted at one imperfectly. The fact as the scientist gave it was more interesting because more accurate. Tennyson on this occasion failed in completeness of interestingness. Nor in this instance was there much room for emotion and so for the expression of emotion. But to be competing in interestingness was, and is, no proper job for a poet. His main job is to express emotion. And this Tennyson could do superbly. Sometimes he expressed it by the picture he gave of the scientific object. Scientists give names to things, mathematicians give hieroglyphics, but poets give pictures. Scientists often try to give pictures too. Very occasionally their pictures seize on us like the greatest things in Dante or Shakespeare: as when Huxley took the crayfish (that 'turmoil of material molecules which are constantly flowing into [it] on the one side, and streaming out on the other') and compared it to the whirlpool three miles below Niagara:

However changeful in the contour of its crest, this wave has been visible, approximately in the same place, and with the same general form, for centuries past. Seen from a mile off, it would appear to be a stationary hillock of water. Viewed closely, it is a typical expression of the conflicting impulses generated by a swift rush of material particles.[1]

But most often the pictures of the scientists merely stupefy us, as those, say, of Jeans do. Tennyson always brings age and immensity within our human reach. The highest pitch to

[1] T. H. Huxley, *The Crayfish: An Introduction to the Study of Zoology*, 1880, p. 85. It is worth remarking that Huxley did not originate this image. He introduced it by saying: 'The parallel between a whirlpool in a stream and a living being, which has often been drawn, is as just as it is striking.' Huxley, convinced of its 'justness', saw to it that his version of the image was as 'striking' as he could make it.

which human words have climbed seems to me that climbed
to in Tennyson's translation of a scrap of the *Iliad*:

> As when in heaven the stars about the moon
> Look beautiful, when all the winds are laid,
> And every height comes out, and jutting peak
> And valley, and the immeasurable heavens
> Break open to their highest. . . .[1]

Homer could not get so high because he had not read the books
Tennyson had read, because his eye had not haunted, as
Tennyson's had, the telescope. Science helped Tennyson to be
a greater poet.[2]

But usually Tennyson did not picture the objects of science
in blank verse. He preferred to picture them in great lung-
emptying lines. And he learned the trick from Shelley.
Shelley was a stimulus to the working-class movement of the
nineteenth century; Shelley taught Swinburne to sing like a
soprano, and for ever and ever; Shelley annoyed Matthew
Arnold for his childish love of what Peacock dubbed 'poetical
impressions'.[3] But for Tennyson, Shelley was the poet of
rhythms like that of

> Worlds on worlds are rolling ever
> From creation to decay.[4]

Printed as one line, it could have gone straight into 'Locksley
Hall'.

Tennyson realised the dream of Wordsworth who said
that the poet could make poetry out of the facts of the botanist,
the chemist, the geologist when he could accept those facts as

---

[1] 'Specimen of a Translation of the Iliad in Blank Verse', ll. 11 ff.

[2] Pater, in his essay on Sir Thomas Browne, noted that 'The really stirring
poetry of science is not in guesses, or facile divinations about it, but in its larger
ascertained truths—the order of infinite space, the slow method and vast results
of infinite time.' (*Appreciations*, p. 155). He was adapting phrases of Tennyson,
which shows that he had him in mind.

[3] op. cit., p. 14.                    [4] *Hellas*, ll. 197 f.

he accepted, say, a sunrise, friendship, children.[1] Tennyson asserted the power of man to hit back at all the light-years and all the aeons. And the scientists could not do without him; some of them still cannot. Though Darwin lost the taste for poetry as he did for music, he regretted the loss. Huxley loved it so much that, returning home after Tennyson's funeral, and rocked into a sort of coma by the train, he commemoratèd the occasion with a poem.[2] It is a remarkably good poem, and was given pride of place among the seven elegies which appeared in the *Nineteenth Century*, elegies by Aubrey de Vere, Roden Noel and so on.[3] The point, however, is not that Huxley's poem is good, but that it exists. Among the scientists of the nineteenth century there were several who tried their hand at poetry, and Charles Daubeny, Professor of Chemistry and Botany at Oxford, collected some of the results.[4] One of the contributors to his anthology is found innocently amusing himself by putting into blank verse the first sentence of Lyell's *Geology*. Fustian as it is, we can take his poem as a symbol of much of the best of nineteenth-century poetry: it exemplifies the contemporary union of scientific discovery with poetry.

[1] In his third shot at a preface for the *Lyrical Ballads* (*The Lyrical Ballads, 1798–1805*, ed. George Sampson, 1944 edition, p. 26).

[2] *Life and Letters*, ed. cit., ii. 338 f.

[3] *Nineteenth Century*, Nov. 1892, pp. 831 ff.

[4] *Fugitive Poems connected with Natural History and Physical Science*, 1869. For a list of contemporary scientific poets twenty years earlier, see *Fraser's Magazine*, 1849, p. 378.

# VIII

## Homage to Tennyson, 1940

FOR K.T.

Bombers, the enemy's loaded arm,
    Flog to bright blood the bones of streets,
    While you worn fatal to the blitz
In room blacked out and over-warm

Humour my sudden bent to hear
    From Tennyson's extent of song
    Whatever lyric-loosened tongue
Liked most to read, in teeth of fear . . .

O laureate rare, they wrong you much
    Who say your sweet is syrup, dub
    Your furnaced silver sillabub,
Your samite sticky to the touch.

You lived too long to suit their taste
    Who resurrect a 'marvellous boy',
    And on the superb promise cloy
Their sentimental sense of waste.

Off-days in eighty years might warble
    Chants for Victoria the Glorious,
    But only knaves keep gilt notorious
And fail to laud the miles of marble.

Your newsprint mask might nod, and say
    The thought of boys and think it men's,
    But not the noble head intense
And pungent with the vigorous bay. . .

What verse could more? your 'lyric cry'
    Of accurate and golden beat,
    Your bells of language loud and sweet
Blazed out the fury of the sky.

# IX
## Wilkie Collins's 'No Name'

NO writer has written novels that are at once so lengthy and so unremittingly exciting as those of Wilkie Collins. Their length, in these days of 'austerity', is a bar no doubt to their reappearance in print. The revival of *No Name* is certainly long overdue; it was last printed, it seems, in the nineties, and that for a novel which, though not as good as *The Woman in White*, is nearly as good as *The Moonstone*. A publisher to-day, looking at *No Name*, must be torn between the length that raises costs and the excitement that ensures purchasers.

The excitement provided by these masterpieces is of two sorts, that of the 'Gothick' novel and that of the detective novel. As an instance of the 'Gothick' sort, one scene in *No Name* stands out. A disused monastic banqueting hall at midnight, with Magdalen Vanstone, the twenty-year-old heroine-villainess disguised as a parlour-maid seeking by candlelight a secret letter, finding it, being discovered:

She roused herself, and pushed [the great sliding-door] further back. . . . She advanced boldly into the gap, and met the night-view of the Banqueting-Hall face to face.

The moon was rounding the southern side of the house. Her paling beams streamed through the nearer windows, and lay in long strips of slanting light on the marble pavement of the Hall. The black shadows of the pediments between each window, alternating with the strips of light, heightened the wan glare of the moonshine on the floor. Towards its lower end, the Hall melted mysteriously into darkness. . . . But one visible object was discernible, besides the gleaming windows and the moon-striped floor. Midway in the last and farthest of the strips of light, the tripod rose erect on its gaunt black legs, like a monster called to life by the moon—a monster rising through the light, and melting invisibly into the upper shadows of the Hall. . . .

She stood motionless in the doorway, with straining eyes, with straining ears . . .[1]

The 'Gothick' of *No Name*, then, gives the authentic shiver. But the excitement that is more usual in a Wilkie Collins comes from the assemblage of such detail as we now associate with that other sort of thriller, the detective novel, a form of which Wilkie Collins must be reckoned both an originating force and, according to good authority, the perfector—'*The Moonstone* is probably the very finest detective story ever written.'[2] As Trollope put it, Wilkie Collins

seems always to be warning me to remember that something happened at exactly half-past two o'clock on Tuesday morning; or that a woman disappeared from the road just fifteen yards beyond the fourth milestone.[3]

Incidents provided with details that are noticeably exact and noticeably numerous are as necessary in a novel by Wilkie Collins as incidents without such detail are necessary, say, in Johnson's *Rasselas*. His exact details, as Trollope's instances

[1] My quotations are taken from the 'first edition', that is, from the parts of *All the Year Round* in which the novel was serialised from 15 March 1862 to 17 January 1863. The differences I have noted between the first text and later ones may be due solely to the practices of the printers concerned.

The novel consists of eight 'scenes' (that is, pieces of the action acted in one place) widely differing in length, each consisting of several chapters. There are also sections headed 'Between the Scenes' which consist for the most part of indirect narrative; when as usual these take the form of letters they are headed 'Progress of the Story through the Post'.

I refer to passages by Scene and chapter. The present quotation is from Scene vii. ch. 4.

[2] Dorothy L. Sayers, in the preface to her *Great Short Stories of Detection, Mystery and Horror*, 1928, p. 25.

[3] All my quotations from Trollope are taken from the *Autobiography* and all but one from ch. xiii on 'On English Novelists of the Present Day'.

suggest, are usually details of the commonplace. This is all to the good: the thrillers that thrill best, or that thrill English readers best,[1] are those that place their action in the houses and streets we live in. In a letter written by Dickens while *No Name* was on the stocks, he advised Wilkie Collins 'to enhance and intensify the power with which Magdalen holds on to her purpose', and to do so by adding 'some touches of comicality'.[2] If Wilkie Collins accepted this technical advice, he accepted it literally: he added 'touches' merely. But he acknowledged handsomely the end Dickens proposed, and his main means of enhancement and intensification were those of placing Magdalen in a milieu not unlike that of comedy, a milieu he built up by selecting from the milieu of a comedy of manners its element of commonplace actuality. For most of the time Magdalen's career is set in the world of a novel of Dickens minus the bright colours and the fun.

In appreciating this milieu, modern readers are at a disadvantage. The action of *No Name* is now a hundred years old; the novel was published in 1862-3 and its story concerned events of the 'forties. In the 'sixties a novel about the 'forties was still more or less contemporary—perhaps the fuss made over Mrs. Lecount's aquarium was the only patch that struck the first readers as antiquated. And even there Collins gave an explanation:

The art of keeping fish and reptiles as domestic pets had not at that time been popularised in England; and Magdalen, on entering the room, started back in irrespressible astonishment and disgust, from the first specimen of an Aquarium that she had ever seen.[3]

---

[1] '[The Englishman] pays great attention . . . to the external details of men and things. [He] likes material exactness in the books he reads; the German and the Frenchman, in different degrees, care little for it in comparison with psychological truth.' (Lion Feuchtwanger, quoted by Dorothy L. Sayers, op. cit., p. 12).

[2] Letter of 24 Jan. 1862.

[3] Scene iii, ch. 2.

But modern readers are not seriously put out. Our attempt to see the action of *No Name* as an action happening round about us does not need to grow into a studious one: we are amply helped by the very homeliness of the detail, by the dogged persistence of the commonplaces of one age into the next. If we do not live among the chairs, tables, doors and windows of the 1840's, we live among their recognisable descendants; fashions in these things do not change the basic pattern; a chair is still something in a room which one person sits down on.

And yet Trollope's complaint is not wholly fair. We cannot accept his words 'he seems always to be warning me', nor must we be unduly impressed by his two instances of the clock-face and the milestone.

To take the two instances first. Both fall into the same category; they both give details with nothing to them except time and space. No detail in actual life is without these qualities of measurement, and so the sting of Trollope's remark lies in the words 'he seems always to be warning me'. It is true that the reader ear-marks certain details as likely to turn out to be among the thousand which as the novel proceeds prove crucial. For instance, the detail of the tripod in that description of the banqueting hall. At long last it achieves its neat little place in the plot, and that place might be suspected as already prepared for it from the attention it receives in the description. In this instance, therefore, Collins may be said to issue a warning; but of course he is far too clever a teller of tales to warn his readers 'always'. And this occasional retentiveness has the pleasantly teasing result that the reader is never certain whether, in noting this or that, he is being clever or a fool—clever if the detail noted turns out to be germinal, a fool if not. Take, for instance, the passage introducing Captain Wragge:

Taking his portrait, from top to toe, the picture of him began with a tall hat, broadly encircled by a mourning band of crumpled crepe. Below the hat was a lean, long, sallow face, deeply pitted with the smallpox, and characterised, very remarkably, by eyes of two different colours—one bilious green, one bilious brown, both sharply intelligent. His hair was iron-grey, carefully brushed round at the temples. His cheeks and chin were in the bluest bloom of smooth shaving;[1] his nose was short Roman; his lips long, thin, and supple, curled up at the corners with a mildly-humourous smile. His white cravat was high, stiff, and dingy; the collar, higher, stiffer, and dingier, projected its rigid points on either side beyond his chin. Lower down, the lithe little figure of the man was arrayed throughout in sober-shabby black. His frock-coat was buttoned tight round the waist, and left to bulge open majestically at the chest. His hands were covered with black cotton gloves, neatly darned at the fingers; his umbrella, worn down at the ferule to the last quarter of an inch, was carefully preserved, nevertheless, in an oilskin case. The front view of him was the view in which he looked oldest; meeting him face to face, he might have been estimated at fifty or more. Walking behind him, his back and shoulders were almost young enough to have passed for five-and-thirty. His manners were distinguished by a grave serenity. When he opened his lips, he spoke in a rich bass voice, with an easy flow of language, and a strict attention to the elocutionary claims of words in more than one syllable. Persuasion distilled from his mildly-curling lips; and, shabby as he was, perennial flowers of courtesy bloomed all over him from head to foot.[2]

What about those odd eyes? Should one remember them for future reference? As it turns out, no. But there are two warts on the back of Magdalen's neck, and, unlike the eyes, they matter to the plot. As marks of identification, they are as invaluable as the strawberry birth-marks in the vulgar novelettes, and much more in evidence. They should furnish, therefore, a vital clue when they belong to a person who undertakes so many disguises. At the crucial moment of the crucial identification, Captain Wragge paints them out—and here is

[1] Close shaving was at that time remarkable. G. T.
[2] Scene i, ch. 2.

one more hooked-in detail: his ability to efface them could not
be more 'natural' since a skill with make-up may be inferred
from his having been Magdalen's manager during her pro-
voncial tour as an actress. There are, then, instances of what
Trollope complained of, but not enough of them to menace
us much.

The details which are more characteristic of Wilkie Collins
are those the importance of which is obvious as soon as they
arise. Usually there is no question of a warning since a warning
implies the existence of an obscurity or deception that will
become clear later. The characteristic details in a Wilkie
Collins story show themselves immediately for what they are
—brilliant moves in a grim game. They are the moves made
by the characters of the story. The characters in a thriller of
Wilkie Collins usually fall into two opposed groups whose sole
job in life is to make detailed arrangements and counter-
arrangements as a means of exasperating and defeating their
opponents. They arrange details that matter, and that matter
not because they have certain qualities and measurements in
time or space that will come to be seen as important, but
because they are arranged as a decisive means to an end. Here
are some of the details arranged on one occasion by Captain
Wragge: he is on Magdalen's side and is instructing Noel
Vanstone how to succeed in marrying the disguised Magdalen
who, if he only knew it, is his arch-enemy:

'I have told you already, my dear sir', he said, modestly, 'that I never
do things by halves. Pardon me for reminding you that we have no time
for exchanging mutual civilities. Are you quite sure about your
instructions? I dare not write them down, for fear of accidents. Try the
system of artificial memory—count your instructions off, after me, on
your thumb and your four fingers. To-day, you tell Mrs. Lecount I
have tried to take you in with my relative's works of Art. To-morrow,
you cut me on the parade. The day after, you refuse to go out, you get

tired of Aldborough, and you allow Mrs. Lecount to make her suggestion [of change of residence]. The next day, you accept the suggestion. And the next day to that, you go to St. Crux. Once more, my dear sir! Thumb—works of Art. Forefinger—cut me on the parade. Middle finger—tired of Aldborough. Third finger—take Lecount's advice. Little finger—off to St. Crux. Nothing can be clearer—nothing can be easier to do. Is there anything you don't understand? Anything that I can explain over again, before you go?'[1]

Or there is the detail of the candles in the scene where Magdalen strikes her strange bargain with her maid Louisa:

'The time has come,' she said to herself, as she sat over the fire ['with a little money lying loose in her lap.'] 'I must sound Louisa first.'

She collected the scattered coins in her lap, and placed them in a little heap on the table—then rose, and rang the bell. The landlady answered it.

'Is my servant down stairs?' inquired Magdalen.

'Yes, ma'am. She is having her tea.'

'When she has done, say I want her up here. Wait a moment. You will find your money on the table—the money I owe you for last week. Can you find it? or would you like to have a candle?'

'It's rather dark, ma'am.'

Magdalen lit a candle. 'What notice must I give you,' she asked, as she put the candle on the table, 'before I leave?'

'A week is the usual notice, ma'am' ...

'Is the money right?'

'Quite right, ma'am. Here is your receipt.'

'Thank you. Don't forget to send Louisa to me, as soon as she has done her tea.'

The landlady withdrew. As soon as she was alone again, Magdalen extinguished the candle, and drew an empty chair close to her own chair, on the hearth. This done, she resumed her former place, and waited until Louisa appeared....

In ten minutes more, Louisa's meek knock was softly audible outside. She was surprised on entering the room, to find no other light in it than the light of the fire.

[1] Scene iv, ch. 9. I have corrected a misprint: 'relatives' is the reading in *All The Year Round,* and is corrected at least as early as the 'New Edition' (the second?) of 1863, the first edition in book form I have been able to consult.

'Will you have the candles, ma'am?' she inquired respectfully.

'We will have candles if you wish for them yourself', replied Magdalen; 'not otherwise. I have something to say to you. When I have said it, you shall decide whether we sit together in the dark or in the light.'

Louisa waited near the door, and listened to those strange words in silent astonishment. . . .[1]

Magdalen has her say, with the result that the erring, miserable, timid Louisa is married to the willing father of her baby, *on condition that* Louisa trains Magdalen in the duties of a parlour maid and agrees to the pious fraud—agreeing that the fraud *is* pious—by which Magdalen becomes employed in the very household where lies the secret letter it behoves her to read. The optional candlelight is part of the strategem to encourage the scared Louisa. The purport of the detail is immediately obvious.

It is the coexistence of the two sorts of detail, the accidental and the willed, which is the characteristic mark of a thriller. And their interplay—their interplay fatal, usually, to one or both of the willers, who cannot arrange everything that matters, or that turns out to matter. However devilish their nature and works, they remain human inevitably, and so lack something both of omniscience and omnipotence. They accomplish wonders of malice, but their structures may fall at the touch of the innocent and simple.

It is Norah not Magdalen who, in the end, lays hold on the lost inheritance. When the story begins the two illegitimate sisters lose a fortune through their father's hairbreadth failure to revise his will, and their mother's to make one. They put their case to the beneficiary, an old estranged relative who is rich enough not to need to inherit their father's £80,000.

[1] Scene vi, ch. 1.

Their plea fails. Norah, the quiet elder one, accepts their dull lot, and after training as a governess, enters on a career that is thankless and even painful. Magdalen, on the other hand, schemes to get the money. But it is Norah who gets it, Norah who never lifts a scheming finger, Norah who having no will to speak of is little more than a measurement in time and place.

Wilkie Collins mixes up the sorts of detail with great ingenuity. There is a neat instance lying behind the instance of the candles. Louisa was appointed Magdalen's maid, not as a move in the great game but because Magdalen's stingy husband, Noel Vanstone, found her the only applicant ready to accept low wages. Her readiness is explained only when Magdalen forces her to confess about her baby, and the same baby is the innocent reason for that other vital link, Louisa's acceptance of Magdalen's apparently crazy conditions. Or, again, there is Mrs. Wragge and her dressmaking. Mrs. Wragge is the one character in the book who is thoroughly comic. She delighted Dickens;[1] she is a lovable, fantastic fool, as successfully laughable as many small characters in the novels of Dickens himself. When she accompanies Magdalen to London, she finds opportunity to indulge her passion for clothes, and buys some Cashmere stuff with which, on all but the last of her reappearances, she is unsuccessfully seeking to make a dress. Inevitably, therefore, she is still at work on it

[1] See Dickens's letter to Wilkie Collins of 20 Sept. 1862, noting that her 'originality . . . without compromise of her probability' is 'a really great achievement.' She also delighted Lewis Carroll:

the White Queen seemed, to my dreaming fancy, gentle, stupid, fat and pale; helpless as an infant; and with a slow, maundering, bewildered air about her, just *suggesting* imbecility, but never quite passing into it; *that* would be, I think, fatal to any comic effect she might otherwise produce. There is a character strangely like her in Mr. Wilkie Collins' novel 'No Name': by two different yet converging paths we have somehow reached the same ideal, and Mrs. Wragg [sic] and the White Queen might have been twin-sisters.

(Lewis Carroll, ' "Alice" on the Stage', in *The Theatre*, 1 April 1887, p. 182).

when Mrs. Lecount nefariously trespasses on her privacy and contrives to draw her—with how smooth a transition!—to bring out a certain dress of Magdalen's which is the crucial means of identifying Magdalen with one of her impersonations.

Trollope did not leave the novels of Wilkie Collins without a word in their praise. He even placed them beside those of George Eliot on the score of their popularity with a public that knows a good thing when it sees it.[1] But his admiration does not outweigh his imperfect sympathy, which is summed up in the remark 'I can never lose the taste of the construction'. Trollope could not have written the novels of Wilkie Collins, any more than Wilkie Collins could have written his. But though the thrillers of the one are thrilling, the novels of the other are 'interesting'—in the general human sense the word bore for Henry James, who laid down the law that to be interesting is a novelist's first duty.[2] We do not put aside a novel by Trollope till we have finished it, any more than we put aside a thriller by Wilkie Collins. And though our interest in a novel by Trollope is tamer, it holds. Which is enough to satisfy the law of Henry James: if interest, like 'beauty' in *The Rape of the Lock*, 'draws us with a single hair' it draws us as surely as by handcuffs. And if the novelist has no lust for giving his readers the peculiar excitement of a thriller by Wilkie Collins (which is the best of its kind) he can attend more completely to other matters that are more important still. When Coleridge drew up a list of the three perfect plots, they were the plots of works that are grounded in human nature and that do not overstep the border-line of what men accept as probable. The conception of the perfect plot has grown more elaborate since Coleridge's day. And the elaboration, so

---

[1] Ch. xi.                    [2] See 'The Art of Fiction'.

far as the plot of *No Name* is concerned, is purchased only at
a high cost of sound human nature and probability—a cost
which we pay readily during our excitement but feel to be
too high on reflection. Trollope described the construction of
the novels as 'most minute and wonderful'. When used in
criticism that word 'wonderful' usually has a taint. Swift
almost always used it in scorn. And so Johnson who applied
to the two pindaric odes of Gray the cant phrase Swift had
used as the title of a pamphlet—'Wonderful Wonder of
Wonders'.[1] On the other hand Johnson gave Gray's 'Elegy'
his veneration, and his dislike of the wonderful odes was
owing to their giving him brilliant insubstantiality, 'glittering
accumulations of ungraceful ornaments',[2] rather than the
solid primary human emotions of the 'Elegy'. The world
of *No Name*, for all its common doors and windows, is not
the world we know. Wilkie Collins could only have made it
so by abandoning what he could do best. He is the arch-
mathematician of story-tellers. I have spoken of two sorts of
detail. But he does not seem interested in telling us how they
differ in the force with which they strike us. He does not value
the details that move us most. A detail which is the silent
consequence of character is snatched into the plot with no
more regard than a detail mechanically possessing measurement. And so we do not look to Wilkie Collins to give us
human beings in the full sense that Trollope does. We look
to him to give us a plot run by human beings where possible,
but when not—and it is often not—by monsters.

It follows that in *No Name* Wilkie Collins shows no sound
sense of morality. There are, to be sure, some fragments of a
moral scheme. But even these fragments exist at variance.
Guilt works no changes in the mind; it goes unpunished by the

[1] *Lives,* iii. 436.  [2] op. cit., iii. 440.

conscience. I say guilt because I am accepting Wilkie Collins's own judgment on the acts of Magdalen Vanstone. He speaks of her as standing between Good and Evil, and choosing Evil. Later on, when her schemes have come to nothing, we hear that

Faintly and more faintly, the inner voices now pleaded with her to pause on the downward way [voices to which Magdalen will not listen]. She turned to the relentless Purpose which was hurrying her to her ruin, and cried to it with the daring of her despair—Drive me on![1]

She chooses Evil—so Wilkie Collins has it—and drives to her ruin. But her ruin turns out very pleasant: she gets not only what she sets out to get, the lost fortune, but, into the bargain, the excellent Mr. Kirke for husband. Meanwhile, of course, she has suffered great misery, but merely the misery of physical exhaustion and the fierce vexation of the frustrated. The end of the book leaves her satisfied in the gained objective. Her only possible complaint is that she did not gain the objective for herself. As I have said, it was the ineffectual Norah who proved effective: she did nothing except be a governess and let Mr. Bartram (to whom the lost legacy had descended) fall in love with her while she was merely sight-seeing in his house, which she would never have heard of but for Magdalen's nefarious residence in it. This mix-up could be made something of by a novelist interested in morality. It admirably represents things as they are, and so offers the novelist the great chance of interesting us afresh in the inscrutable and leaving us as he found us, puzzled by it. Faced with the tangle of his own incidents Wilkie Collins, we feel, should himself be puzzled! He would be, if he paused to think. Not choosing to think he has no right to call Magdalen's course 'Evil' with or without a capital; he could only have that

[1] Scene vi, ch. i.

right if he were prepared to allow that evil, in some cases, has pleasant consequences, or consequences seemingly pleasant. The only moral we can draw from *No Name* is one that we know from his smug preface Wilkie Collins did not intend— the moral that evil is the best policy because, though it may fail directly, it succeeds indirectly. Instead, he pipes that 'evil brings ruin'. The reason for his moralising use of the word evil can only be guessed at: it may have pleased those of his readers who felt easier in their consciences if the novels they yielded to claimed to be edifying; it may have been welcome because it added another dark colour to his lowering canvas; or it may have been a token of the homage which a writer of thrillers pays to the great novelists, a twinge of aspiration towards the philosophy that moves in the great novels, in the novels, say, of Thackeray and George Eliot.

As for his making a psychological study of the situation of Norah and Magdalen, that also was out of the question. Materials existed for one—to miss an inheritance by narrow accidents invites one to hanker, hope and covet with all the appearances of justification. Henry James with his dread of taking too much would have made ten thousand stories out of the materials of *No Name*. Wilkie Collins is not interested in Norah. He is a novelist racing on from factual point to point: and so racing on with Magdalen, the arch-contriver of incident. Like her, he never inspects the landscape, the fenny landscape, of the mind. For him as for her the mind is a will choosing an objective and an intellect making the means to arrive at it.

# X

## Henry James and his Limitations

ONE thing can be taken for granted about Henry James: in his novels and stories he created what we call a 'world'. That world is the world of wealthy people who are American or English or of various Western European countries; they live in exquisite surroundings, and have their share of human problems, some of which are due to the clash between the different civilisations which have shaped them.

## II

It is common, however, to find critics speaking as if this world, vast as it is, is all that James can show. Here, for instance, are some of the well-known charges that Mr. E. M. Forster has brought against him—perhaps I ought rather to say *once* brought against him, since it is possible that Mr. Forster has changed his mind since 1927:

[his] characters, besides being few in number, are constructed on very stingy lines. They are incapable of fun, of rapid motion, of carnality, and of nine-tenths of heroism. Their clothes will not take off, the diseases that ravage them are anonymous, like the sources of their income, their servants are noiseless or resemble themselves; no social explanation o the world we know is possible for them, for there are no stupid people in their world, no barriers of language, and no poor. Even their sensations are limited. They can land in Europe and look at works of art and at each other, but that is all.[1]

It is delightful to see charges delivered with so much wit. But charges are charges. These, as it happens, can be refuted by the

[1] *Aspects of the Novel*, 1927, pp. 205 f.

simple method of ocular demonstration. Especially from the earlier work (James's first story appeared in 1865, when he was twenty-one, and by 'earlier work' I mean work done before 1887 when he temporarily left off writing fiction for writing plays). The world of the wealthy, which is the world James has particularly made his own, he made his own mainly in the later work, and one cannot help suspecting that it is only the later work that is familiar to his unsympathetic critics.

Surely Mr. Forster, when he brought up those charges, could not have recollected *The Princess Casamassima*, a work serialised in 1885-6. Hyacinth Robinson, its hero, is the unacknowledged bastard of an aristocrat; he lives in Pentonville, works in Soho, and in his spare time is an active inner member of an underground organisation planning violent revolution. As a child he is taken by his adoptress, a dressmaker, to visit his dying mother, who is in prison for the murder of her lover. Much of the subject-matter of the book resembles that of novels by Dickens, George Eliot and Gissing rather than that of novels by the Henry James Mr. Forster has in mind, novels like *The Ambassadors* or *The Golden Bowl*. But let it have a chance or two of speaking for itself:

[Paul Muniment, Hyacinth's friend, and himself] came oftener [to the 'Sun and Moon'] this second winter, for the season was terribly hard; and as, in that lower world, one walked with one's ear nearer the ground, the deep perpetual groan of London misery seemed to swell and swell, and form the whole undertone of life. The filthy air came into the place in the damp coats of silent men, and hung there till it was brewed to a nauseous warmth, and ugly, serious faces squared themselves through it, and strong-smelling pipes contributed their element in a fierce, dogged manner which appeared to say that it now had to stand for everything— for bread and meat and beer, for shoes and blankets and the poor things at the pawnbroker's and the smokeless chimney at home. Hyacinth's colleagues seemed to him wiser then, and more permeated with

R

intentions boding ill to the satisfied classes; and though the note of popularity was still most effectively struck by the man who could demand oftenest, unpractically, 'What the plague am I to do with seventeen shillings?' it was brought home to our hero on more than one occasion that revolution was ripe at last. . . .[1]

In the description of an earlier political meeting in the same pub we get this:

There were men who kept saying, 'Them was my words in the month of February last, and what I say I stick to—what I say I stick to;' and others who perpetually inquired of the company, 'And what the plague am I to do with seventeen shillings—with seventeen shillings? What am I to do with them—will ye tell me that?' an interrogation which, in truth, usually ended by eliciting a ribald reply. There were still others who remarked, to satiety, that if it was not done to-day it would have to be done to-morrow, and several who constantly proclaimed their opinion that the only way was to pull up the Park rails again,—just to pluck them straight up. A little shoemaker, with red eyes and a grayish face, whose appearance Hyacinth deplored, scarcely ever expressed himself but in the same form of words: 'Well are we in earnest or ain't we in earnest?—that's the thing I want to know.' He was terribly in earnest himself, but this was almost the only way he had of showing it; and he had much in common (though they were always squabbling) with a large, red-faced man, of uncertain attributes and stertorous breathing, who was understood to know a good deal about dogs, had fat hands, and wore on his forefinger a big silver ring, containing some one's hair (Hyacinth believed it to be that of a terrier, snappish in life.) He had always the same refrain: 'Well, now, are we just starving, or ain't we just starving? I should like the v'ice of the company on that question.'[2]

And there are the enquiries made by Captain Sholto, tactless

---

[1] *Princess Casamassima*, ch. xxi, text of first edition, *The Atlantic Monthly*, February, 1886, p. 170. The revisions for the collected edition include one made in the interests of violence: 'What the hell am I to do with half a quid?'

[2] Op. cit., ch. xxi, February, 1886, p. 168. Revision produced more violence, of which the salient instance is 'And what the plague am I to do with seventeen bob—with seventeen bloody bob?'

and only temporarily left-wing, when he visits the Muniments at their home in Camberwell:

'Now, how many families would there be in such a house as this, and what should you say about the sanitary arrangements? Would there be others on this floor—what is it, the third, the fourth?—beside yourselves, you know, and should you call it a fair specimen of a tenement of its class?'[1]

Or there is this piece of dialogue which might have been written by William Morris, or by any political novelist at any time since:

'I think you are much better than I, and I know very few people so good as you', Lady Aurora remarked, blushing, not for her opinions, but for her timidity. It was easy to see that, though she was original, she would have liked to be even more original than she was. She was conscious, however, that such a declaration might appear rather gross to persons who did n't see exactly how she meant it, so she added, as quickly as her hesitating manner permitted, to cover it up, 'You know there's one thing you ought to remember, apropos of revolutions and changes and all that sort of thing; I just mention it because we were talking of some of the dreadful things that were done in France. If there were to be a great disturbance in this country—and of course one hopes there won't—it would be my impression that the people would behave in a different way altogether.'

'What people do you mean?' Hyacinth allowed himself to inquire.

'Oh, the upper class, the people that have got all the things.'

'We don't call them the people', observed Hyacinth, reflecting the next instant that his remark was a little primitive.

'I suppose you call them the wretches, the villains!' Rose Muniment suggested, laughing merrily.

'All the things, but not all the brains', her brother said.

'No, indeed, are n't they stupid?' exclaimed her ladyship. 'All the same, I don't think they would go abroad.'

'Go abroad?'

'I mean like the French nobles, who emigrated so much. They would

[1] Op. cit., ch. xv, January, 1886, p. 80. The only verbal revision changed 'specimen' to 'example'.

stay at home and resist; they would make more of a fight. I think they would fight very hard.'

'I'm delighted to hear it, and I'm sure they would win!' cried Rosy.

'They wouldn't collapse, don't you know', Lady Aurora continued. 'They would struggle till they were beaten.'

'And you think they would be beaten in the end?' Hyacinth asked.

'Oh, dear, yes', she replied, with a familiar brevity at which he was greatly surprised. 'But of course one hopes it won't happen.'

'I infer from what you say that they talk it over a good deal among themselves, to settle the line they will take', said Paul Muniment.[1]

All I need add to these quotations is that the book contains Millicent Henning, a Cockney shop girl who makes the reader accept her as actual—she is as actual as Arabella in *Jude the Obscure*.

To take another instance, there is that very different novel *The Bostonians*, a work serialised simultaneously with *The Princess*. Its heroine, Verena Tarrant, a girl of negligible education, is endowed with the gift of speaking 'inspirationally' before large audiences on the subject of the rights of women. She comes of what in England would be called lower-middle-class parents, and to the description of her home conditions Henry James allots some of that 'solidity of specification' he had recommended the year before in his 'Art of Fiction'. The result is like Gissing, a Gissing gone cheerful by virtue of a spirited intellect. This, for instance, is the beginning of an account of Mrs. Tarrant:

even Verena, who, filially, was much less argumentative than in her civic and, as it were, public capacity, had a perception that her mother was queer. She was queer, indeed—a flaccid, relaxed, unhealthy, whimsical woman, who still had a capacity to cling. What she clung to was 'society', and a position in the world which a secret whisper told her

---

[1] Op. cit., ch. viii, November, 1885, pp. 581 f. Almost all the revisions are designed to improve the conversational tone: e.g., each 'they would' becomes 'they'd'.

she had never had, and a voice more audible reminded her she was in danger of losing. To keep it, to recover it, to reconsecrate it, was the ambition of her heart; this was one of the many reasons why Providence had judged her worthy of having so wonderful a child. Verena was born not only to lead their common sex out of bondage, but to remodel a visiting-list which bulged and contracted in the wrong places, like a country-made garment. As the daughter of Abraham Greenstreet, Mrs. Tarrant had passed her youth in the first Abolitionist circles, and she was aware how much such a prospect was clouded by her union with a young man who had begun life as an itinerant vendor of lead-pencils (he had called at Mr. Greenstreet's door in the exercise of this function), had afterwards been for a while a member of the celebrated Cayuga community, where there were no wives, or no husbands, or something of that sort (Mrs. Tarrant could never remember), and had still later (though before the development of the healing faculty) achieved distinction in the spiritualistic world.[1]

These are instances from the earlier work. But the later also has its place, if less often and less spaciously, for the lower-middle class. In 1891 came 'Brooksmith', the story of a butler who is as good as finished by the death of his employer, and whom the 'I' of the story finds ill in dingy lodgings 'in a short sordid street in Marylebone':

The room into which I was shown was above the small establishment of a dyer and cleaner who had inflated kid gloves and discoloured shawls in his shop-front. There was a great deal of grimy infant life up and down the place, and there was a hot, moist smell within, as of the 'boiling' of dirty linen. Brooksmith sat with a blanket over his legs at a clean little window, where, from behind stiff bluish-white curtains, he could look across at a huckster's and a tinsmith's and a small greasy public-house. He had passed through an illness and was convalescent, and his mother, as well as his aunt, was in attendance on him. I liked the mother, who was bland and intensely humble, but I didn't much fancy the aunt, whom I connected, perhaps unjustly, with the opposite public-

---

[1] *The Bostonians*, ch. x, *The Century Magazine*, March, 1885, p. 698. James made no revisions, since he did not include the work in the collected edition.

house (she seemed somehow to be greasy with the same grease), and whose furtive eye followed every movement of my hand, as if to see if it were not going into my pocket. It didn't take this direction—I couldn't, unsolicited, put myself at that sort of ease with Brooksmith. Several times the door of the room opened, and mysterious old women peeped in and shuffled back again. I don't know who they were; poor Brooksmith seemed encompassed with vague, prying, beery females.[1]

A year later came *Sir Dominick Ferrand* (under its original title, *Jersey Villas*). In that 'long short' story Peter Baron, the young, poor, free-lance journalist, strikes up an acquaintance with a fellow lodger, Mrs. Ryves, and with her infant son Sidney:

it all went fast, for the little boy had been almost as great a help as the piano. Sidney haunted the door-step of No. 3 ; he was eminently sociable, and had established independent relations with Peter, a frequent feature of which was an adventurous visit upstairs, to picture books criticised for not being all geegees and walking sticks happily more conformable. The young man's window, too, looked out on their acquaintance; through a starched muslin curtain it kept his neighbor before him, made him almost more aware of her comings and goings than he felt he had a right to be. He was capable of a shyness of curiosity about her, and of dumb little delicacies of consideration. She did give a few lessons; they were essentially local, and he ended by knowing more or less what she went out for and what she came in from. She had almost no visitors, only a decent old lady or two, and, every day, poor dingy Miss Teagle, who was also ancient and who came humbly enough to góverness the infant of the parlors [Mrs. Ryves occupied the parlour floor of the house]. Peter Baron's window had always, to his sense, looked out on a good deal of life, and one of the things it had most shown him was that there is nobody so bereft of joy as not to be able to command, for twopence, the services of somebody less joyous. Mrs. Ryves was a struggler (Baron

---

[1] *The Lesson of the Master* [etc.], 1892, pp. 197 f. I have not seen the text of the first edition, that in *Harper's Weekly*, 2 May, 1891. James's most striking revision was made for the sake of avoiding verbal repetition, gaining allusiveness and improving the characterisation of the narrator; 'I liked the nearer relative . . . but I had my doubts of the remoter. . . .' (*Daisy Miller* [etc.], 1922, p. 326.)

scarcely liked to think of it), but she occupied a pinnacle for Miss
Teagle, who had lived on—and from a noble nursery—into a period of
diplomas and humiliation.[1]

Or again this is the Peter who has just bought a second-hand
desk, and has discovered in its secret cavity a batch of letters
which severely compromise the high reputation of a late
diplomatist:

He was too nervous to eat, and he forgot even to dine; he forgot to light
his candles, he let his fire go out, and it was in the melancholy chill of the
late dusk that Mrs. Bundy [his landlady], arriving at last with his lamp,
found him extended moodily upon his sofa. She had been informed that
he wished to speak to her, and, as she placed on the malodorous luminary
an oily shade of green pasteboard she expressed the friendly hope that
there was nothing wrong with his 'ealth.[2]

And so the paragraph ends. James reserves his strongest stroke
of 'realism' to the end, but the hold on the whole small scene
is, as always in his work, masterly: how much we learn from
that 'arriving', although she knew he wanted to speak to her,
'*at last* with his lamp'; how much we learn about the whole
place from the periphrasis for 'lamp' and its 'oily' shade.

Evidence might be called in from 'The Real Thing' (1893),
or 'In the Cage' (1898), the story of a telephone girl, or 'The
Papers' (1903), the story of two young Fleet Street journalists
with its description of tea-shops (with their 'greasy white
slabs, repeatedly mopped with moist grey cloths by young
women in black uniforms'). Instead I go to 1909, towards the
close of James's career, and quote one passage from 'The
Bench of Desolation'. Herbert Dodd has paid the spirited
Kate Cookham almost the whole £300 she has demanded as
her due after his breach of promise. And he has turned for

---

[1] Text of first edition, *The Cosmopolitan*, July 1892, pp. 318 f. Later editions do
not show much verbal change.
[2] Op cit., August, p. 433. The later revisions are negligible.

comfort to the tame Nan Drury; he is now recalling his wedding and his married life:

That memory referred itself to the dark days of old Drury's smash, the few weeks between his partner's dastardly flight and Herbert's own comment on it in the form of his standing up with Nan for the nuptial benediction of the Vicar of St. Bernards on a very cold, bleak December morning and amid a circle of seven or eight long-faced, red-nosed, and altogether dowdy persons. Poor Nan herself had struck him as red-nosed and dowdy by that time, but this only added, in his then, and indeed in his lasting view, to his general and his particular morbid bravery. He had cultivated ignorance, there were small inward immaterial luxuries he could scrappily cherish even among other, and the harshest, destitutions; and one of them was represented by this easy refusal of his mind to render to certain passages of his experience, to various ugly images, names, associations, the homage of continued attention. That served him, that helped him; but what happened when, a dozen dismal years having worn themselves away, he sat single and scraped bare again, as if his long wave of misfortune had washed him far beyond everything and then conspicuously retreated, was that, thus stranded by tidal action, deposited in the lonely hollow of his fate, he felt even sustaining pride turn to nought and heard no challenge from it when old mystifications, stealing forth in the dusk of the day's work done, scratched at the door of speculation and hung about, through the idle hours, for irritated notice.

The evenings of his squalid clerkship were all leisure now, but there was nothing at all near home on the other hand, for his imagination, numb and stiff from its long chill, to begin to play with. Voices from far off would quaver to him therefore in the stillness; where he knew for the most recurrent, little by little, the faint wail of his wife. He had become deaf to it in life, but at present, after so great an interval, he listened again, listened and listened, and seemed to hear it sound as by the pressure of some weak broken spring. It phrased for his ear her perpetual question, the one she had come to at the last as under the obsession of a discovered and resented wrong, a wrong withal that had its source much more in his own action than anywhere else. 'That you did n't make *sure* she could have done anything, that you did n't make sure and that you were too afraid!'—this commemoration had ended by playing such a part in Nan's finally quite contracted consciousness as to exclude everything else.[1]

After all this the drift of Mr. Forster's charges seems ungrateful.

## III

BEFORE going further we might distinguish some of the degrees to which James participates in his stories. The writing of fiction never allows the author to put into his work a self that is as actual as the self he puts into his letters, perhaps into his essays. Even when he breaks into his story as Chaucer or Thackeray does, the intrusive self is a fictional version of the actual self. Into the stories of James, then, there is no intrusion of the James who wrote the prefaces. But that apart, the self in the stories is as near the self of the actual, historical Henry James as a fictional self can ever be. And this cannot but make for some limitation. In the earlier stories the fictional self exists in particular, and in the later exists in general. But in the earlier stories the particular self existing in the 'I' that tells them is not yet a self that is strongly personal: the actual James was not yet so thoroughly the unusual self he had become by the time he kept himself out of his novels as a particular presence using 'I'. His intrusions into his earlier stories attract little attention. If the 'I' is fastidious at times there is nothing extraordinary in a fastidiousness that does not like marble-topped tables and the grey cloths that swab them. Nor must we confuse any limitation of taste in the narrator with a limitation of experience: what he does not like is not excluded from his experience. But just because it is an 'I' who

---

[1] Text of first edition, *Putnam's Magazine*, November 1909, p. 154. A few changes of punctuation were made later, and a few verbal ones: 'struck him as' became 'came to affect him as scarce other than', 'old mystifications' became 'its mystifications', and 'commemoration' (possibly a misprint) became 'communication'.

tells the story and an 'I' who is not one of the main actors, there is inevitably a limitation, which is a technical limitation. To write in the first person is to forgo the omniscience available to narrative in the third person. And by often choosing a narrator within the action James cut out, at one stroke, the very opportunities for providing something of what Mr. Forster charges him with omitting—a third party is permitted to see only what the public, against which James protested, allowed a contemporary novelist to write of. The adoption of the narrator within the frame was a clever move for making its limits as acceptable as possible to the artistic conscience. But even here, as I shall come to show, the limits imposed by the public were not too maiming.

So much for the earlier stories. In the later the presence of the fictional self is a general presence, except at scattered points when James writes such avuncular phrases as 'our hero'. But never was general presence felt more strongly. In the later work the presence of the self is pervasively pungent as that of musk. And for this I offer the following as explanation.

James's experience of phenomena was abnormally gay, eager, thorough, sensitive and expert: 'Try to be one of the people on whom nothing is lost' was one of his major tenets. But what he took in from the external world could hardly have been taken in more critically. The young Matthew Arnold laid it down that the poet 'must begin with an Idea of the world in order not to be prevailed over by the world's multitudinousness'.[1] James, who had an even stronger horror of being overwhelmed, was saved in part by having 'an idea',[2]

---

[1] *Arnold to Clough*, p. 97.

[2] 'One does nothing of value in art or literature unless one has some general ideas'; and James goes on to show their value outside art and literature: 'and if one has a few such, constituting a motive and a support, those flippancies and vulgarities (abusive reviews in newspapers) are the last thing one troubles about.' (*The Notebooks*, ed. F. O. Matthiessen and K. B. Murdock, 1947, p. 69).

and in part, by having something else quite as co-ordinating—his own instinct for what matched. He was not overwhelmed because he could find a use for a great deal of the multitudinousness. From the start his own nature exercised its aristocratic right to sort to a pip the innumerable seized particulars, to bring them into the Jamesian scheme, to tint them to his liking. And as the exercise proceeded, his prose came to resemble, sentence by sentence, the poetry of a lyric poet: it came to be so much his own as all that. Coleridge had noted the capacity of the imagination for reducing multiplicity to unity. The act performed by James's imagination, however, seemed scarcely an act of reduction since the particulars retained were so numerous. But though they are numerous, they always hang beautifully together.

The result is that the presence of the agent is always as salient in his work as the presence of any of his scenes or characters. This is the effect which is usual in narrative poems written by romantic poets: Porphyrio and Madeleine, the feast of delicacies and the Gothic window all flow out from their centre in Keats. But we do not expect it of a novelist, especially of a novelist who can convince us that his characters are actual people. Virginia Woolf (who learned, and lifted, many things large and small from James and paid her thanks so warmly)[1] could do it, but only narrowly—only, that is, when the character was to all intents and purposes Virginia Woolf under the name of Mrs. Dalloway or Mrs. Ramsay. James often did it in this narrow way: his narratives contain many characters who, except in so far as they are named otherwise and act otherwise, were almost himself. But he brought it off also when the characters did not resemble himself. It is a remarkable feat to have created this double awareness in us,

[1] See the essays on James in *The Death of a Moth*.

the awareness of himself and at the same time (to take two
very small and so more telling instances from a single novel)
Madame Goldoni and the Prince Casamassima. The power
that affected this co-ordination was a combination of several
qualities: a sense of the appearance of things (as lively as that
of the French impressionists, but often taking in as much
matter, scene by scene, as a picture of Rubens), an intelligence
(like that of his admired Matthew Arnold), and a sympathy
for human beings, particularly for women (as tender and
understanding as the sympathy of George Eliot, whose
innumerable discoveries about mind and body taught James
a great deal, supplementing what he learned from Thackeray's).

As James's career unfolded, the presence in the writing
obtruded itself more and more. This personal domination
came to work mainly in three ways: in style, in contrivance
and in morality. The later style of James is, as I have said,
notoriously his own—so much his own as sometimes to be
scarcely English: whereas the style of the earlier work
whispers, or even sings or whistles 'The style is the man, and
the man Henry James', the style of the later work warbles or
rumbles it. When James says anything in the later work, he
seems to be playing an organ in a cathedral: whether the music
played is 'light quirks' or plainsong, the same immense
echo swoops and envelops it. And as time went on this style
got in the way of the humanity of his characters. Humanity
they have, and have it complete. But it is James who expresses
much of it for them. They have all the wonderful advantages
of being recognisably his creatures. But just because they are
recognisably human beings also we wish they were allowed
to be more wholly themselves even though at the price of
some unpresentableness, unselfconsciousness, stupidity. If
James the novelist is not so great as George Eliot or Tolstoy

it is because he is too much himself. It is here that, by the standard of George Eliot and Tolstoy, he shows a limitation.

IV

THE charge which to novel readers seems the most stinging is that which denies carnality to James's characters. (I shall understand the term *carnality* in its strongest sense, and confine what I say to that: there is no need to demonstrate that James makes his characters eat and doze).

By 'carnality' Mr. Forster means something more than the carnality implied in James's statements that such and such sexual relationships are in being. When a government official, his pen poised over the printed form, puts the questions 'married or single? Any children?' and gets the answers 'married: x children' the questioner and the answerer speak, as we say, 'without thinking', without visualising, without starting up any inner experience: carnality is implied for the workaday intellect but is not explored by the imagination either on its physical or psychological sides. But when the word *married* is used in a novel, it suggests both a physical and a psychological relationship. Many novelists have dealt freely with the psychological relationship. They have explored it freely, not leaving it to mere suggestion. But not many of them have done the same by the physical relationship: or not so directly and explicitly as, say, D. H. Lawrence dealt with a sexual relationship in *Lady Chatterley's Lover*, the novel in which he explores carnality as directly as a biography of Livingstone shows us the exploration of another dark continent. Obviously the psychological side of sexual relationships has always been part of the permissible and demanded subject-matter of stories, but at certain times 'the climate of opinion' has made it risky or impossible for the novelist to explore the carnal side directly. Whenever this proscription was in force, the novelist relied on suggestion to 'give body', as we might say, to his assurances; and he did not find it difficult to suggest pretty well everything, certainly everything that mattered.

James, on this count, occupies a unique position among novelists. When Mr. Forster charged him with failing to supply his characters with carnality, he cannot have meant that James failed to notify us that they are having their share of sexual life. For if questioned by a government official, a high proportion of them would answer 'married' and, if questioned closely, say in court, a remarkably high proportion of the married would have to own to 'unsocial' sexual relationships: a great many of his married characters are given as having sexual relationships outside marriage. Indeed his favourite subjects are the twin ones of publicity and adultery.

Mr. Forster, then, cannot mean that carnality is absent from the stated object of the writings: he can mean only that James does not treat it so as to satisfy the reader's imagination (for the purposes of criticism, the reader must be postulated as the 'normal' reader). By 'satisfy the imagination' I mean satisfy the imagination as, say, George Eliot satisfies it: in *Middlemarch* she tells us enough about Dorothea's relationship with Mr. Casaubon and with Will Ladislav, about Rosamond's relationship with Lydgate, to make us feel we know everything; Mrs. Cadwallader, who being inside the book knew less than we, had no doubt she knew everything, and in advance: marrying Casaubon, she prophesies, will be like going into a nunnery. It was impossible to do more than suggest at the time when George Eliot, and James, were writing. But in most stories it is not necessary to do more at any time. To do

more may be to spoil what has been done already, to transgress the literary conventions which, so far, have been duly
observed. To do more may be to solicit the reader to break
away from the imagined scene into action on his own account,
into non-literary experience. This is what spoils *Lady
Chatterley's Lover* as literature: at certain points in the novel
the reader transfers his interest from the novel to himself,
which, of course, is the effect of pornographical literature.
That effect is avoided when (if the age permits him to) a writer
goes further as a necessary matter of plot, as when, for example,
Shakespeare goes further in *Othello*. But Shakespeare, like
Chaucer, can go where he likes. He is in control, whatever
crops up: he sees his play steadily and sees it whole.

If George Eliot's novels are taken as the standard for the
representation and suggestion of carnality in novels, can we
say, as Mr. Forster does, that those of James fall below it?

Again, I think we must distinguish between the earlier and
the later work.

In the earlier, James satisfies the standard completely. Take
the scene at the end of the *Portrait of a Lady* (1880). The
repeatedly rejected Caspar Goodwood makes one last attempt,
this time to keep Isabel from returning to her husband in
Rome: he surprises her as she is sitting in the garden. I quote a
part of the scene, using the text of the first edition:

'. . . I understand all about it: you are afraid to go back. You are
perfectly alone; you don't know where to turn. Now it is that I want you
to think of me.'

'To think of you?' Isabel said, standing before him in the dusk. The
idea of which she had caught a glimpse a few moments before now
loomed large. She threw back her head a little; she stared at it as if it had
been a comet in the sky.

'You don't know where to turn; turn to me! I want to persuade you to
trust me', Goodwood repeated. And then he paused a moment, with

his shining eyes. 'Why should you go back—why should you go through that ghastly form?'

'To get away from you!' she answered. But this expressed only a little of what she felt. The rest was that she had never been loved before. It wrapped her about; it lifted her off her feet.

At first, in rejoinder to what she had said, it seemed to her that he would break out into greater violence. But after an instant he was perfectly quiet; he wished to prove that he was sane, that he had reasoned it all out. 'I wish to prevent that, and I think I may, if you will only listen to me. It's too monstrous to think of sinking back into that misery. It's you that are out of your mind. Trust me as if I had the care of you. Why shouldn't we be happy—when it's here before us, when it's so easy? I am yours for ever—for ever and ever. Here I stand; I'm as firm as a rock. What have you to care about? You have no children; that perhaps would be an obstacle. As it is, you have nothing to consider. You must save what you can of your life; you mustn't lose it all simply because you have lost a part. It would be an insult to you to assume that you care for the look of the thing—for what people will say—for the bottomless idiocy of the world! We have nothing to do with all that; we are quite out of it; we look at things as they are. You took the great step in coming away; the next is nothing; it's the natural one. I swear, as I stand here[,] that a woman deliberately made to suffer is justified in anything in life—in going down into the streets, if that will help her! I know how you suffer, and that's why I am here. We can do absolutely as we please; to whom under the sun do we owe anything? What is it that holds us—what is it that has the smallest right to interfere in such a question as this? Such a question is between ourselves—and to say that is to settle it! Were we born to rot in our misery—were we born to be afraid? I never knew *you* afraid! If you only trust me, how little you will be disappointed! The world is all before us—and the world is very large. I know something about that.'

Isabel gave a long murmur, like a creature in pain; it was as if he were pressing something that hurt her. 'The world is very small', she said, at random; she had an immense desire to appear to resist. She said it at random, to hear herself say something; but it was not what she meant. The world, in truth, had never seemed so large; it seemed to open out, all round her, to take the form of a mighty sea, where she floated in fathomless waters. She had wanted help, and here was help; it had come in a rushing torrent. I know not whether she believed everything that he said; but she believed that to let him take her in his arms would be the next best thing to dying. This belief, for a moment, was a kind of rapture, in which she felt herself sinking and sinking. In the movement she seemed to beat with her feet, in order to catch herself, to feel something to rest on.

'Ah, be mine as I am yours!' she heard her companion cry. He had suddenly given up argument, and his voice seemed to come through a confusion of sound.

This however, of course, was but a subjective fact, as the metaphysicians say; the confusion, the noise of waters, and all the rest of it, were in her own head. In an instant she became aware of this. 'Do me the greatest kindness of all', she said. 'I beseech you to go away!'

'Ah, don't say that. Don't kill me!' he cried.

She clasped her hands; her eyes were streaming with tears.

'As you love me, as you pity me, leave me alone!'

He glared at her a moment through the dusk, and the next instant she felt his arms about her, and his lips on her own lips. His kiss was like a flash of lightning; when it was dark again she was free. She never looked about her; she only darted away from the spot. There were lights in the windows of the house; they shone far across the lawn. In an extraordinarily short time—for the distance was considerable—she had moved through the darkness (for she saw nothing) and reached the door. Here only she paused. She looked all about her; she listened a little; then she put her hand on the latch. She had not known where to turn; but she knew now. There was a very straight path.[1]

---

[1] *Portrait of a Lady* in *Macmillan's Magazine*, November 1881, pp. 18 f. James revised the novel for its inclusion in the collected edition. The revisions are worth noting in detail. I have italicised the major additions—the italics given to single pronouns are James's. They show him as still further exploring Isabel's emotions:

'. . . I understand all about it: you're afraid to go back. You're perfectly alone; you don't know where to turn. *You can't turn anywhere; you know that perfectly.* Now it is therefore that I want you to think of *me*.'

'To think of "you"?' Isabel said, standing before him in the dusk. The idea of which she had caught a glimpse a few moments before now loomed large. She threw back her head a little; she stared at it as if it had been a comet in the sky.

'You don't know where to turn. Turn straight to *me*,' Goodwood repeated.

Or this from *The Bostonians:* Verena, getting deeper and deeper in love with Basil Ransom, is proportionately retreating from the passionate masterfulness of her young patron, Olive Chancellor:

There was no candle in any window, and when she pushed in and stood in the hall, listening a moment, her step awakened no answering

And then he paused with his shining eyes. 'Why should you go back—why should you go through that ghastly form?'

'To get away from *you*!' she answered. But this expressed only a little of what she felt. The rest was that she had never been loved before. *She had believed it, but this was different; this was the hot wind of the desert, at the approach of which the others dropped dead, like mere sweet airs of the garden.* It wrapped her about; it lifted her off her feet, *while the very taste of it, as of something potent, acrid and strange, forced open her set teeth.*

At first, in rejoinder to what she had said, it seemed to her that he would break out into greater violence. But after an instant he was perfectly quiet; he wished to prove he was sane, that he had reasoned it all out. 'I want to prevent that, and I think I may, if you'll only for once listen to me. It's too monstrous of you to think of sinking back into that misery, *of going to open your mouth to that poisoned air.* [I omit the rest of this paragraph and all the next, in which the changes are small].

'Ah, be mine as I'm yours!' she heard her companion cry. He had suddenly given up argument, and his voice seemed to come, *harsh and terrible,* through a confusion of vaguer sounds.

This however, of course, was but a subjective fact, as the metaphysicians say; the confusion, the noise of waters, all the rest of it, were in her own *swimming* head. In an instant she became aware of this. 'Do me the greatest kindness of all', she *panted.* 'I beseech you to go away!'

'Ah, don't say that. Don't kill me!' he cried.

She clasped her hands; her eyes were streaming with tears. 'As you love me, as you pity me, leave me alone!'

He glared at her a moment through the dusk, and the next instant she felt his arms about her and his lips on her own lips. His kiss was like white lightning, *a flash that spread, and spread again, and stayed; and it was extraordinarily as if, while she took it, she felt each thing in his hard manhood that had least pleased her, each aggressive fact of his face, his figure, his presence, justified of its intense identity and made one with this act of possession. So had she heard of those wrecked and under water following a train of images before they sink.* But when darkness returned she was free. She never looked about her; she only darted from the spot. There were lights in the windows of the house; they shone far across the lawn. In an extraordinarily short time—for the distance was considerable—she moved through the darkness (for she saw nothing) and reached the door. Here only she paused. She looked all about her; she listened a little; then she put her hand on the latch. She had not known where to turn; but she knew now. There was a very straight path.

sound. Her heart failed her; Verena's staying out in a boat from ten o'clock in the morning till nightfall was too unnatural, and she gave a cry, as she rushed into the low, dim parlor (darkened on one side, at that hour, by the wide-armed foliage, and on the other by the veranda and trellis), which expressed only a wild personal passion, a desire to take her friend in her arms again on any terms, even the most cruel to herself. The next moment she started back, with another and a different exclamation, for Verena was in the room, motionless, in a corner,— the first place in which she had seated herself on reëntering the house,— looking at her with a silent face which seemed strange, unnatural, in the dusk. Olive stopped short, and for a minute the two women remained as they were, gazing at each other in the dimness. After that, too, Olive still said nothing; she only went to Verena and sat down beside her. She didn't know what to make of her manner; she had never been like that before. She was unwilling to speak; she seemed crushed and humbled. This was almost the worst—if anything could be worse than what had gone before; and Olive took her hand with an irresistible impulse of compassion and reassurance. From the way it lay in her own she guessed her whole feeling—saw it was a kind of shame, shame for her weakness, her swift surrender, her insane gyration, in the morning. Verena expressed it by no protest and no explanation; she appeared not even to wish to hear the sound of her own voice. Her silence itself was an appeal—an appeal to Olive to ask no questions (she could trust her to inflict no spoken reproach); only to wait till she could lift up her head again. Olive understood, or thought she understood, and the wofulness of it all only seemed the deeper. She would just sit there and hold her hand; that was all she could do; they were beyond each other's help in any other way now. Verena leaned her head back and closed her eyes, and for an hour, as nightfall settled in the room, neither of the young women spoke. Distinctly, it was a kind of shame. After a while the parlor-maid, very casual, in the manner of the servants at Marmion, appeared on the threshold with a lamp; but Olive motioned her frantic- ally away. She wished to keep the darkness. It was a kind of shame.[1]

Surely the only limitation in such passages is the limitation

---

[1] *The Bostonians*, ch. xxxix, *The Century Magazine*, January 1886, pp. 345 f. James, as I have said above, did not include a reprint of *The Bostonians* in the first collected edition. It was therefore never revised.

which finds no place for the vocabulary of physiology or for the vocabulary of smoke-room stories and limericks. In other words, no limitation that is relevant. Private scenes like these, both in actual life and in novels, do not permit the presence of doctors and jokers, even if the participants are doctors or jokers at other times. At moments of such passion in such circumstances, people like Goodwood and Isabel, Verena and Olive, feel, think, act and speak (if they speak at all) with the limitations which James has observed, limitations which D. H. Lawrence himself would have found it necessary to observe if he had been writing about these characters in these situations, and had 'remained faithful' to them. Whether the novelist be allowed to remain as particularly and completely faithful to his characters in scenes of closer physical contact depends, as I have said, on the age in which he is writing. But if he has remained faithful up to the point at which such scenes begin, that is all that is necessary, and, as I have suggested, all that is usually desirable. If he shows he can touch the carnal, he need not go on to show that he can do more than touch it, especially since the frequent penalty of proceeding further is to cease to write literature in any proper sense of the term, and willy-nilly to herd with the pornographers.

## V

AFTER this we cannot, I think, hold that James's work altogether deserves to be classed with the British and American fiction pilloried by Maud Blessingbourne and Colonel Voyt in 'The Story in it'. I select the following from the dialogue in Chapter II:

'Yes, when I read a novel I mostly read a French one', [Maud] had said to Voyt in answer to a question about her usual practice; 'for I seem with it to get hold more of the real thing—to get more life for my money...'

'... But if you can't read the novel of British and American manufacture, heaven knows I'm at one with you. It seems really to show our sense of life as the sense of puppies and kittens. ... [The French sense of life] *is* one; you can make it out. ... They do what they feel, and they feel more things than we. They strike so many more notes, and with so different a hand. When it comes to any account of a relation say between a man and a woman—I mean an intimate or a curious or a suggestive one—where are we compared to them? They don't exhaust the subject, no doubt ... but we don't touch it, don't even skim it. It's as if we denied its existence, its possibility....'[1]

Colonel Voyt speaking of English and American fiction might be Mr. Forster himself speaking of James's! 'The Story in it' was first printed in 1903. Twenty years earlier had come 'The Art of Fiction' where James in his own person had already made a plea for more freedom than was allowed him by his public. Meanwhile he himself was busy using what freedom he had. And it was enough. The sense of life shown in his novels was not that of puppies and kittens. Assuredly he did more than skim the passions of men.

## VI

IN the earlier work of James, then, the imagination of the reader feels satisfied on the score of carnality.

But if not so much in the later novels for due reasons, and reasons which win our respect. For though in these novels carnality exists, it exists to be put in its place. As instances of this, I will speak of two late novels, and their heroines.

Now that James's notebooks have been published we can see him deliberately ruling out carnality from *The Wings of a Dove* so far as Millie, 'the dove', was concerned. But not

[1] *Daisy Miller ... and Other Tales*, ed. 1922, pp. 374 f.

because of any general fear of it. With some embarrassment as intruders on an author talking to himself, we can now see James building up his story in advance of writing it:

[Millie] learns that she has but a short time to live. . . . The idea of a young man who meets her, who, knowing her fate, is terribly touched by her, and who conceives the idea of saving her as far as he can—little as that may be. . . . The young man, in his pity, wishes he could make her taste of happiness, give her something that it breaks her heart to go without having known. That 'something' can only be—of course—the chance to love and to be loved. . . . I see him as having somehow to risk something, to lose something, to sacrifice something in order to be kind to her, and to do it without a reward, for the poor girl, even if he loved her, has no life to give him in return: no life and no personal, no physical surrender, for it seems to me that one must represent her as too ill for *that* particular case.

And what follows on this shows James as fearless as he is masterly: there is no shrinking but equally no yielding:

It has bothered me in thinking of the little picture—this idea of the physical possession, the brief physical, passional rapture which at first appeared essential to it; bothered me on account of the ugliness, the incongruity, the nastiness, *en somme*, of the man's 'having' a sick girl:

and the final reason:

also on account of something rather pitifully obvious and vulgar in the presentation of such a remedy for her despair—and such a remedy only. 'Oh, she's dying without having had it? Give it to her and let her die'— that strikes me as sufficiently second-rate. Doesn't a greater prettiness, as well as a better chance for a story, abide in her being already too ill for that, and in his being able merely to show her some delicacy of kindness, let her think that they might have loved each other *ad infinitum* if it hadn't been too late. . . .[1]

During the course of the planning, then, carnality was faced and rejected in the scrupulous interests of the story. The only matter open, therefore, to criticism is the sort of story that

[1] *Notebooks*, ed. cit., pp. 169 f.

calls for such rejection. On planes so high as this I shrink from playing the adjudicator. And before encouraging others to do so I would ask them to see the interests that James, so far as his heroine goes, has more at heart than carnality. We can put the chief of his interests in this way: that he wishes to illustrate a remark dropped by Colonel Voyt in 'The Story in it', the remark that describes passion as 'the enemy to behaviour'.[1] For in these late novels, more even than in the earlier, James is as constructive a moralist as he is a searching psychologist. His late stories exist first and foremost, as do all his stories, to be 'interesting', but part of their interestingness lies in their showing us people painfully seeking to live well, to heal rather than hurt, to set subtle wrongs to rights, and to do it all by the humane wisdom and kindness which is what James meant by 'behaviour'. In *The Golden Bowl* the good to be done can only be done well (that is with good 'behaviour') if done by means of renunciations which include carnal renunciations. Prince Amerigo is married to Maggie Verver, and Charlotte, the young wife of her father, is his mistress. In order to work things back to their former innocence Maggie has to tame in herself passions of body and mind which at moments are 'vertiginous'. As in this passage:

She continued to walk and continued to pause; she stopped afresh for the look into the smoking-room, and by this time—it was as if the recognition had of itself arrested her—she saw as in a picture, with the temptation she had fled from quite extinct [the temptation to smash up the false relationships], why it was she had been able to give herself from the first so little to the vulgar heat of her wrong. She might fairly, as she watched them, have missed it as a lost thing; have yearned for it, for the straight vindictive view, the rights of resentment, the rages of jealousy, the protests of passion, as for something she had been cheated of not least: a range of feelings which for many women would have meant so much,

[1] Ed. cit., p. 377.

but which for *her* husband's wife, for her father's daughter, figured nothing nearer to experience than a wild eastern caravan, looming into view with crude colours in the sun, fierce pipes in the air, high spears against the sky, all a thrill, a natural joy to mingle with, but turning off short before it reached her and plunging into other defiles. She saw at all events why horror itself had almost failed her; the horror that, foreshadowed in advance, would by her thought have made everything that was unaccustomed in her cry out with pain; the horror of finding evil seated all at its ease where she had only dreamed of good; the horror of the thing hideously *behind*, behind so much trusted, so much pretended, nobleness, cleverness, tenderness. It was the first sharp falsity she had known in her life, to touch at all or be touched by; it had met her like some bad-faced stranger surprised in one of the thick-carpeted corridors of a house of quiet on a Sunday afternoon; and yet, yes, amazingly, she had been able to look at terror and disgust only to know that she must put away from her the bitter-sweet of their freshness. The sight, from the window, of the group so constituted, *told* her why, told her how, named to her, as with hard lips, named straight *at* her, so that she must take it full in the face, that other possible relation to the whole fact which alone would bear upon her irresistibly. It was extraordinary: they positively brought home to her that to feel about them in any of the immediate, inevitable, assuaging ways, the ways usually open to innocence outraged and generosity betrayed, would have been to give them up, and that giving them up was, marvellously, not to be thought of. She had never, from the first hour of her state of acquired conviction, given them up so little as now; though she was, no doubt, as the consequence of a step taken a few minutes later, to invoke the conception of doing that, if might be, even less. She had resumed her walk. . . .[1]

In face of passages like this we can allow Mr. Forster's categories to fight among themselves: Maggie, to whom he denies both heroism and carnality, is heroic because she suppresses carnality. That sort of suppression is not common: Maggie did *not* claim 'the rights of resentment, the rages of jealousy, the protests of passion', or the 'range of feeling that

---

[1] *The Golden Bowl*, 1923 edition, ii. 209 f.

for most women would have meant so much', or 'the ways usually open to innocence outraged and generosity betrayed'. For Maggie, as for Millie, carnality is ruled out expressly, as 'second-rate', as standing, from the point of view of the narrator and his moral values, in the way of something he rated as more precious. The narrator must take the consequences, as I have said, of having these saints-in-the-making for the characters on whom he throws his loveliest light. He must take the consequences of writing stories so minutely and psychologically moral. And also the consequences of writing stories so immensely Jamesian in the writing. But his limitations are ones he has chosen for himself. Like all of us in the completeness of their resources, his choicest characters differ from most of us in trying to organise those resources in the interests of their neighbours.

# ABBREVIATIONS

*Apologia* = *Newman's Apologia pro Vita Sua*, ed. Wilfred Ward, edn. 1931.

*Appreciations* = Walter Pater, *Appreciations with an Essay on Style*, 1889.

*Arnold to Clough* = *Letters of Matthew Arnold to Arthur Hugh Clough*, ed. Howard Foster Lowry, Oxford, 1932.

*Biographia Literaria* = S. T. Coleridge, *Biographia Literaria*, ed. J. Shawcross, 2 vols., Oxford, 1907.

*Culture and Anarchy* = Matthew Arnold, *Culture and Anarchy*, ed. J. Dover Wilson, Cambridge, 1935.

*Essays in Criticism* = Matthew Arnold, *Essays in Criticism*, 1865.

*Essays in Criticism: Second Series* = Matthew Arnold, *Essays in Criticism. Second Series*, 1895.

*Letters* = *Letters of Matthew Arnold 1844-1888*, ed. G. W. E. Russell, 2 vols., 1895.

*Letters* = *The Letters of John Keats*, ed. M. B. Forman, edn. 1947.

*Letters* = *Letters and Correspondence of John Henry Newman during his Life in the English Church*, ed. Anne Mozley, 2 vols., 1891.

*Lives of the Poets* = Samuel Johnson, *Lives of the English Poets*, ed. George Birkbeck Hill, 3 vols., Oxford, 1905.

*Mixed Essays* = Matthew Arnold, *Mixed Essays*, 1879.

*On Translating Homer* = Matthew Arnold, *On Translating Homer. Three Lectures Given at Oxford*, 1861.

*Tennyson and his Friends* = *Tennyson and His Friends*, ed. Hallam, Lord Tennyson, 1911.

*The New Republic* = *The New Republic; or, Culture, Faith, and Philosophy in an English Country House* [by W. H. Mallock], 2 vols., 1877.

*The Renaissance* = Walter Pater, *Studies in the History of the Renaissance*, 1873.

Twickenham ed. = *The Twickenham Edition of the Poems of Alexander*

*Pope*, general editor John Butt, 1939, in progress.

*Works* = *The Complete Works of John Ruskin*, ed. E. T. Cook and Alexander Wedderburn, 39 vols., 1903-12.

*Note on Newman's works.* All references to works of Newman, unless it is stated otherwise, are to the works as they appear in the uniform edition, which Newman brought out between 1868 and 1881. Later printings have repeated the text which is there finally established.

# INDEX

T